BOOK 2 – INSTITUTIONAL INVESTORS, CAPITAL MARKET EXPECTATIONS, ECONOMIC CONCEPTS, AND ASSET ALLOCATION

Readings and Learning Outcome Statements 3

Study Session 5 – Portfolio Management for Institutional Investors 8

Self-Test – Portfolio Management for Institutional Investors............................... 60

Study Session 6 – Capital Market Expectations in Portfolio Management.............. 63

Study Session 7 – Economic Concepts for Asset Valuation in Portfolio Management.. 119

Self-Test – Economic Concepts 148

Study Session 8 – Asset Allocation 151

Self-Test – Asset Allocation 214

Formulas... 219

Index 221

SCHWESERNOTES™ 2014 CFA LEVEL III BOOK 2: INSTITUTIONAL INVESTORS, CAPITAL MARKET EXPECTATIONS, ECONOMIC CONCEPTS, AND ASSET ALLOCATION

©2013 Kaplan, Inc. All rights reserved.

Published in 2013 by Kaplan Schweser.

Printed in the United States of America.

ISBN: 978-1-4277-4916-1 / 1-4277-4916-7

PPN: 3200-4017

READINGS AND
LEARNING OUTCOME STATEMENTS

READINGS

The following material is a review of the Institutional Investors, Capital Market Expectations, Economic Concepts, and Asset Allocation principles designed to address the learning outcome statements set forth by CFA Institute.

STUDY SESSION 5

Reading Assignments
Portfolio Management for Institutional Investors, CFA Program 2014 Curriculum, Volume 2, Level III

    15. Managing Institutional Investor Portfolios   page 8
    16. Linking Pension Liabilities to Assets   page 52

STUDY SESSION 6

Reading Assignment
Capital Market Expectations in Portfolio Management, CFA Program 2014 Curriculum, Volume 3, Level III

    17. Capital Market Expectations   page 63

STUDY SESSION 7

Reading Assignments
Economic Concepts for Asset Valuation in Portfolio Management, CFA Program 2014 Curriculum, Volume 3, Level III

    18. Equity Market Valuation   page 119

STUDY SESSION 8

Reading Assignments
Asset Allocation, CFA Program 2014 Curriculum, Volume 3, Level III

    19. Asset Allocation   page 151

Learning Outcome Statements (LOS)

Study Session 5

The topical coverage corresponds with the following CFA Institute assigned reading:

15. Managing Institutional Investor Portfolios

The candidate should be able to:

a. contrast a defined-benefit plan to a defined-contribution plan and discuss the advantages and disadvantages of each from the perspectives of the employee and the employer. (page 9)

b. discuss investment objectives and constraints for defined-benefit plans. (page 9)

c. evaluate pension fund risk tolerance when risk is considered from the perspective of the 1) plan surplus, 2) sponsor financial status and profitability, 3) sponsor and pension fund common risk exposures, 4) plan features, and 5) workforce characteristics. (page 10)

d. prepare an investment policy statement for a defined-benefit plan. (page 11)

e. evaluate the risk management considerations in investing pension plan assets. (page 13)

f. prepare an investment policy statement for a defined-contribution plan. (page 14)

g. discuss hybrid pension plans (e.g., cash balance plans) and employee stock ownership plans. (page 14)

h. distinguish among various types of foundations, with respect to their description, purpose, source of funds, and annual spending requirements. (page 15)

i. compare the investment objectives and constraints of foundations, endowments, insurance companies, and banks. (page 16)

j. prepare an investment policy statement for a foundation, an endowment, an insurance company, and a bank. (page 16)

k. contrast investment companies, commodity pools, and hedge funds to other types of institutional investors. (page 29)

l. discuss the factors that determine investment policy for pension funds, foundations, endowments, life and nonlife insurance companies, and banks. (page 30)

m. compare the asset/liability management needs of pension funds, foundations, endowments, insurance companies, and banks. (page 28)

n. compare the investment objectives and constraints of institutional investors given relevant data, such as descriptions of their financial circumstances and attitudes toward risk. (page 30)

The topical coverage corresponds with the following CFA Institute assigned reading:

16. Linking Pension Liabilities to Assets

The candidate should be able to:

a. contrast the assumptions concerning pension liability risk in asset-only and liability-relative approaches to asset allocation. (page 52)

b. discuss the fundamental and economic exposures of pension liabilities and identify asset types that mimic these liability exposures. (page 53)

c. compare pension portfolios built from a traditional asset-only perspective to portfolios designed relative to liabilities and discuss why corporations may choose not to implement fully the liability mimicking portfolio. (page 56)

STUDY SESSION 6

The topical coverage corresponds with the following CFA Institute assigned reading:

17. Capital Market Expectations

The candidate should be able to:

a. discuss the role of, and a framework for, capital market expectations in the portfolio management process. (page 63)

b. discuss challenges in developing capital market forecasts. (page 64)

c. demonstrate the application of formal tools for setting capital market expectations, including statistical tools, discounted cash flow models, the risk premium approach, and financial equilibrium models. (page 69)

d. explain the use of survey and panel methods and judgment in setting capital market expectations. (page 80)

e. discuss the inventory and business cycles, the impact of consumer and business spending, and monetary and fiscal policy on the business cycle. (page 81)

f. discuss the impact that the phases of the business cycle have on short-term/long-term capital market returns. (page 82)

g. explain the relationship of inflation to the business cycle and the implications of inflation for cash, bonds, equity, and real estate returns. (page 84)

h. demonstrate the use of the Taylor rule to predict central bank behavior. (page 86)

i. evaluate 1) the shape of the yield curve as an economic predictor and 2) the relationship between the yield curve and fiscal and monetary policy. (page 87)

j. identify and interpret the components of economic growth trends and demonstrate the application of economic growth trend analysis to the formulation of capital market expectations. (page 88)

k. explain how exogenous shocks may affect economic growth trends. (page 90)

l. identify and interpret macroeconomic, interest rate, and exchange rate linkages between economies. (page 91)

m. discuss the risks faced by investors in emerging-market securities and the country risk analysis techniques used to evaluate emerging market economies. (page 92)

n. compare the major approaches to economic forecasting. (page 93)

o. demonstrate the use of economic information in forecasting asset class returns. (page 95)

p. evaluate how economic and competitive factors affect investment markets, sectors, and specific securities. (page 95)

q. discuss the relative advantages and limitations of the major approaches to forecasting exchange rates. (page 98)

r. recommend and justify changes in the component weights of a global investment portfolio based on trends and expected changes in macroeconomic factors. (page 100)

STUDY SESSION 7

The topical coverage corresponds with the following CFA Institute assigned reading:
18. **Equity Market Valuation**
    The candidate should be able to:
    a. <u>explain</u> the terms of the Cobb-Douglas production function and <u>demonstrate</u> how the function can be used to model growth in real output under the assumption of constant returns to scale. (page 119)
    b. <u>evaluate</u> the relative importance of growth in total factor productivity, in capital stock, and in labor input given relevant historical data. (page 121)
    c. <u>demonstrate</u> the use of the Cobb-Douglas production function in obtaining a discounted dividend model estimate of the intrinsic value of an equity market. (page 123)
    d. <u>critique</u> the use of discounted dividend models and macroeconomic forecasts to estimate the intrinsic value of an equity market. (page 123)
    e. <u>contrast</u> top-down and bottom-up approaches to forecasting the earnings per share of an equity market index. (page 128)
    f. <u>discuss</u> the strengths and limitations of relative valuation models. (page 130)
    g. <u>judge</u> whether an equity market is under-, fairly, or over-valued using a relative equity valuation model. (page 130)

STUDY SESSION 8

The topical coverage corresponds with the following CFA Institute assigned reading:
19. **Asset Allocation**
    The candidate should be able to:
    a. <u>explain</u> the function of strategic asset allocation in portfolio management and <u>discuss</u> its role in relation to specifying and controlling the investor's exposures to systematic risk. (page 151)
    b. <u>compare</u> strategic and tactical asset allocation. (page 152)
    c. <u>discuss</u> the importance of asset allocation for portfolio performance. (page 152)
    d. <u>contrast</u> the asset-only and asset/liability management (ALM) approaches to asset allocation and <u>discuss</u> the investor circumstances in which they are commonly used. (page 152)
    e. <u>explain</u> the advantage of dynamic over static asset allocation and <u>discuss</u> the trade-offs of complexity and cost. (page 153)
    f. <u>explain</u> how loss aversion, mental accounting, and fear of regret may influence asset allocation policy. (page 153)
    g. <u>evaluate</u> return and risk objectives in relation to strategic asset allocation. (page 154)
    h. <u>evaluate</u> whether an asset class or set of asset classes has been appropriately specified. (page 158)
    i. <u>select</u> and <u>justify</u> an appropriate set of asset classes for an investor. (page 182)
    j. <u>evaluate</u> the theoretical and practical effects of including additional asset classes in an asset allocation. (page 159)
    k. <u>demonstrate</u> the application of mean–variance analysis to decide whether to include an additional asset class in an existing portfolio. (page 160)
    l. <u>describe</u> risk, cost, and opportunities associated with nondomestic equities and bonds. (page 162)

©2013 Kaplan, Inc.

m. <u>explain</u> the importance of conditional return correlations in evaluating the diversification benefits of nondomestic investments. (page 165)

n. <u>explain</u> expected effects on share prices, expected returns, and return volatility as a segmented market becomes integrated with global markets. (page 166)

o. <u>explain</u> the major steps involved in establishing an appropriate asset allocation. (page 167)

p. <u>discuss</u> the strengths and limitations of the following approaches to asset allocation: mean–variance, resampled efficient frontier, Black–Litterman, Monte Carlo simulation, ALM, and experience based. (page 168)

q. <u>discuss</u> the structure of the minimum-variance frontier with a constraint against short sales. (page 180)

r. <u>formulate</u> and <u>justify</u> a strategic asset allocation, given an investment policy statement and capital market expectations. (page 182)

s. <u>compare</u> the considerations that affect asset allocation for individual investors versus institutional investors and <u>critique</u> a proposed asset allocation in light of those considerations. (page 189)

t. <u>formulate</u> and <u>justify</u> tactical asset allocation (TAA) adjustments to strategic asset class weights, given a TAA strategy and expectational data. (page 192)

The following is a review of the Institutional Investors principles designed to address the learning outcome statements set forth by CFA Institute. This topic is also covered in:

Managing Institutional Investor Portfolios

Exam Focus

It is important to read Topic Review 10 prior to studying this session to review the basic framework, structure, and approach to the investment policy statement (IPS). This topic review extends that process to institutional portfolios. Study sessions 4 and 5 together have been the most tested topic areas for the Level III exam. Be prepared to spend one to two hours of the morning constructed response portion of the exam on IPS questions and related issues.

Warm-Up: Pension Plan Terms

General Pension Definitions

- *Funded status* refers to the difference between the present values of the pension plan's assets and liabilities.
- *Plan surplus* is calculated as the the value of plan assets minus the value of plan liabilities. When plan surplus is positive the plan is *overfunded* and when it is negative the plan is *underfunded*.
- *Fully funded* refers to a plan where the values of plan assets and liabilities are approximately equal.
- *Accumulated benefit obligation* (ABO) is the total present value of pension liabilities to date, assuming no further accumulation of benefits. It is the relevant measure of liabilities for a terminated plan.
- *Projected benefit obligation* (PBO) is the ABO plus the present value of the additional liability from projected future employee compensation increases and is the value used in calculating funded status for ongoing (not terminating) plans.
- *Total future liability* is more comprehensive and is the PBO plus the present value of the expected increase in the benefit due current employees in the future from their service to the company between now and retirement. This is not an accounting term and has no precise definition. It could include such items as possible future changes in the benefit formula that are not part of the PBO. Some plans may consider it as supplemental information in setting objectives.
- *Retired lives* is the number of plan participants currently receiving benefits from the plan (retirees).
- *Active lives* is the number of currently employed plan participants who are not currently receiving pension benefits.

DEFINED-BENEFIT PLANS AND DEFINED-CONTRIBUTION PLANS

LOS 15.a: Contrast a defined-benefit plan to a defined-contribution plan and discuss the advantages and disadvantages of each from the perspectives of the employee and the employer.

CFA® Program Curriculum, Volume 2, page 434

In a **defined-benefit** (DB) retirement plan, the sponsor company agrees to make payments to employees after retirement based on criteria (e.g., average salary, number of years worked) spelled out in the plan. As future benefits are accrued by employees, the employer accrues a liability equal to the present value of the expected future payments. This liability is offset by plan assets which are the plan assets funded by the employer's contributions over time. A plan with assets greater (less) than liabilities is termed overfunded (underfunded). The employer bears the investment risk and must increase funding to the plan when the investment results are poor.

In a **defined-contribution** (DC) plan, the company agrees to make contributions of a certain amount as they are earned by employees (e.g., 1% of salary each month) into a retirement account owned by the participant. While there may be vesting rules, generally an employee legally owns his account assets and can move the funds if he leaves prior to retirement. For this reason we say that the plan has **portability**. At retirement, the employee can access the funds but there is no guarantee of the amount. In a *participant directed* DC plan, the employee makes the investment decisions and in a *sponsor directed* DC plan, the sponsor chooses the investments. In either case, the employee bears the investment risk and the amount available at retirement is uncertain in a DC plan. The firm has no future financial liability. This is the key difference between a DC plan and a DB plan. In a DB plan, the sponsor has the investment risk because a certain future benefit has been promised and the firm has a liability as a result. A firm with a DC plan has no liability beyond making the agreed upon contributions.

A **cash balance plan** is a type of DB plan in which individual account balances (accrued benefit) are recorded so they can be portable. A **profit sharing plan** is a type of DC plan where the employer contribution is based on the profits of the company. A variety of plans funded by an individual for his own benefit, grow tax deferred, and can be withdrawn at retirement (e.g., individual retirement accounts or IRAs) are also considered defined contribution accounts.

LOS 15.b: Discuss investment objectives and constraints for defined-benefit plans.

CFA® Program Curriculum, Volume 2, page 436

The objectives and constraints in the IPS for a defined-benefit plan are the standard ones you have learned. The objectives of risk and return are jointly determined. The constraints can be separated into the plan's time horizon, tax and regulatory status, liquidity needs, legal and regulatory constraints, and unique circumstances of the plan that would constrain investment options.

Analysis of these objectives and constraints, along with a discussion of the relevant considerations in establishing them, is covered in the next two LOS.

LOS 15.c: <u>Evaluate</u> pension fund risk tolerance when risk is considered from the perspective of the 1) plan surplus, 2) sponsor financial status and profitability, 3) sponsor and pension fund common risk exposures, 4) plan features, and 5) workforce characteristics.

CFA® Program Curriculum, Volume 2, page 437

Several factors affect the risk tolerance (ability and willingness to take risk) for a defined benefit plan.

- **Plan surplus.** The greater the plan surplus, the greater the ability of the fund to withstand poor/negative investment results without increases in funding. Thus a positive surplus allows a higher risk tolerance and a negative surplus reduces risk tolerance. A negative surplus might well increase the desire of the sponsor to take risk in the hope that higher returns would reduce the need to make contributions. This is not acceptable. Both the sponsor and manager have an obligation to manage the plan assets for the benefit of the plan beneficiaries. Compared to foundations and endowments, which may be managed aggressively, DB plans will range from low to moderately above-average risk tolerance. A negative surplus may increase the willingness of the sponsor to take risk, but this willingness does not change or outweigh the fact that the plan is underfunded and the fund risk tolerance is lowered by a negative surplus.

- **Financial status and profitability.** Indicators such as debt to equity and profit margins indicate the financial strength and profitability of the sponsor. The greater the strength of the sponsor, the greater the plan's risk tolerance. Both lower debt and higher profitability indicate an ability to increase plan contributions if investment results are poor.

- **Sponsor and pension fund common risk exposures.** The higher the correlation between firm profitability and the value of plan assets, the less the plan's risk tolerance. With high correlation, the fund's value may fall at the same time that the firm's profitability falls and it is least able to increase contributions.

- **Plan features.** Provisions for early retirement or for lump-sum withdrawals decrease the duration of the plan liabilities and, other things equal, decrease the plan's risk tolerance. Any provisions that increase liquidity needs or reduce time horizon reduce risk tolerance.

- **Workforce characteristics.** The lower the average age of the workforce, the longer the time horizon and, other things equal, this increases the plan's risk tolerance. The higher the ratio of retirees drawing benefits to currently working plan participants, the greater the liquidity requirements and the lower the fund's risk tolerance. Conversely, when the ratio of active lives to retired lives is higher the plan's risk tolerance is higher.

LOS 15.d: Prepare an investment policy statement for a defined-benefit plan.

CFA® Program Curriculum, Volume 2, page 439

The elements of an IPS for a defined benefit fund are not unlike those for IPS or other investment funds.

The objectives for risk and return are jointly determined with the risk objective limiting the return objective. The factors affecting risk tolerance discussed for the previous LOS should be considered in determining the risk tolerance objective included in an IPS for a defined benefit plan fund.

While these factors determine the relative risk tolerance for plan assets, they do not address the issue of how risk should be measured for a DB plan and the form that a risk objective should take. As already noted, from a firm risk standpoint the correlation of operating results and plan results is important. If operating results and pension results are positively correlated, the firm will find it necessary to increase plan contributions just when it is most difficult or costly to do so.

The primary objective of a DB plan is to meet its obligation to provide promised retirement benefits to plan participants. The risk of not meeting this objective is best addressed using an **asset/liability management** (ALM) framework. Under ALM, risk is measured by the variability (standard deviation) of plan surplus. Alternatively, many plans still look at risk from the perspective of assets only and focus on the more traditional standard deviation of asset returns.

> **For the Exam:** ALM is a major topic in the Level III material. Expect it to occur on the exam, perhaps more than once. This topic review does not discuss it in any detail as it is covered elsewhere. In a general IPS question on any portfolio with definable liabilities, it is appropriate to mention the desirability of looking at return in terms of maintaining or growing the surplus and risk as variability of surplus. Do not make it the focus of the answer; move on and address the rest of the issues relevant to the question. Also be prepared for a question that does test the details of ALM found in other parts of the curriculum.

Another approach to setting a risk objective for a DB plan focuses on its **shortfall risk** (the probability that the plan asset value will be below some specific level or have returns below some specific level) over a given time horizon. Shortfall risk may be estimated for a status at some future date of fully funded (relative to the PBO), fully funded with respect to the total future liability, funded status that would avoid reporting a liability (negative surplus position) on the firm's balance sheet, or funded status that would require additional contribution requirements of regulators or additional premium payments to a pension fund guarantor. Alternative or supplemental risk objectives may be included to minimize the volatility of plan contributions or, in the case of a fully or over-funded plan, minimizing the probability of having to make future plan contributions.

DB Plan Return Objective

The ultimate goal of a pension plan is to have pension assets generate return sufficient to cover pension liabilities. The specific return requirement will depend on the plan's risk tolerance and constraints. At a minimum the return objective is the discount rate used to compute the present value of the future benefits. If a plan were fully funded, earns the discount rate, and the actuarial assumptions are correct, the fully funded status will remain stable. It is acceptable to aim for a somewhat higher return that would grow the surplus and eventually allow smaller contributions by the sponsor. Objects might include:

- *Future pension contributions.* Return levels can be calculated to eliminate the need for contributions to plan assets.
- *Pension income.* Accounting principles require pension expenses be reflected on sponsors' income statements. Negative expenses, or pension income, can also be recognized. This also leads the sponsor to desire higher returns, which will reduce contributions and pension expense.

Recognize these may be goals of the sponsor and are legitimate plan objectives if not taken to excess. The return objective is limited by the appropriate level of risk for the plan and pension plans should not take high risk.

DB Plan Constraints

Liquidity. The pension plan receives contributions from the plan sponsor and makes payments to beneficiaries. Any net outflow represents a liquidity need. Liquidity requirements will be affected by:

- *The number of retired lives.* The greater the number of retirees receiving benefits relative to active participants, the greater the liquidity that must be provided.
- *The amount of sponsor contributions.* The smaller the corporate contributions relative to retirement payments, the greater the liquidity needed.
- *Plan features.* Early retirement or lump-sum payment options increase liquidity requirements.

Time horizon. The time horizon of a defined-benefit plan is mainly determined by two factors:

1. If the plan is terminating, the time horizon is the termination date.

2. For an ongoing plan, the relevant time horizon depends on characteristics of the plan participants.

   The time horizon for a going concern defined-benefit plan is often long term. Legally it may have an infinite life. However, the management of the current plan assets and the relevant time horizon of the portfolio depend on the characteristics of the current plan participants and when distributions are expected to be made. Some sponsors and managers view going concern plans as a multistage time horizon, one for active lives and one for retired lives, essentially viewing the portfolio as two sub portfolios. The active lives portion of the plan will have a time horizon associated with expected term to retirement. The retired lives portion will have a time horizon as a function of life expectancy for those currently receiving benefits.

Taxes. Most retirement plans are tax exempt and this should be stated. There are exceptions in some countries or some portions of return are taxed, but others are not. If any portions are taxed, this should be stated in the constraint and considered when selecting assets.

Legal and regulatory factors. In the United States, the Employee Retirement Income Security Act (ERISA) regulates the implementation of defined-benefit plans. The requirements of ERISA are consistent with the CFA program and modern portfolio theory in regard to placing the plan participants first and viewing the overall portfolio after considering diversification effects. Most countries have applicable laws and regulations governing pension investment activity. The key point to remember is that when formulating an IPS for a pension plan, the adviser must incorporate the regulatory framework existing within the jurisdiction where the plan operates. Consultation with appropriate legal experts is required if complex issues arise. A pension plan trustee is a **fiduciary** and as such must act solely in the best interests of the plan participants. A manager hired to manage assets for the plan takes on that responsibility as well.

Unique circumstances. There are no unique issues to generalize about. Possible issues include:

- A small plan may have limited staff and resources for managing the plan or overseeing outside managers. This could be a larger challenge with complex alternative investments that require considerable due diligence.
- Some plans self impose restrictions on asset classes or industries. This is more common in government or union-related plans.

LOS 15.e: <u>Evaluate</u> the risk management considerations in investing pension plan assets.

CFA® Program Curriculum, Volume 2, page 449

Another dimension of DB plan risk is its affect on the sponsor. These plans can be large with the potential to affect the sponsoring company's financial health. The company needs to consider two factors.

1. *Pension investment returns in relation to the operating returns of the company.* This is the issue of correlation of sponsor business and plan assets considered earlier, now viewed from the company's perspective. The company should also favor low correlation to minimize the need for increasing contributions during periods of poor performance. The plan should avoid investing in the sponsor company (which is often illegal) and in securities in the same industry or otherwise highly correlated with the company.

2. *Coordinating pension investments with pension liabilities.* This is the ALM issue. By focusing on managing the surplus and stability of surplus, the company minimizes the probability of unexpected increases in required contributions.

Professor's Note: This will be discussed in great detail elsewhere. At its simplest this means matching the plan asset and liability durations using fixed-income investments. In a more sophisticated fashion, a closer match may be achieved by using real rate bonds and equity as a portion of the assets. ALM will also lead to a surplus efficient frontier and a minimum variance surplus portfolio. For now just realize the Level III material is highly integrated and questions normally draw from multiple LOS and study sessions—keep studying.

LOS 15.f: <u>Prepare</u> an investment policy statement for a defined-contribution plan.

CFA® Program Curriculum, Volume 2, page 451

Constructing the IPS for a sponsor-directed DC plan is similar to that for other DB plans, but simpler. Here we will distinguish between the IPS for a DB plan and the IPS for a participant directed DC plan. With a participant directed DC plan, there is no one set of objectives and constraints to be considered since they may be different over time and across participant accounts. The IPS for this type of plan deals with the sponsor's obligation to provide investment choices (at least three under ERISA) that allow for diversification and to provide for the free movement of funds among the choices offered. Additionally, the sponsor should provide some guidance and education for plan participants so they can determine their risk tolerance, return objectives, and the allocation of their funds among the various investment choices offered. When the sponsor offers a choice of company stock, the IPS should provide limits on this as a portfolio choice to maintain adequate diversification (think Enron).

So overall the IPS for a participant directed DC plan does not relate to any individual participant or circumstance, but outlines the policies and procedures for offering the choices, diversification, and education to participants that they need to address their own objectives of risk and return, as well as their liquidity and time horizon constraints. The management of the individual participant balances and setting their objectives and constraints in the participant directed plan would be handled like any other O&C for an individual.

In contrast, a sponsor-directed DC plan would be treated like a DB plan. However, there is no specified future liability to consider in setting the objectives and constraints. Otherwise, the analysis process would be similar to a DB plan.

HYBRID PLANS AND ESOPS

LOS 15.g: <u>Discuss</u> hybrid pension plans (e.g., cash balance plans) and employee stock ownership plans.

CFA® Program Curriculum, Volume 2, page 455

Cash balance plan. A cash balance plan is a type of defined-benefit plan that defines the benefit in terms of an account balance. In a typical cash balance plan, a participant's account is credited each year with a pay credit and an interest credit. The pay credit is usually based upon the beneficiary's age, salary, and/or length of employment, while the interest credit is based upon a benchmark such as U.S. Treasuries. These features are similar to DC plans.

However, and more like DB plans, the sponsor bears all the investment risk because increases and decreases in the value of the plan's investments (due to investment decisions, interest rates, etc.) do not affect the benefit amounts promised to participants. At retirement, the beneficiary can usually elect to receive a lump-sum distribution, which can be rolled into another qualified plan, or receive a lifetime annuity.

Employee stock ownership plans (ESOPs). An ESOP is a type of defined-contribution benefit plan that allows employees to purchase the company stock, sometimes at a discount from market price. The purchase can be with before- or after-tax dollars. The final balance in the beneficiary's account reflects the increase in the value of the firm's stock as well as contributions during employment. ESOPs receive varying amounts of regulation in different countries.

At times the ESOP may purchase a large block of the firm's stock directly from a large stockholder, such as a founding proprietor or partner who wants to liquidate a holding. An ESOP is an exception to the general aversion to holding the sponsor's securities in a retirement plan. It does expose the participant to a high correlation between plan return and future job income.

FOUNDATIONS

LOS 15.h: Distinguish among various types of foundations, with respect to their description, purpose, source of funds, and annual spending requirements.

CFA® Program Curriculum, Volume 2, page 456

From an investment management perspective and a typical set of objectives and constraints, foundations and endowments are going to be treated the same. The terms are frequently used interchangeably, though in the United States there are nuances of legal distinction. In general **foundations** are grant-making entities funded by gifts and an investment portfolio. **Endowments** are long-term funds owned by a non-profit institution (and supporting that institution). Both are not for profit, serve a social purpose, generally are not taxed if they meet certain conditions, are often perpetual, and unlike pension plans may well and should pursue aggressive objectives.

Figure 1 contains a summary of the characteristics of the four basic types of foundations.[1]

---

1. Based upon Exhibit 2, "Managing Institutional Investor Portfolios," by R. Charles Tschampion, CFA, Laurence B. Siegel, Dean J. Takahashi, and John L. Maginn, CFA, from *Managing Investment Portfolios: A Dynamic Process*, 3rd edition, 2007 (CFA Institute, 2014 Level III Curriculum, Reading 15, Vol. 2, p. 457).

Figure 1: Types of Foundations and Their Important Characteristics

Type of Foundation	Description	Purpose	Source of Funds	Annual Spending Requirement
Independent	Private or family	Grants to charities, educational institutions, social organizations, etc.	Typically an individual or family, but can be a group of interested individuals	5% of assets; expenses cannot be counted in the spending amount
Company sponsored	Closely tied to the sponsoring corporation	Same as independent; grants can be used to further the corporate sponsor's business interests	Corporate sponsor	Same as independent foundations
Operating	Established for the sole purpose of funding an organization (e.g., a museum, zoo, public library) or some ongoing research/medical initiative		Same as independent	Must spend at least 85% of dividend and interest income for its own operations; may also be subject to spending 3.33% of assets
Community	Publicly sponsored grant-awarding organization	Fund social, educational, religious, etc. purposes	General public, including large donors	None

LOS 15.i: <u>Compare</u> the investment objectives and constraints of foundations, endowments, insurance companies, and banks.

LOS 15.j: <u>Prepare</u> an investment policy statement for a foundation, an endowment, an insurance company, and a bank.

CFA® Program Curriculum, Volume 2, page 458

Foundation Objectives

Risk. Because there are no contractually defined liability requirements, foundations may be more aggressive than pensions on the risk tolerance scale. If successful in earning higher returns the foundation can increase its social funding in the future. If unsuccessful the foundation suffers and can fund less in the future. In either case the benefit and risk are symmetrically borne. The board of the foundation (and manager) will generally consider the time horizon and other circumstances of the foundation in setting the risk tolerance.

Return. Time horizon is an important factor. If the foundation was created to provide perpetual support, the preservation of real purchasing power is important. One useful guideline is to set a minimum return equal to the required payout plus expected inflation and fund expenses. This might be done by either adding or compounding the return elements. (Note: this issue is discussed under endowments).

Foundation Constraints

Time horizon. Except for special foundations required to spend down their portfolio within a set period, most foundations have infinite time horizons. Hence, they can usually tolerate above-average risk and choose securities that tend to offer high returns as well as preservation of purchasing power.

Liquidity. A foundation's anticipated spending requirement is termed its **spending rate**. Many countries specify a minimum spending rate, and failure to meet this will trigger penalties. For instance the United States has a 5% rule to spend 5% of previous year assets. Other situations may follow a **smoothing rule** to average out distributions.

For ongoing foundations there is generally a need to also earn the inflation rate to maintain real value of the portfolio and distributions. Earning the required distribution and inflation can be challenging with conflicting interpretations for risk. It may argue for high risk to meet the return target or less risk to avoid the downside of disappointing returns.

Many organizations find it appropriate to maintain a fraction of the annual spending as a cash reserve in the portfolio.

Tax considerations. Except for the fact that investment income of private foundations is currently taxed at 1% in the United States, foundations are not taxable entities. One potential concern relates to *unrelated business income*, which is taxable at the regular corporate rate. On average, tax considerations are not a major concern for foundations.

Legal and regulatory. Rules vary by country and even by type of foundation. In the United States most states have adopted the Uniform Management Institutional Funds Act (UMIFA) as the prevailing regulatory framework. Most other regulations concern the tax-exempt status of the foundation. Beyond these basics, foundations are free to pursue the objectives they deem appropriate.

> *Professor's Note: We are discussing foundations and endowments as two different institution types, as done in the CFA text. There may someday be a question on the exam regarding the subtle, technical differences. We do not believe that has yet occurred. The way they are managed and the issues to consider are overwhelmingly consistent. Read both sections together and then apply what is taught.*

ENDOWMENTS AND SPENDING RULES

Endowments are legal entities that have been funded for the expressed purpose of *permanently* funding the endowment's institutional sponsor (a not for profit that will receive the benefits of the portfolio). The intent is to preserve asset principal value in perpetuity and to use the income generated for budgetary support of specific activities. Universities, hospitals, museums, and charitable organizations often receive a substantial portion of their funding from endowments. Spending from endowments is usually earmarked for specific purposes and spending fluctuations can create disruptions in the institutional recipient's operating budget.

Most endowments (and foundations) have spending rules. In the United States, foundations have a minimum required spending rule but endowments can decide their spending rate, change it, or just fail to meet it.

Three forms of spending rule are as follows:

- **Simple spending rule.**

    The most straightforward spending rule is spending to equal the specified spending rate multiplied by the beginning period market value of endowment assets:

    $$\text{spending}_t = S(\text{market value}_{t-1})$$

    where:
    S = the specified spending rate

- **Rolling 3-year average spending rule.**

    This modification to the simple spending rule generates a spending amount that equals the spending rate multiplied by an average of the three previous years' market value of endowment assets. The idea is to reduce the volatility of what the portfolio must distribute and of what the sponsor will receive and can spend:

    $$\text{spending}_t = \left(\text{spending rate}\right)\left(\frac{\text{market value}_{t-1} + \text{market value}_{t-2} + \text{market value}_{t-3}}{3}\right)$$

- **Geometric spending rule.**

    The rolling 3-year rule can occasionally produce unfortunate consequences. Consider a case of dramatic, steady decline in market value for three years. It would require a high distribution in relation to current market value. The geometric spending rule gives some smoothing but less weight to older periods. It weights the prior year's spending level adjusted for inflation by a smoothing rate, which is usually between 0.6 and 0.8, as well as the previous year's beginning-of-period portfolio value:

    $$\text{spending}_t = (R)(\text{spending}_{t-1})(1 + I_{t-1}) + (1 - R)(S)(\text{market value}_{t-1})$$

    where:
    R = smoothing rate
    I = rate of inflation
    S = spending rate

Endowment Objectives

Risk. Risk tolerance for an endowment is affected by the institution's dependence on funding from the endowment portfolio to meet its annual operating budget. Generally, if the endowment provides a significant portion of the institution's budget, ability to tolerate risk is diminished. The endowment is concerned not only with portfolio volatility but also spending volatility. (The real purpose of the smoothing rules is to allow more risk and portfolio volatility but smooth distributions to the institution, allowing the institution to better plan and budget.)

Because the time horizon for endowments is usually infinite, the risk tolerance of most endowments is relatively high. The need to meet spending requirements and keep up with inflation can make higher risk appropriate.

Like a foundation, the ultimate decision is up to the board (and manager).

Return. As previously indicated, one of the goals of creating an endowment is to provide a permanent asset base for funding specific activities. Attention to preserving the real purchasing power of the asset base is paramount.

A total return approach is typical. The form of return, income, realized, or unrealized price change is not important. If the return objective is achieved, in the long run the distributions will be covered. It is not necessary in any one year that the amount earned equal the distribution. However the long-term nature also requires the inflation rate be covered (earned as well). The inflation rate used is not necessarily the general inflation rate but should be the rate reflecting the inflation rate relevant to what the endowment spends. For example if the spending for health care is the objective and health care inflation is 6%, use 6%.

While it is typical to add the spending rate, relevant inflation rate, and an expense rate if specified, others argue for using the higher compound calculation. Monte Carlo simulation can analyze path dependency and multiple time periods to shed some light on this issue. For example if the asset value declines and the spending amount is fixed, the distribution disproportionately reduces the size of the portfolio available. This suggests the return target be set somewhat higher than is conventionally done.

Endowment Constraints

Time horizon. Because the purpose of most endowment funds is to provide a permanent source of funding, the time horizon for endowment funds is typically perpetual.

Liquidity requirements. The liquidity requirements of an endowment are usually low. Only emergency needs and current spending require liquidity. However, large outlays (e.g., capital improvements) may require higher levels of liquidity.

Tax considerations. Endowments are generally tax exempt. There are exceptions and these might occur and be described in a given situation. In the United States, some assets generate unrelated business income. In that case, Unrelated Business Income Tax

(UBIT) may have to be paid. If a case does include details on taxation, note this as a tax constraint and consider the after-tax return of that asset.

Legal and regulatory considerations. Regulation is limited. Foundations and endowments have broad latitude to set and pursue their objectives. In the United States, 501(c)(3) tax regulations require earnings from tax-exempt entities not be used for private individuals. Most states have adopted the Uniform Management Institutional Fund Act (UMIFA) of 1972 as the governing regulation for endowments. If no specific legal considerations are stated in the case, for U.S. entities, state UMIFA applies. Other countries may have other laws.

Unique circumstances. Due to their diversity, endowment funds have many unique circumstances. Social issues (e.g., defense policies and racial biases) are typically taken into consideration when deciding upon asset allocation. The long-term nature of endowments and many foundations have lead to significant use of alternative investments. The cost and complexity of these assets should be considered. They generally require active management expertise.

INSURANCE COMPANIES

Insurance companies sell policies that promise a payment to the policyholder if a covered event occurs during the life (term, period of coverage) of the policy. With life insurance that event would be the death of the beneficiary. With automobile insurance that might be an accident to the automobile. In exchange for insurance coverage the policyholder pays the insurer a payment (premium). Those funds are invested till needed for payouts and to earn a return for the company.

Historically there were **stock companies** owned by shareholders seeking to earn a profit for the shareholders and **mutuals** owned by the policyholder and operated only for the benefit of the policyholders. In recent years many mutuals have been **demutualized** and become stock companies.

LIFE INSURANCE COMPANIES

Life insurance companies sell insurance policies that provide a death benefit to those designated on the policy when the covered individual dies. A variety of types of life insurance exist that may have different time horizons and liquidity needs. It is common to segregate the investment portfolio by type of policy (line of business) and invest to match the needs of that product. Some of the important policy types and implications for portfolio management include:

- **Whole life or ordinary life** generally requires a level payment of premiums over multiple years to the company and provides a fixed payoff amount at the death of the policyholder. These policies often include a cash value allowing the policyholder to terminate the policy and receive that cash value. Alternatively the policyholder may be able to borrow the cash value. The cash value builds up over the life of the policy at a **crediting rate**.

    There are portfolio implications to these features. The company faces competitive pressure to offer higher crediting rates to attract customers, which creates a need for higher return on the portfolio. In addition, **disintermediation risk** occurs during periods of high interest rates when policyholders are more likely to withdraw cash value causing increased demand for liquidity from the portfolio. High rates are also likely to be associated with depressed market values in the portfolio. While duration of whole life is usually long, the combination of policy features and volatile interest rates makes the duration and time horizon of the liabilities more difficult to predict. Overall, competitive market factors and volatile interest rates have led to shortening the time horizon and duration of the investment portfolio.

- **Term life** insurance usually provides insurance coverage on a year by year basis leading to very short duration assets to fund the short duration liability.
- **Variable life**, **universal life**, and **variable universal life** usually include a cash value build up and insurance (like whole life), but the cash value buildup is linked to investment returns. The features are less likely to trigger early cash withdrawals but increase the need to earn competitive returns on the portfolio to retain and attract new customers.

Life Insurance Company Objectives

Risk. Public policy views insurance company investment portfolios as *quasi-trust funds*. Having the ability to pay death benefits when due is a critical concern. The National Association of Insurance Commissioners (NAIC) directs life insurance companies to maintain an asset valuation reserve (AVR) as a cushion against substantial losses of portfolio value or investment income. Worldwide the movement is towards risk-based capital, which requires the company to have more capital (and less financial leverage) the riskier the assets in the portfolio.

- **Valuation risk** and ALM will figure prominently in any discussion of risk, and interest rate risk will be the prime issue. Any mismatch between duration of assets and of liabilities will make the surplus highly volatile as the change in value of the assets will not track the change in value of liabilities when rates change. The result is the duration of assets will be closely tied to the duration of liabilities.
- **Reinvestment risk** will be important for some products. For example, annuity products (sometimes called guaranteed investment contracts or GICS) pay a fixed amount at a maturity date. (Effectively they are like a zero-coupon bond issued by the company.) The company must invest the premium and build sufficient value to pay off at maturity. As most assets in the portfolio will be coupon-bearing securities, the accumulated value in the portfolio will also depend on the reinvestment rate as the coupon cash flow comes into the portfolio.

ALM is the prime tool for controlling both of these risks. The risk objective will typically state the need to match asset and liability duration or closely control any mismatch.

Other risk issues are:

- **Cash flow volatility.** Life insurance companies have a low tolerance for any loss of income or delays in collecting income from investment activities. Reinvesting interest on cash flow coming in is a major component of return over long periods. Most companies seek investments that offer minimum cash flow volatility.

- **Credit risk.** Credit quality is associated with the ability of the issuers of debt to pay interest and principal when due. Credit analysis is required to gauge potential losses of investment income and has been one of the industry's strong points. Controlling credit risk is a major concern for life insurance companies and is often managed through a broadly diversified portfolio.

Traditionally life insurance company portfolios were conservatively invested but business competition increases the pressure to find higher returns.

Return. Traditionally insurance companies focused on a minimum return equal to the actuaries' assumed rate of growth in policyholder reserves. This is essentially the growth rate needed to meet projected policy payouts. Earn less and the surplus will decline. More desirable is to earn a **net interest spread**, a return higher than the actuarial assumption. Consistent higher returns would grow the surplus and give the company competitive advantage in offering products to the market at a lower price (i.e., lower premiums).

While it is theoretically desirable to look at total return it can be difficult to do in the insurance industry. Regulation generally requires liabilities to be shown at some version of book value. Valuing assets at market value but liabilities at book value can create unintended consequences.

The general thrust is to segment the investment portfolio by significant line of business and set objectives by the characteristics of that line of business. The investments are heavily fixed-income oriented with an exception. The surplus may pursue more aggressive objectives such as stock, real estate, and private equity.

Life Insurance Company Constraints

Liquidity. Volatility and changes in the marketplace have increased the attention life insurance companies pay to liquidity issues. There are two key issues:

- Companies must consider **disintermediation risk** as previously discussed. This has led to shorter durations, higher liquidity reserves, and closer ALM matching. Duration and disintermediation issues can be interrelated. Consider a company with asset duration exceeding liability duration. If interest rates rise, asset value will decline faster than liability value. If the company needs to sell assets to fund payouts it would be doing so at relatively low values and likely a loss on the asset sale. A mismatch of duration compounds the problem of disintermediation.
- **Asset marketability risk** has also become a larger consideration. Traditionally life insurance companies held relatively large portions of the portfolio in illiquid assets. The increased liquidity demands on the portfolios have lead to greater emphasis on liquid assets.

The growth of derivatives has lead many companies to look for derivative-based risk management solutions.

Time horizon. Traditionally long at 20–40 years, it has become shorter for all the reasons discussed previously. Segmentation and duration matching by line of business is the norm.

Tax considerations. Life insurance companies are taxable entities. Laws vary by country but often the return up to the actuarial assumed rate is tax free and above that is taxed. The reality is quite complex and tax laws are changing. Ultimately after-tax return is the objective.

> *Professor's Note: Again remember the CFA exam does not teach or presume you are a tax or legal expert. Only state what you are taught and remember if a case brings up complex issues to state the need to seek qualified advice. Candidates are expected to know when to seek help, not to know what the advice will be. Hint: for the legal constraint for insurance companies, generally state complex and extensive.*

Legal and regulatory constraints. Life insurance companies are heavily regulated. In the United States, it is primarily at the state level. These regulations are very complex and may not be consistent by regulator. Regulations often address the following:

- **Eligible investments** by asset class are defined and percentage limits on holdings are generally stated. Criteria such as the minimum interest coverage ratio on corporate bonds are frequently specified.
- In the United States, the **prudent investor rule** has been adopted by some states. This replaces the list of eligible investments approach discussed in the bullet above in favor of portfolio risk versus return. (Essentially modern portfolio theory as the risk is portfolio risk including correlation effects).
- Valuations methods are commonly specified (and are some version of book value accounting). Because the regulators do consider these valuations, it limits the ability to focus on market value and total return of the portfolio.

These regulatory issues do significantly affect the eligible investment for and the asset allocation of the portfolio.

Unique circumstances. Concentration of product offerings, company size, and level of surplus are some of the most common factors impacting each company.

Non-Life Insurance Companies

> *Professor's Note: Non-life companies include health, property and casualty, and surety companies. Treat them like life companies except where specific differences are discussed.*

Non-life insurance is very similar to life insurance. ALM is crucial to both. It differs from life insurance in a several areas:

- While the product mix is more diverse, the liability durations are shorter. The typical policy covers one year of insurance.
- However there is often a **long tail** to the policy. A claim could be filed and take years to process before payout. Think of a contentious claim that is litigated for years before payout.

- Many non-life policies have **inflation risk**. The company may insure replacement value of the insured item creating less certain and higher payoffs on claims. In contrast life insurance policies are typically for a stated face value.
- Life insurance payouts are generally very predictable in amount but harder to predict in timing. Non-life is hard to predict in both dimensions of amount and timing.
- Non-life insurers have an **underwriting or profitability cycle**. Company pricing of policies typically varies over a 3- to 5-year cycle. During periods of intense business competition, prices on insurance are reduced to retain business. Frequently the prices are set too low and lead to losses as payouts on the policies occur. The company then must liquidate portfolio assets to supplement cash flow.
- Non-life business risk can be very concentrated geographically or with regard to specific events (which will be discussed under risk).

The conclusion will be that the operating results for non-life insurance companies are more volatile than for life insurance companies, duration is shorter, liquidity needs are both larger and less predictable.

Non-Life Insurance Company Objectives

Risk. Like life companies, non-life companies have a quasi-fiduciary requirement and must be invested to meet policy claims. However, the payoffs on claims are less predictable. For example a company that insures property in a specific area that is then hit with severe weather can experience sudden high claims and payouts. Also there is inflation risk if the payout is based on replacement cost of the insured item. Key considerations are:

1. The *cash flow characteristics* of non-life companies are often erratic and unpredictable. Hence, risk tolerance, as it pertains to loss of principal and declining investment income, is quite low.

2. The *common stock-to-surplus ratio* has been changing. Traditionally the surplus might have been invested in stock. Poor stock market returns in the 1970s and regulator concerns lead to reduced stock holdings. Bull markets in the 1990s only partially reversed this trend.

 Professor's Note: The underlying issue is that the non-life business is both cyclical and erratic in profitability and cash flow. The investment portfolio seeks to smooth profitability and provide for unpredictable liquidity needs. Unfortunately there is no obvious way to do this.

Return. Historically a non-life company acted like two separate companies, an insurance company and an investment company. Investment returns were not factored into calculating policy premiums charged for insurance. Things have changed but there is still a mix of factors affecting the return requirement: the competitive pricing of the insurance product, need for profitability, growth of surplus, tax issues, and total return.

Complicating factors impacting non-life insurance company return objectives that do not arise for life insurance companies include:

- **Competitive pricing policy.** High-return objectives allow the company to charge lower policy premiums and attract more business, but when high returns are earned the companies tend to cut premiums. (Essentially this is the underwriting cycle).
- **Profitability.** Investment income and return on the investment portfolio are primary determinants of company profitability. They also provide stability to offset the less stable underwriting cycle of swings in policy pricing. The company seeks to maximize return on the capital and surplus consistent with appropriate ALM.
- **Growth of surplus.** Higher returns increase the company's surplus. This allows the company to expand the amount of insurance it can issue. Alternative investments, common stocks, and convertibles have been used to seek surplus growth.
- **After-tax returns.** Non-life insurance companies are taxable entities and seek after-tax return. At one time differential taxation rules in the United States led to advantages in holding tax-exempt bonds and dividend paying stocks. Changes in regulation have reduced this.
- **Total return.** Active portfolio management and total return are the general focus for at least some of the portfolio. Interestingly the returns earned across companies are quite varied. This reflects wider latitude by non-life regulators, a more varied product mix, varying tax situations, varying emphasis in managing for total return or for income, and differing financial strength of the companies.

Non-Life Insurance Company Constraints

Liquidity needs are high given the uncertain business profitability and cash flow needs. The company typically 1) holds significant money market securities such as T-bills and commercial paper, 2) holds a laddered portfolio of highly liquid government bonds, and 3) matches assets against known cash flow needs.

Time horizon is affected by two factors. It is generally short due to the short duration of the liabilities.

However, there can be a subsidiary issue to consider in the United States. The asset duration (time horizon) tends to cycle with swings from loss to profit in the underwriting cycle and decreasing or increasing use of tax-exempt bonds. In periods of loss, the company will use taxable bonds and owe no taxes. When profitable, the company may switch to tax-exempt bonds but the tax-exempt bonds generally have a very steep yield curve. There is a strong incentive to purchase longer maturities for better yield.

Tax considerations. Non-life insurance companies are taxable entities. Applicable tax rules in the United States have been changing. After-tax return is the objective.

Legal and regulatory constraints. Regulatory considerations are less onerous for non-life insurance companies than for life insurance companies. An asset valuation reserve (AVR) is not required, but risk-based capital (RBC) requirements have been established. Non-life companies are given considerable leeway in choosing investments compared to life insurance companies.

Unique circumstances. There are no generalizations to make.

Conclusion

The portfolio is first structured for liquidity needs. A portfolio of bonds and stocks is used to increase return. The management of the portfolio must be coordinated with the company's business needs.

BANKS

> **For the Exam:** A bank IPS is somewhat unique. It is driven by the fundamentals of the banking business and derives from the role of the investment portfolio in that business. This review is not really about managing a bank portfolio but about the IPS. It may not reflect the approach of every bank, but it is the approach for exam questions.

The objectives and constraints of a bank's securities portfolio derive from its place in the overall asset liability structure of the bank. Banks are in business to take in deposits (liabilities), make loans (assets), and make a profit primarily from a spread off the interest earned on assets less paid on liabilities. A potential problem exists in the relationship between a bank's assets and liabilities. Liabilities are mostly in the form of short-term deposits, while assets (loans) can be fairly long term in nature and illiquid. The loans also generally offer returns higher than can be earned on the securities in which banks invest and are riskier. This leads to a significant mismatch in asset-liability durations, liquidity, and quality.

The bank's security portfolio is a residual use of funds (i.e., excess funds that have not been loaned out or are required to be held as reserves against deposits). While it is desirable to earn an attractive return on the portfolio, the primary purpose of the securities portfolio is to address the mismatch of liabilities (deposits) and the primary assets (loans).

Duration, Credit Risk, Income, and Liquidity

It is generally easier and timelier to adjust the characteristics of the investment portfolio than it is to adjust the characteristics of the liabilities or of the other assets (the loans). Generally the investment portfolio manager adjusts the bank's investment portfolio duration such that overall **asset duration** is kept in the desired relationship to **liability duration**.

In theory if a manager forecasts increasing interest rates, she can decrease the duration of the portfolio to set the overall asset duration below the liability duration. If the interest rate prediction is correct, the assets will decline less than the liabilities for an economic gain. The reality is this is very risky and is not done or done in very limited fashion for banks. Bank leverage is very high with very low equity capital to assets. Thus the primary goal is to adjust the duration of the portfolio such that overall duration of assets matches liability duration.

In addition to duration management, a bank uses its security portfolio to manage the **credit risk** and **diversification** of its assets. For example, a bank's loans can become geographically concentrated. To offset the associated credit risk and lack of diversification, management can minimize the credit risk and maximize diversification using the securities portfolio.

Loans are relatively illiquid and the investment portfolio will emphasize very liquid securities to compensate. In general the bank investment portfolio is heavily or exclusively short-term government securities.

Lastly, the bank securities portfolios can generate **income** for the bank, but this should be a consideration after the other items discussed here have been addressed.

Bank Risk Measures

> *Professor's Note: Banks are heavily regulated and the regulators define various reporting measures for the bank. Following is a brief discussion of some of them. VAR is discussed extensively in other parts of the curriculum and is a common source of questions.*

 Leverage adjusted duration gap (LADG) receives only a passing comment in the CFA text and no math is covered. It is just duration of assets versus liabilities taking into account that they will not be of equal size. The concept of asset versus liability duration is asset liability management (ALM), and it is very important on the exam. LADG is just a specialized application of ALM used by some bank regulators.

Both assets and liabilities are sensitive to changing interest rates. Banks must continually monitor their interest rate risk. Value at risk (VAR) is one commonly used tool. Regulators often define and specify calculation methodology, set minimum target levels, and impose restrictions if targets are not met.

Leverage-adjusted duration gap is another such regulatory tool. It is defined as the duration of the bank's assets less the *leveraged* duration of the bank's liabilities:

$$\text{LADG} = D_{assets} - \left(\frac{L}{A}\right) D_{liabilities}$$

where:
LADG = leverage adjusted duration gap
D_{assets} = duration of the bank's assets
$D_{liabilities}$ = duration of the bank's liabilities
$\dfrac{L}{A}$ = leverage measure (market value of liabilities over market value of assets)

LADG should predict the theoretical change in fair market value of bank equity capital if interest rates change. If LADG is:

- Zero, equity should be unaffected by interest rate changes.
- Positive, equity change is inverse to rates (e.g., rates up equity down).
- Negative, equity value moves in the same direction as rates.

The Bank IPS

Bank Objectives

Risk. The acceptable risk should be set in an ALM framework based on the effect on the overall bank balance sheet. Banks usually have a below-average risk tolerance because they cannot let losses in the security portfolio interfere with their ability to meet their liabilities.

Return. The return objective for the bank securities portfolio is to earn a positive interest spread. The interest spread is the difference between the bank's cost of funds and the interest earned on loans and other investments.

Bank Constraints

Liquidity. A bank's liquidity needs are driven by deposit withdrawals and demand for loans as well as regulation. The resulting portfolio is generally short and liquid.

Time horizon. The time horizon is short and linked to the duration of the liabilities.

Taxes. Banks are taxable entities. After-tax return is the objective.

Legal and regulatory. Banks in industrialized nations are highly regulated. Risk-based capital (RBC) guidelines require banks to establish RBC reserves against assets; the riskier the asset, the higher the required capital. This tilts the portfolio towards high-quality, short-term, liquid assets.

Unique. There are no particular general issues.

Asset/Liability Management for Institutional Investors

LOS 15.m: Compare the asset/liability management needs of pension funds, foundations, endowments, insurance companies, and banks.

CFA® Program Curriculum, Volume 2, page 439

ALM is the preferred framework for evaluation portfolios with definable, measurable liabilities. Focusing on asset return and risk is not sufficient. The focus should be on surplus and surplus volatility. At a minimum, asset and liability duration should be matched to stabilize surplus. Depending on risk tolerance, active management through defined deviations in asset and liability duration might be used to exploit expected changes in interest rates.

Hint: this is discussed in multiple study sessions and perhaps best covered in fixed income with numeric calculations.

DB pension plans, insurance companies, and banks are the most suited to the ALM approach.

INVESTMENT COMPANIES

LOS 15.k: Contrast investment companies, commodity pools, and hedge funds to other types of institutional investors.

CFA® Program Curriculum, Volume 2, page 498

The institutional portfolios discussed up to now manage money for a particular entity (e.g., a bank or an insurance company). Categorizing by group offers useful insights. All DB plans have similarities in their objectives and share common issues of analysis. In contrast, **investment companies**, **commodity pools**, and **hedge funds** are institutional investors but are just intermediaries that pool and invest money for groups of investors and pass the returns through to those investors. Unlike other institutional investors it is not possible to generalize about their policy statements.

- **Investment companies** are **mutual funds** and invest in accord with their prospectus. There are mutual funds, for example, to fit just about any equity or fixed-income investment style, from small-cap growth funds to large-cap value funds to funds that invest exclusively in one of a variety of sectors or industries.
- **Commodity pools** invest in commodity-related futures, options contracts, and related instruments.
- **Hedge funds** are highly diverse. Grouping all hedge fund types under the same general heading explains virtually nothing about what each fund does. Hedge funds gather money from institutional and wealthy individual investors and construct various investment strategies aimed at identifying and capitalizing on mispriced securities.

All three of these pool money from a group of investors and pursue the stated objective of the portfolio.

INVESTMENT POLICIES OF INSTITUTIONAL INVESTORS

LOS 15.l: <u>Discuss</u> the factors that determine investment policy for pension funds, foundations, endowments, life and nonlife insurance companies, and banks.

LOS 15.n: <u>Compare</u> the investment objectives and constraints of institutional investors given relevant data, such as descriptions of their financial circumstances and attitudes toward risk.

CFA® Program Curriculum, Volume 2, pages 436, 437

LOS 15.l and 15.n are summarized in Figure 2.

Figure 2: Factors Affecting Investment Policies of Institutional Investors

			Institutional Investor Type			
IPS Component	*Defined-Benefit Plans*	*Foundations*	*Endowment Funds*	*Life Insurance Companies*	*Non-Life Insurance Companies*	*Commercial Banks*
Objectives *Return*	Actuarial rate. A capital gains focus when the fund has low liquidity needs and younger workers. An income focus (duration matching) when there are high liquidity needs and older workers.	Private foundations must generate 5% plus management expenses plus inflation. Total return is appropriate.	Total return approach. The return objective must be balanced between a need for high current income and long-term protection of principal.	*Fixed-income segment:* "spread management" and actuarial assumptions. *Surplus segment:* capital gains.	*Fixed income:* maximize the return for meeting claims. *Equity segment:* grow the surplus/ supplement funds for liability claims.	Return is determined by the cost of funds. Primarily concerned with earning a positive interest rate spread.
Risk Tolerance	Depends on surplus, age of workforce, time horizon, and company balance sheet.	Moderate to high, depending on spending rate and time horizon.	Moderate to high, depending on spending needs.	*Fixed-income segment:* conservative. *Surplus segment:* aggressive.	*Fixed-income segment:* conservative. *Surplus segment:* aggressive.	Banks are primarily concerned with meeting their liabilities and other liquidity needs and cannot suffer losses in the securities portfolio. Tend to have below-average risk tolerance.

Figure 2: Factors Affecting Investment Policies of Institutional Investors (Continued)

		Institutional Investor Type					
	IPS Component	*Defined-Benefit Plans*	*Foundations*	*Endowment Funds*	*Life Insurance Companies*	*Non-Life Insurance Companies*	*Commercial Banks*
Constraints	*Liquidity*	Depends on age of workforce and retired lives proportion.	Some hold a percentage of annual distribution amount as a cash reserve.	Some hold a percentage of annual distribution amount as a cash reserve.	*Fixed-income portion:* relatively high. *Surplus segment:* nil.	*Fixed-income portion:* relatively high. *Surplus segment:* nil.	Liquidity is also relative to liabilities. Banks need continuing liquidity for liabilities and new loans.
	Time Horizon	Long if going concern. Short if terminating plan.	Long, usually infinite.	Long, usually infinite.	Getting shorter.	Short due to the nature of claims.	Time horizon tends to be short to intermediate because of mostly short-term liabilities.
	Legal Regulatory	ERISA/ prudent expert rule.*	Few. Prudent investor rule applies.	Low. Prudent investor rule typically applies.	High, especially on the state level/prudent investor rule.	Moderate, but increasing/ prudent investor rule.	Must meet regulatory requirements for liquidity, reserves, and pledging. Usually with short-term treasuries.
	Taxes	None	Few	None	High	High	Banks are taxable entities, so taxes must be considered.
	Unique Needs	Surplus, age of workforce, time horizon, and company balance sheet affect policy.	Foundation specific. Moral/ ethical concerns may restrict certain securities.	Restrictions on certain securities/ asset classes common due to nature of funds.	Must distinguish between strategies for the fixed-income segment and the surplus segment.	The financial status of the firm; the management of investment risk and liquidity requirements influence IPS.	Varies from bank to bank. May need to use securities portfolio as diversification tool and/or to provide liquidity.

*The *prudent investor rule* requires a fiduciary to "prudently" invest trust assets as if they were his own based on the knowledge the fiduciary has at the time and considering only the needs of the trust's beneficiaries.

The *prudent expert rule* requires that the fiduciary manage the portfolio with the care, skill, prudence, and diligence, under the circumstances then prevailing, that a prudent investor would use. It extends the prudent investor rule beyond prudence by suggesting a higher level of expertise.

KEY CONCEPTS

LOS 15.a

Plan Type	Advantages to the Employee	Advantages to the Firm	Disadvantages to the Employee	Disadvantages to the Firm
Defined Benefit	No investment risk. Stable retirement income.	Possible pension income. Ability to support stock with some investment in company stock.	Early termination risk. Usually a vesting period. Restricted withdrawal of funds. Adverse affect on diversification because both job and pension are linked to health of employer.	Investment risk. Regular funding obligation. Early retirement and other options can increase liquidity requirements. Highly regulated by governments. Extra resources needed to fulfill due diligence.
Defined Contribution	Own all personal contributions. Once vested, own all sponsor contributions. Assets easily transferred to another plan. Can diversify portfolio to suit needs. Lowers taxable income.	No financial liability other than matching provisions. No investment risk. Lower liquidity requirements. Fewer resources required. Fewer regulations.	Investment risk. Must monitor and make necessary reallocation decisions. Restricted withdrawal of funds.	Usually legally required to have an IPS that addresses how the plan will help participants meet their objectives and constraints (e.g., types and number of investment alternatives, advice).

LOS 15.b

The two objectives are:
- Risk.
- Return.

The five constraints are:
- Time horizon.
- Taxes.
- Liquidity.
- Legal and regulatory factors.
- Unique circumstances.

In determining the investment objectives, it is helpful to first determine the plan sponsor's risk tolerance before the determination of the return objective. Pension plans are typically tax exempt.

LOS 15.c

Underfunded plans indicate a liability funding shortfall. Although there may be a willingness to take greater investment risk, the underfunded status dictates a decreased ability to take risk.

Sponsor financial status can be indicated by the sponsor's balance sheet. Profitability can be indicated by the sponsor's current or pro forma financials. Lower debt ratios and higher current and expected profitability indicate better capability of meeting pension liabilities and, therefore, imply greater ability to take risk. The opposite is also true.

Common risk exposure is measured by the correlation between the firm's operating characteristics and pension asset returns. The higher the correlation between firm's operations and pension asset returns, the lower the risk tolerance. The opposite is also true.

Plan features offer participants the option of either retiring early or receiving lump-sum payments from their retirement benefits. Plans that offer early retirement or lump-sum payments essentially decrease the time horizon of the retirement liability and increase the liquidity requirements of the plan. Therefore, the ability to assume risk is decreased.

Workforce characteristics relate to the age of the workforce and the ratio of active lives to retired lives. In general, the younger the workforce, the greater the ratio of active to retired lives will be. This increases the ability to take risk when managing pension assets. The opposite is also true.

LOS 15.d

IPS for Defined-Benefit Plan

Return: Minimum return requirement is determined by actuarial rate. If liquidity needs are low and workers young, use a capital gains focus; for high-liquidity needs and older workers, use an income focus (duration matching). Also consider the number of retirees the plan must support.

Risk tolerance: Depends on surplus, age of workforce, time horizon, and company balance sheet. For example, a surplus indicates a higher risk tolerance.

Liquidity: Consider the age of workforce and retired lives population. Income is required to meet payments to retirees, but contributions are available for longer-term investments.

Time horizon: Same as for liquidity. In addition, the horizon is long if the plan is a going concern but short if it is a terminating plan.

Taxes: Usually tax exempt.

Legal/regulatory: ERISA and the prudent expert rule apply. The plan must be managed for the sole benefit of plan participants.

Unique circumstances: Could include insufficient resources to perform due diligence on complex investments, special financial concerns related to the sponsor firm or the fund, socially responsible investing requirements, et cetera.

LOS 15.e

If the performance of the plan assets and firm operations are highly correlated:

- When pension assets are generating high returns with high operating profits, the probability of the firm having to make a contribution is low. If a contribution is necessary, the amount will be low. The ability to make contributions is high when the plan is fully funded or overfunded. Therefore, the fund is better able to meet benefit payments, which positively impacts firm valuation due to a lowered negative pension expense.
- When pension assets are generating low returns with low operating profits, the probability of the firm having to make a pension contribution is high. The firm's ability to make contributions is low at the same time that the plan is underfunded. An underfunded status means that there is a decreased ability to meet retirement payments, which negatively impacts firm valuation due to increased pension expense.

LOS 15.f

In a defined-contribution plan, the plan employer does not establish the investment goals and constraints; rather, the employee decides her own risk and return objectives. Therefore, the employee bears the risk of the investment results. Consequently, the investment policy statement (IPS) for a defined-contribution plan describes the investment alternatives available to the plan participants. This IPS becomes a document of governing principles instead of an IPS for an individual. Some of the issues addressed in the IPS would be:

- Making a distinction between the responsibilities of the plan participants, the fund managers, and the plan sponsor.
- Providing descriptions of the investment alternatives available to the plan participants.
- Providing criteria for monitoring and evaluation of the performance of the investment choices.
- Providing criteria for selection, termination, and replacement of investment choices.
- Establishing effective communication between the fund managers, plan participants, and the plan sponsor.

LOS 15.g

A cash balance plan is a defined-benefit plan that defines the benefit in terms of an account balance, which the beneficiary can take as an annuity at retirement or as a lump sum to roll into another plan. In a typical cash balance plan, a participant's account is credited each year with a pay credit and an interest credit. The pay credit is typically based upon the beneficiary's age, salary, and/or length of employment, and the interest credit is based upon a benchmark such as U.S. Treasuries. Rather than an actual account with a balance, the cash balance is a paper balance only and represents a future liability for the company.

An employee stock ownership plan (ESOP) is a type of defined-contribution benefit plan that allows employees to purchase the company stock. The purchase can be with before- or after-tax dollars and the final balance in the beneficiary's account reflects the increase in the value of the firm's stock as well as contributions during employment.

LOS 15.h
Foundations

Type of Foundation	Description	Purpose	Source of Funds	Annual Spending Requirement
Independent	Private or family	Grants to public groups	Individual or family	5% of assets
Company sponsored	By a corporation	Public and company grants	Corporate sponsor	5% of assets
Operating	Established to fund an organization (e.g., museum, zoo, or some ongoing research/medical initiative)	Individual or family	At least 85% of dividend and interest income for operations
Community	Publicly sponsored	Grants to public groups	General public	None

LOS 15.i, j, l, n
Defined-Benefit Plans
Return: Actuarial rate.

Risk tolerance: Depends on surplus, age of workforce, time horizon, and balance sheet.

Liquidity: Depends on age of workforce and retired lives proportion.

Time horizon: Long, if going concern. Short, if terminating plan.

Legal/regulatory: ERISA/prudent expert rule.

Tax considerations: None.

Unique circumstances: Surplus, age of workforce, time horizon, and balance sheet.

Foundation IPS
Return: Depends on time horizon stated for the foundation.

Risk tolerance: Moderate to high, depending on spending rate and time horizon. Usually more aggressive than pension funds.

Liquidity: Some foundations choose to hold a portion of the annual distribution amount as a cash reserve.

Time horizon: Usually infinite.

Tax considerations: Not taxable with the exception on investment income from private foundations in the United States (1%).

Legal/regulatory: Few—many states in the United States have adopted the Uniform Management Institutional Funds Act as the regulatory framework. Prudent investor rule generally applies.

Endowment IPS

Return: Usually funded for the purpose of permanently funding an activity. Preserve asset base and use income generated for budget needs. No specific spending requirement. Balance the need for high current income with long-term protection of principal. Ensure purchasing power is not eroded by inflation. May use total approach or strive to minimize spending level volatility.

Risk tolerance: Linked to relative importance of the fund in the sponsor's overall budget picture. Inversely related to dependence on current income. Exposure to market fluctuation is a major concern. Infinite life means that overall risk tolerance is generally high.

Liquidity: Usually low but may be high if large outlays are expected.

Time horizon: Usually infinite.

Tax considerations: Income is tax exempt.

Legal/regulatory: Few—many states in the United States have adopted the Uniform Management Institutional Funds Act as the regulatory framework. Prudent investor rule generally applies.

Unique needs: Diverse and endowment specific.

Life Insurance Company IPS

Return: Three components: (1) minimum required rate of return—statutory rate set by actuarial assumptions, (2) enhanced margin rates of return or "spread management," and (3) surplus rates of return, where surplus equals total assets – total liabilities.

Risk tolerance: Specific factors include (1) how market volatility adversely impacts asset valuation, (2) a low tolerance of any loss of income or delays in collecting income, (3) reinvestment risk is a major concern, and (4) credit quality is associated with timely payment of income and principal.

Liquidity: There are three primary concerns to address: disintermediation, asset-liability mismatches, and asset marketability risk.

Time horizon: Traditionally 20–40 years but progressively shorter as the duration of liabilities has decreased due to increased interest rate volatility and competitive market factors.

Tax considerations: Taxes are a major consideration. Policyholder's share is not taxed; funds transferred to the surplus are taxed.

Legal/regulatory: Heavily regulated at the state level. Regulations relate to eligible investments, prudent person rule, and valuation methods.

Unique needs: Diversity of product offerings, company size, and level of asset surplus.

Non-Life Insurance Company IPS

Return: Greater uncertainty regarding claims, but they're not as interest rate sensitive. Fixed-income component should maximize the return for meeting claims. Equity segment should grow the surplus/supplement funds for liability claims. Impacted by competitive pricing policy, profitability, growth of surplus, after-tax returns, and total return.

Risk tolerance: Risk must be tempered by the liquidity requirements. Inflation risk is a big concern because of replacement cost policies. Cash flow characteristics are unpredictable. Many companies have self-imposed ceilings on the common stock to surplus ratio.

Liquidity: Relatively high.

Time horizon: Short, due to nature of claims.

Tax considerations: Taxes play an important role—frequent contact with tax counsel is advised.

Legal/regulatory: Considerable leeway in choosing investments. Regulations less onerous than for life insurance companies.

Unique needs: The financial status of the firm and the management of the investment risk and liquidity requirements influence the IPS.

Bank IPS

Return: The return objective for the bank's securities portfolio is primarily to generate a positive interest rate spread.

Risk: The most important concern is meeting liabilities, and the bank cannot let losses in the securities portfolio interfere with that. Therefore, its tolerance for risk is below average.

Time horizon: Bank liabilities are usually fairly short term, so securities in the portfolio should be of short to intermediate maturity/duration.

Liquidity: Because banks require regular liquidity to meet liabilities and new loan requests, the securities must be liquid.

Tax: Banks are taxable entities.

Legal/regulatory: Banks are highly regulated and are required to maintain liquidity, reserve requirements, and pledge against certain deposits.

Unique circumstances: Some potential unique circumstances include lack of diversification or lack of liquidity in the loan portfolio.

LOS 15.m

Pension funds: For a defined-benefit plan, surplus management is key. Managers usually attempt to match durations of assets and liabilities to minimize the volatility of the surplus. Managers always minimize the risk of the asset portfolio while meeting return requirements. For a defined-contribution plan, once annual contributions are met, the sponsor's only remaining obligations are monitoring the plan and providing sufficient investment alternatives for participants. Beneficiaries manage their own assets.

Foundations: Generally have to meet all funding requirements (grants and operating expenses) through investment earnings.

Endowments: Typically, the overall goal is to preserve assets while meeting spending requirements.

Insurance companies: Life and non-life are taxable entities. They segment their general portfolio to match assets to liabilities according to interest rate risk (duration), return, and credit risk.

Banks: The bank's primary objective is meeting its liabilities by earning a positive interest rate spread so that the portfolio allocation is determined using an asset-liability framework.

LOS 15.k

Investment companies, **commodity pools**, and **hedge funds** are institutional investors but are just intermediaries that pool and invest money for underlying investors and pass the returns through to their investors. Unlike other institutional investors it is not possible to generalize about their policy statements.

Investment companies gather funds from investors and invest the pooled funds based upon advertised objectives and constraints.

Commodity pools are similar to mutual funds but invest in pools of commodity futures and options contracts.

Hedge funds gather funds from institutional and wealthy individual investors and construct various investment strategies aimed at identifying and capitalizing on mispriced securities.

In summary, the primary difference between investment companies, commodity pools, and hedge funds and the institutional investors is the source and use of their invested funds. Pension plans, insurance companies, endowments, foundations, and banks all invest their own assets to meet various funding requirements, while the latter group collects funds from investors and invests the funds to meet their investors' needs.

CONCEPT CHECKERS

1. Alexander Ellington, President of Ellington Foods, has contacted your firm to discuss the company's defined-benefit pension plan. He has provided the following information about the company and its pension plan:
    *   Ellington Foods has annual sales of $300 million.
    *   The annual payroll is about $100 million.
    *   The average age of the workforce is 43 years.
    *   30% of the plan participants are now retired.
    *   Company profits last year were $10 million and have been growing at 10% annually. The Ellington Foods pension plan has $80 million in assets and is currently overfunded by 10%.
    *   The duration of the plan's liabilities is 15 years.
    *   The discount rate applied to liabilities is 6%.
    *   Fund trustees wish to maintain 5% of plan assets in cash.

    Ellington would like to achieve a rate of return of 7% on its pension fund (which is less than the 9% that the fund has historically achieved). Ellington would like to be able to reduce contributions to the pension fund and possibly increase employee benefits.

    A. **Formulate** and **justify** investment policy objectives for the Ellington Foods pension plan in the following three areas (use the following template):
        i.   Return objective.
        ii. Risk tolerance.
        iii. Time horizon.

    Template for Question 1A

Investment Policy Statement Elements for Ellington Foods Pension Plan	
Element	Discussion
i. Return objective	
ii. Risk tolerance	
iii. Time horizon	

    B. **State** whether the original allocation to each asset class (as shown in the table) should be lower, the same, or higher for the Ellington Foods pension plan. **Justify** your response with reference to each of the asset classes (use the following template):

Original Allocation
Ellington Foods Pension Plan

Asset Class	Original Allocation (%)	Expected Total Return (%)
T-bills	5	4
U.S. intermediate-term bonds (5-year duration)	30	6
U.S. long-term bonds (20-year duration)	15	7
U.S. equities	50	12
International developed market equities	0	13
Emerging market equities	0	16

Template for Question 1B

Ellington Foods Pension Plan's Asset Allocation			
Asset Class and Original Allocation	**Circle the change (lower/same/higher) and justify your response. STATE YOUR ASSUMPTIONS CLEARLY.**		
U.S. Treasury bills (5%)	LOWER	SAME	HIGHER
U.S. intermediate-term bonds (5-year duration) (30%)	LOWER	SAME	HIGHER
U.S. long-term bonds (20-year duration) (15%)	LOWER	SAME	HIGHER
U.S. equities (50%)	LOWER	SAME	HIGHER
Developed market equities (0%)	LOWER	SAME	HIGHER
Emerging market equities (0%)	LOWER	SAME	HIGHER

2. Ellington appreciated your advice but decided to handle the situation "in house." The company also decided to stay with the original allocation. Assume ten years have passed and Ellington has returned to you for advice. The average age of the workforce is now 51 years. Sixty percent of the plan participants are now retired. The duration of the plan's liabilities is four years. The fund is currently underfunded by 20%. The discount rate applied to the liabilities is 9%. Company profits have been in decline for the past two years but are expected to turn around in the upcoming year. Given the updated information:

    A. **Formulate** and **justify** investment policy objectives for the Ellington Foods Pension Plan in the following three areas (use the following template):
        i.   Return objective.
        ii. Risk tolerance.
        iii. Time horizon.

    Template for Question 2A

Investment Policy Statement Elements Ellington Foods Pension Plan	
Element	**Discussion**
i. Return objective	
ii. Risk tolerance	
iii. Time horizon	

3. **Describe** a defined-contribution pension plan. Be sure to **discuss** all aspects of such a plan.

4. Aid to the Homeless is a nonprofit organization that provides funding throughout the Washington D.C. area to run shelters for the homeless. The Cassidy Endowment Fund provides a large portion of the Aid to the Homeless's operating budget. The endowment fund was set up by the Cassidy family as a way to leave a legacy to their father. He was a wealthy entrepreneur throughout his lifetime but suffered from dementia in old age and consequently lived out his last days wandering the streets of D.C. as a homeless person. The fund has assets totaling $5 million, and directors of the endowment anticipate a spending rate of 6%. Inflation is expected to be 3% annually.

A. **Formulate** and **justify** investment policy objectives for the Cassidy Endowment Fund in the following three areas (use the following template):
   i. Return objective.
   ii. Risk tolerance.
   iii. Time horizon.

Template for Question 4A

Investment Policy Statement Elements Cassidy Endowment Fund	
Element	Discussion
i. Return objective	
ii. Risk tolerance	
iii. Time horizon	

B. From the following asset allocations, **select** the one allocation that best serves the needs of the Endowment Fund and **justify** its selection by maximizing the following three criteria simultaneously (use the following template):
  i.   Return objective.
  ii. Diversification.
  iii. Efficiency.

Asset Classes	Expected Total Return	Cash Flow Yield	Portfolios			
			A	B	C	D
U.S. stocks	12%	2.0%	20%	40%	35%	20%
Non-U.S. stocks	15%	1.5%	15%	20%	15%	0%
U.S. corporate bonds	8%	8.0%	20%	0%	25%	40%
U.S. Treasury bonds	7%	7.0%	5%	0%	20%	35%
Real estate	10%	4.0%	10%	20%	0%	0%
U.S. Treasury bills	4%	4.0%	30%	20%	5%	5%
Expected total return			8.8%	10.6%	10.1%	8.3%
Expected yield (cash flow)			4.2%	2.7%	4.5%	6.3%
Sharpe measure			0.20	0.21	0.26	0.27

Template for Question 4B

Investment Policy Statement Elements Cassidy Endowment Fund	
Selected Portfolio	Discussion
	Return objectives:
	Diversification:
	Efficiency:

5. U.S.-based Liles Insurance Company has recently decided to segment its portfolio into those assets used to meet liabilities and those assets considered surplus. George Baxter, CFO, has drafted his proposal for the asset allocation for the surplus portfolio, which appears below. He has contacted your firm to establish an IPS and to review the proposed asset allocation for its surplus portfolio. The surplus portfolio contains $200 million of the firm's $800 million in total assets.

Proposed Allocation—Liles Life Insurance Surplus Portfolio

Asset Class	Proposed Allocation (%)	Expected Return (%)
Cash	10	4
U.S. intermediate bonds (5-year duration)	5	6
U.S. long-term bonds (20-year duration)	45	7
U.S. equities	25	12
Developed market equities	15	13
Equity REITs	0	14
Venture capital	0	22

A. **Formulate** and **justify** investment policy objectives and constraints for Liles Insurance Company Surplus Portfolio in the following three areas (use the template for Question 5A):
    i.   Return objective.
    ii. Risk tolerance.
    iii. Liquidity requirements.

Template for Question 5A

Investment Policy Statement Elements Liles Insurance Company Surplus Portfolio	
Element	Discussion
i. Return objective	
ii. Risk tolerance	
iii. Liquidity requirements	

B. **State** whether the current allocation to each asset class as shown in the
previous table should be lower, the same, or higher for the Surplus Portfolio
of Liles Insurance Company. **Justify** your response with reference to each of
the asset classes (use the template for Question 5B):

Template for Question 5B

Liles Insurance Company Surplus Portfolio Asset Allocation		
Asset Class and Original Allocation	**Circle the change (lower/same/higher) and justify your response. STATE YOUR ASSUMPTIONS CLEARLY.**	
Cash (10%)	LOWER SAME HIGHER	
U.S. intermediate-term bonds (5-year duration) (5%)	LOWER SAME HIGHER	
U.S. long-term bonds (20-year duration) (45%)	LOWER SAME HIGHER	
U.S. equities (25%)	LOWER SAME HIGHER	
Developed market equities (15%)	LOWER SAME HIGHER	
Equity REITS (0%)	LOWER SAME HIGHER	
Venture capital (0%)	LOWER SAME HIGHER	

6.   The asset-liability management committee (ALCO) for First Southern Piedmont Bank (FSPB) will implement an IPS and oversee its securities portfolios. Based in Southern North Carolina, nearly 80% of FSPB's loans are in or around the Winston-Salem area. There has been an influx of deposits lately and a reduction in the demand for new loans, and managers are finding themselves with a considerable amount of excess cash. From the information provided, construct an appropriate IPS, including *two* objectives and *five* constraints for FSPB's securities portfolio.

ANSWERS – CONCEPT CHECKERS

1. A. Investment policy statement elements, Ellington Foods pension fund.

    i. *Return objective.* The return requirement must at least equal the actuarial assumption of 6%. A desired return level of 7% has been expressed and is less than the fund's average return of 9%. The fund is currently overfunded by 10%, which allows the company to reduce its contributions. As the firm continues to earn more than the actuarially determined required return, the ability of the fund to tolerate risk will also rise.

    ii. *Risk tolerance.* The fund has above-average ability to tolerate risk for at least three reasons. First, the average employee age of 43 is probably relatively young. Next, 30% retired lives gives a ratio of better than two active lives for each retired life. Third, the plan is overfunded by 10%.

    iii. *Time horizon.* The plan's time horizon is long term. Assuming a retirement age of 65 and an average age of 43, the average employee will work another 22 years. Unless stated otherwise, we assume a perpetual life for the plan.

> *Professor's Note: Visualize passage of each of the next 20 years. As each year passes, some employees retire, but it will take over 20 years for half of the currently active employees to do so. This means that, even with no growth in active employment numbers, the relatively low percentage of retired lives combined with the relatively low average age translates into a long time horizon before the ratio of active to retired lives falls to 1.0.*

For the Exam: Average can be a relative term. In this case, it implies a comparison to pension plans of firms in comparable industries. When you see an overfunded pension plan, it is generally fair to assume the fund has above-average ability to tolerate risk. Using average workforce age to determine ability to tolerate risk, however, depends upon the average age for comparable pension plans. On the Level III exam, candidates have customarily been given the average employee age and funded status of a pension plan and the industry and have been asked to determine what the data suggest. For example, if Ellington's average age is 43 and the industry average age is 45, this would not (by itself) indicate the plan has above-average ability to tolerate risk.

As time passes, the average age of active employees will change; some employees leave, new employees are hired, and some employees retire. Average employee age is, therefore, a snapshot in time that indicates the plan's time horizon and liquidity needs at that point in time. In general, the lower the average age, the longer the investment time horizon (this usually translates into a greater use of equities) and the lower the liquidity needs. As employees age and the ratio of active to retired lives falls, the plan's liquidity needs increase and the ability to tolerate risk falls. Note, however, that as active employees age and retire, retired employees also age. It is the rate of active employee retirements relative to retired employee deaths combined with the growth of the firm (i.e., new active employees contributing to the plan) that determines how quickly the ratio of active to retired lives falls.

B. Ellington Foods pension fund's asset allocation.

U.S. T-bills/cash (5%); SAME. Comply with trustees' wishes for 5% cash.

U.S. intermediate-term bonds (5-year duration) (30%); LOWER. Intermediate-term bonds tend to be less volatile than longer-term bonds and should represent a substantial portion of the pension fund allocation. However, with a younger workforce producing a longer-term liability stream, a shift away from assets with a shorter duration is warranted.

U.S. long-term bonds (20-year duration) (15%); HIGHER. With a younger workforce producing a longer-term liability stream, a higher allocation is recommended for assets with a longer duration.

U.S. equities (50%); LOWER. Although a substantial portion of the portfolio should contain equities in order to achieve the goals of reducing company contributions and possibly enhancing employee benefits, the equity portion of the portfolio should be distributed across categories within the equity asset class in order to achieve maximum diversification and possibly to enhance returns.

Developed market equities (0%); HIGHER. Developed market equities offer the opportunity for enhanced returns coupled with further diversification potential and should be represented in the pension portfolio.

Emerging market equities (0%); HIGHER. Emerging market equities are expected to return 16% and should be included in the portfolio. Emerging markets usually have a low correlation with developed markets, which helps to provide enhanced diversification benefits.

2. A. Investment policy statement elements for Ellington Foods pension fund.

i. *Return objective.* To maintain at least its current funded status, the fund needs to generate at least the actuarially determined rate of 9%. The fact that the fund is currently underfunded by 20% would ordinarily call for enhanced returns. However, the workforce is advanced in age, and a majority of the plan participants are now retired. In addition, company profits have been in decline for the past two years, which may indicate an inability for the company to increase contributions. The company must make every attempt to increase current contributions and will have to increase contributions in upcoming years.

ii. *Risk tolerance.* The risk tolerance (i.e., ability) of the plan has decreased dramatically over the past ten years. A surplus has been replaced with a deficit while the average age of the workforce has increased, a larger proportion of the workforce is now retired, and the duration of the plan's liabilities has decreased significantly. Thus, at exactly the time they need higher returns, the fund has below-average ability to tolerate risk.

iii. *Time horizon.* The time horizon has decreased due to the shortening of the duration of the plan's liabilities (i.e., the aging of the workforce). The plan remains a going concern, which requires a focus on the longer term while addressing the shorter-term needs, which are currently a major concern for the pension plan.

3.   Employers make regular contributions to the plan on behalf of qualified employees. Employees are sometimes required to match a certain percentage of the employer's contribution. For example, the employer may contribute 5% of the employee's gross annual salary to the plan as long as the employees contribute 2.5% of their gross annual salary. The 2.5% contribution is typically handled as a pretax payroll deduction.

Employers like defined-contribution plans because all investment risk is shifted to the employees. Plan participants typically make their own portfolio decisions. They are offered a "menu" of investment options from which they can create their portfolios.

In a participant-directed defined-contribution plan (DCP), the firm:

i.   Must offer sufficient choices to facilitate diversification.

ii. Must provide the ability for participants to switch funds across choices.

iii. Must keep contributions of company stock at a level that will not overweight the participant portfolios and reduce the benefits of diversification.

Because in a DCP the firm (sponsor) is not associated with the investments, per se, the IPS is more of a set of guidelines. The plan sponsor, rather than charged with meeting benefits, must oversee and help employees/participants in their retirement planning. Objectives and constraints for the DCP are determined by plan participants. The sponsor will typically establish a board or committee to oversee the retirement plan. This board will:

i.   See that participants have sufficient educational opportunities to facilitate investment decisions.

ii. Provide descriptions of all investment opportunities.

iii. Select and periodically evaluate fund managers.

iv. Generally oversee the plan and its participants.

4.   A.   Investment policy statement elements, Cassidy Endowment Fund.

i.   *Return objective.* The fund's return objective should focus on a total return approach. Return should equal the maximum spending rate plus an adjustment for expected inflation. In this situation, the return requirement would be 9% in order to achieve a 6% spending rate and protect the corpus against the 3% inflation forecast.

Alternatively: $(1.06)(1.03) - 1 = 9.18\%$. To incorporate management fees (if present in the question), include them in the compounded rate:
$(1 + \text{spending rate})(1 + \text{inflation})(1 + \% \text{ fees}) - 1$

ii. *Risk tolerance.* The fund's risk tolerance is below average. In general, endowments have a high tolerance for risk based on their long time horizon. In the case of the Cassidy Endowment Fund, the Aid to the Homeless organization relies heavily on contributions from the endowment to fund a large portion of its operating budget. Therefore, the endowment cannot tolerate much fluctuation in its investments without adversely affecting the funding to the Aid to the Homeless organization. Thus, the endowment has a below-average risk tolerance.

iii. *Time horizon.* The time horizon for the Cassidy Endowment Fund is very long (infinite). Most endowment funds are established to perpetually support the budget of the sponsored organization. The case indicates that Cassidy's endowment fund will continue indefinitely.

B. Selected Portfolio—C.

Return objectives. In order to achieve the total return objective, Portfolio C is expected to generate sufficient return to meet both the spending rate and inflation. Portfolios A and D fail to meet the 9% return requirement. Portfolio B achieves the return target but is poorly diversified.

Diversification. Portfolio C best achieves the required diversification goal. Allocations to both domestic and nondomestic stocks as well as corporate and treasury bonds are present. Portfolios A and D also show promise from a diversification standpoint, although D excludes a vital asset class, international equity. Portfolio B does not contain any debt securities, which is the most efficient way to produce income.

Efficiency. Efficiency is measured through the use of the Sharpe measure, which measures excess return to total risk. From an efficiency standpoint, Portfolio C has the second-highest Sharpe measure, only slightly surpassed by Portfolio D. Portfolios A and B have efficiency measures considerably lower than C and D.

5. A. Investment policy statement elements for Liles Insurance Company surplus portfolio.

   i. *Return objective.* The return objective for Liles Insurance Company surplus portfolio is to achieve growth. The primary requirement for the surplus portfolio is to achieve higher returns through portfolio growth. Equity-oriented investments, including venture capital, are typically used to achieve this objective.

   ii. *Risk tolerance.* The risk tolerance for Liles Insurance Company is relatively high. Because these funds are not supporting a specific liability, the risk tolerance for the surplus portfolio is relatively high. This higher risk tolerance, if rewarded with higher returns, allows life insurance companies to expand insurance volume.

   iii. *Liquidity requirements.* The liquidity requirements for the surplus portion of the life insurance company are very low. The purpose of the surplus portfolio is to generate growth. Liquidity needs are typically met through the segment of the portfolio used to meet liabilities.

   B. Liles Insurance Company surplus portfolio asset allocation.

   Cash (10%); LOWER. The need for cash in the *surplus* segment of a life insurance company is very low. The goal of the surplus segment is to earn competitive returns, which is not typically accomplished by holding cash.

   U.S. intermediate-term bonds (5-year duration) (5%); SAME. Having a small presence of fixed-income securities would be wise in the surplus segment for diversification purposes. The current level seems reasonable.

   U.S. long-term bonds (20-year duration) (45%); LOWER. Longer-term bonds provide higher returns than intermediate-term bonds over the long term. However, the lower proportion is recommended given that the main objective of the surplus portfolio is to grow the principal.

U.S. equities (25%); HIGHER. The surplus portfolio should be geared toward equity-type investments. The proportion of domestic equities should be increased in order to generate additional growth in principal.

Developed market equities (15%); SAME. The developed market equities are expected to produce slightly higher returns than the U.S. equities and may provide diversification benefits. An allocation of 15% seems reasonable for achieving the objectives of the surplus portfolio. The company may want to consider currency hedging should it decide to retain or increase this allocation.

Equity REITS (0%); HIGHER. Equity REITS provide diversification benefits and an opportunity for enhanced return. The asset class is currently not included in the current asset allocation and should be added.

Venture capital (0%); HIGHER. Venture capital is an appropriate part of a surplus segment investment strategy. The current allocation does not include venture capital. Given its high expected return, the company should consider venture capital as a part of the surplus segment portfolio.

6. From the information provided, we have no reason to assume FSPB has any remarkable characteristics that would distinguish it from other banks.

Objectives:

Return. The return objective for the portfolio is to generate a positive interest rate spread.

Risk. Because the liabilities are certain, the securities must be low risk. FSPB has a below-average risk tolerance.

Constraints:

Time horizon. Liabilities are short term, so securities in the portfolio should be of short-to-intermediate maturity/duration.

Taxes. FSPB is a taxable entity, so tax consequences must be considered in selecting securities.

Liquidity. FSPB requires liquidity to meet depositor withdrawals and new loan requests, so the securities must be liquid.

Legal and regulatory. Through bank regulations, FSPB is required to maintain liquidity, meet reserve requirements, and meet pledging requirements.

Unique. Due to their high concentration of loans in the Winston-Salem area (i.e., high geographic and possibly even industry concentration), FSPB should utilize its securities portfolio to provide diversification.

The following is a review of the Portfolio Management for Institutional Investors principles designed to address the learning outcome statements set forth by CFA Institute. This topic is also covered in:

LINKING PENSION LIABILITIES TO ASSETS

EXAM FOCUS

This topic review is an important extension of the application of asset liability management to pension plans. It quickly reviews and discards asset-only management as inadequate. It then turns to a form of ALM, the liability-relative approach, as a more appropriate way to select assets that will mimic the future behavior of the liabilities and minimize the variability of plan surplus. ALM is an important theme in the Level III material and has regularly appeared on the exam. Be prepared.

ASSET-ONLY AND LIABILITY-RELATIVE ASSET ALLOCATION

LOS 16.a: Contrast the assumptions concerning pension liability risk in asset-only and liability-relative approaches to asset allocation.

CFA® Program Curriculum, Volume 2, page 526

Under an **asset-only approach**, a pension fund focuses on selecting efficient portfolios. It does not attempt to explicitly hedge the risk of the liabilities. This approach ignores the fact that a future liability is subject to market-related risk. Market risk arises from interest rate risk, inflation risk, or from an exposure to economic growth. For example, if a firm does extraordinarily well due to the economy, its wages paid may grow and the firm's future pension liabilities will increase. A failure to recognize the risk in the liabilities could lead to a portfolio that does not adequately satisfy the liabilities.

A more appropriate asset allocation approach would recognize *economic liability*. This approach recognizes the various exposures and components of the pension liability, as will be discussed later. In this **liability-relative approach**, the portfolio is chosen for its ability to mimic the liability (i.e., the portfolio will have a high correlation with the liability).

In the asset-only approach, the risk-free investment is the return on cash. In a liability-relative approach, the risk-free investment is a portfolio that is highly correlated with and mimics the liability in performance. The pension fund manager must construct this portfolio by decomposing the liability into its various exposures. An asset mix which most closely tracks these exposures can then be selected as the benchmark portfolio. This approach could also be relevant to non-pension obligations, such as meeting insurance liabilities and retirement planning.

PENSION LIABILITY EXPOSURES

LOS 16.b: Discuss the fundamental and economic exposures of pension liabilities and identify asset types that mimic these liability exposures.

CFA® Program Curriculum, Volume 2, page 526

Many pension managers measure their pension liability through duration management. This approach focuses on short-term changes in the liability relative to changes in interest rates. This approach is valid when pension risk is short-term, as in the case of firms near bankruptcy. For ongoing plans, it is superior to asset-only, but liability-relative management is better.

Most pension plans are ongoing and the more appropriate liability modeling captures the risk of the fund not satisfying short-term obligations as well as the risk of not satisfying the longer-term liabilities. A better understanding of pension liabilities requires a decomposition of the liabilities' risk exposures. This will help the portfolio manager determine the appropriate discount rate for pension liabilities.

Professor's Note: Throughout this coming discussion the "benchmark" means the asset mix that will most closely track the changes in the liabilities and minimize the variability of surplus. It provides a reference point for future evaluation of performance. An active manager can choose to deviate from the benchmark, seeking to add value, but this is more risky.

Market Exposures Due to Accrued Benefits

To decompose the liability's exposures, the pension obligation should first be separated into that due to *inactive* and that due to *active participants*. Inactive participants are no longer increasing their future benefits through continuing employment with the firm. They could be retirees who have started drawing benefits or those no longer employed by the firm who are owed a future benefit but are not yet drawing benefits (the deferreds). The future benefits for inactive participants could be:

- fixed, not increasing with inflation, making nominal bonds the optimal benchmark;
- fully indexed to inflation making real rate (real return) bonds such as Treasury Inflation Protected Securities (TIPS) the optimal benchmark;
- or partially indexed, making a combination of real rate and nominal bonds appropriate.

Active participants are those currently working for the firm. The obligations to these employees can be separated into that owed for past service and that owed for future service. The obligations for past service are analyzed like those for inactive participants and matched with real rate and nominal bonds based on whether or not the past service benefits are linked to inflation. The retirement payments owed to inactive participants and the payments for past service to active participants constitute *accrued benefits*.

Market Exposures Due to Future Benefits

In the case where a pension plan is frozen, no future benefits will be accrued and the plan's only liability is that which has accrued. In this case, the liability-mimicking portfolio is one consisting of nominal and inflation-indexed bonds. Most pensions, however, are ongoing and have obligations for future benefits.

Future benefits are those from wages to be earned in the future, by existing employees as well as new entrants into the plan. Although future benefits are long-term in nature and do not affect the plan's short-term risk, their effect on the plan's funded status and the ability to hedge these liabilities must be considered.

The first component of future benefits is wages to be earned in the future. Given a known growth rate in wages, one can calculate the expected amount of future benefits. The present value of this amount is referred to as the *future wage liability*, which along with the accrued benefits represents the projected benefit obligation under U.S. Financial Accounting Standards and the defined benefit obligation under international standards.

The growth in future wages can be decomposed into a portion equal to the rate of inflation and any additional real growth over and above inflation. The liability linked to wages that will increase with inflation will require real return bonds as a benchmark; however, the future benefits associated with those wages may or may not be inflation indexed so some nominal bonds may also be needed for the benchmark.

Wage growth arising from real growth is due to increases in labor productivity. This productivity will be reflected in GDP, which is strongly correlated with the stock market. The liability associated with wage increases over and above inflation can be best mimicked with stocks.

There can also be future benefits not funded with assets, more difficult to calculate, and not modeled in the benchmark. For example, there could be unplanned changes in the plan features that increase benefits and new participants who enter the plan. These are not funded with current assets or reflected in the projected liabilities, so they are not reflected in the benchmark. Essentially, the plan sponsor must pay for these with contributions and the earnings on those future contributions.

Non-Market Exposures

The exposures discussed so far are market exposures as they are related to inflation, interest rates, and economic growth. Pensions are also subject to non-market exposures referred to as *liability noise*. These exposures can be divided into two parts: that due to plan demographics and that due to model uncertainty. The former exposure is affected primarily by the number of participants and can be estimated using statistical models. It is more predictable when the number of participants is larger. The latter exposure is less predictable and is different for inactive versus active participants.

Recall that inactive participants can be divided into retirees (i.e., currently receiving benefits) and deferreds (i.e., not working for the company but not yet eligible for benefits). The source of liability noise arising from retirees is the mortality assumption. If the mortality assumption is incorrect, the pension plan will be responsible for the retirees' benefits for a different period of time than that modeled. Unfortunately, there are no financial products that can hedge this risk, although some are being developed. For deferreds, there is risk from the mortality risk (longevity risk) as well as uncertainty arising from when retirement occurs. The sooner the deferreds retire, the smaller the benefit paid for a longer period of time. Thus, for deferreds, there is uncertainty in the timing and amount of liability as well as longevity risk. For these reasons, the liability noise associated with deferreds is larger and less easily hedged than that for retirees.

The liability noise arising from active participants is even greater than that from deferreds. These participants are often many years from retirement and there is much uncertainty regarding the plan's future obligation.

In Figure 1, we summarize the exposures of a pension plan and the assets needed to satisfy them. We assume that the accrued benefits are not indexed to inflation. If they are indexed to inflation, then real return bonds would be used. Recall that term structure risk is the interest rate risk of parallel and nonparallel shifts in the yield curve.

> **For the Exam:** Focus on the first three plan segments (indicated with *) because they are the pension's primary emphasis in the liability-relative portfolio.

Figure 1: Pension Liability Exposures

Pension Plan Segment	Market or Non-Market Exposure	Risk Exposure	Liability Mimicking Assets
Modeled in the Benchmark			
*Inactive- and active-accrued	Market	Term structure	• Nominal bonds for benefits not linked to inflation. • Real return bonds for benefits linked to inflation
*Active-future wage growth	Market	Term structure	Nominal bonds
	Market	Inflation	Real return bonds
	Market	Economic growth	Equities
Generally Not Modeled in the Benchmark			
Active-future service rendered	Market	Similar to wage growth but more uncertain	Not typically funded
Active-future participants	Market	Very uncertain	Not typically funded
Liability noise-demographics	Non-market	Plan demographics	Not easily hedged
Liability noise-inactive	Non-market	Model uncertainty & longevity risk	Not easily hedged or modeled
Liability noise-active	Non-market	Model uncertainty & longevity risk	Not easily hedged or modeled

THE LIABILITY-RELATIVE APPROACH IN PRACTICE

LOS 16.c: Compare pension portfolios built from a traditional asset-only perspective to portfolios designed relative to liabilities and discuss why corporations may choose not to implement fully the liability mimicking portfolio.

CFA® Program Curriculum, Volume 2, page 526

In terms of satisfying their future liability over time, the best portfolio for a pension plan will be a liability-mimicking portfolio consisting of nominal bonds, real return bonds, and stocks. The weights in these assets will be determined by the proportion of future obligations relative to accrued, inflation indexing of the benefits, and the plan status (e.g., whether it is frozen or growing). If the workforce is younger, more will be allocated to equities. If there is a significant amount of benefits that is indexed to inflation, inflation-indexed bonds are used more than nominal bonds. If the plan is frozen, there are no future obligations and nominal bonds would dominate the portfolio.

The liability-mimicking, low-risk portfolio, however, will be costly and, by construction, will not provide a return (i.e., accrue value) in excess of the liabilities. Recall that the liability from future service rendered and future participants is uncertain and is not modeled or funded. An investment in the low-risk portfolio, therefore, requires future cash payments by the sponsor to satisfy these obligations.

For pension plans, the best use of the low-risk portfolio is as a benchmark. Outperforming the benchmark will ensure that the majority of the pension's obligations are met. The optimum for pensions is to outperform the benchmark, while minimizing the risk of not being able to meet their obligations.

In the traditional asset-only approach, the portfolio is usually composed of 60–70% equities with the rest in short- and medium-duration nominal bonds. In a liability-relative approach, derivatives can be used to hedge the market-related exposure of the pension. For example, term structure risk is typically the largest plan exposure and can be hedged with bond futures contracts. Derivatives are relatively inexpensive and free up capital for use in a higher expected return portfolio component. Thus, the liability-mimicking portfolio is typically composed of derivatives, long duration bonds, inflation-indexed bonds, and equities, as well as other components dedicated to generating an efficient return.

KEY CONCEPTS

LOS 16.a

Under an asset-only approach, a pension fund focuses on selecting efficient portfolios. It does not attempt to explicitly hedge the risk of the liabilities. This approach ignores the fact that a future liability is subject to market-related risk. Market risk arises from interest rate risk, inflation risk, or from exposure to economic growth.

In the liability-relative approach, the portfolio is chosen for its ability to mimic the liability (i.e., the portfolio will have a high correlation with the liability). If pension liabilities are correctly modeled, this will create the portfolio with the lowest surplus variability.

LOS 16.b

A pension fund is exposed to market and non-market related risks. If the benefits paid are not indexed to inflation, the appropriate liability-mimicking assets are nominal bonds. If the benefits paid are indexed to inflation, the appropriate liability-mimicking assets are inflation-indexed bonds. If the benefits correspond with growth in the firm and economy, the appropriate liability-mimicking assets are equities. Many liabilities are a mixture of these exposures and will require a mix of these assets.

The retirement payments to inactive participants and the payments to active participants for past service constitute accrued benefits. If the benefits are not indexed to inflation, they will be hedged with nominal bonds.

A pension's future obligations are those arising due to wages to be earned in the future and new entrants into the plan. The first component is typically hedged with equities, nominal bonds, and real bonds, while the latter component is uncertain and not easily modeled or funded.

Non-market exposures (liability noise) can be divided into two parts: those that are due to plan demographics and those that are due to model uncertainty. These exposures are not easily hedged.

LOS 16.c

The traditional asset-only portfolio is usually predominantly equities with the remainder in short- and medium-duration nominal bonds. The liability-mimicking portfolio is typically composed of derivatives, long duration bonds, inflation-indexed bonds, and equities, as well as other components dedicated to generating an efficient return.

The liability-mimicking, low-risk portfolio is costly and does not provide a return in excess of the liabilities.

CONCEPT CHECKERS

1. Correlations are important in both the asset-only approach and the liability-relative approach to investing, but they are used differently in each approach. **Discuss** the differences.

2. Suppose a pension fund decides to begin indexing the benefits to inflation. What changes would one expect to see in her portfolio, if it is a liability-mimicking portfolio?

3. When comparing an asset-only approach portfolio and a liability-relative approach portfolio, which portfolio would be *more likely* to contain derivative contracts?

©2013 Kaplan, Inc.

ANSWERS – CONCEPT CHECKERS

1. In an asset-only approach, investments are chosen to have a low correlation with firm assets. In a liability-relative approach, the focus is on hedging the pension liabilities, so investments are chosen to have a high correlation with the liabilities.

2. The pension fund would shift its assets from nominal bonds into inflation-indexed (real return) bonds in order to hedge the inflation-indexed benefits.

3. The liability-relative approach portfolio would be more likely invested in derivatives. This approach focuses on hedging the pension liabilities and might use derivatives to hedge the pension's market-related risks. This would free up capital to pursue higher expected returns.

    The asset-only approach does not explicitly hedge the pension liabilities and would be more likely invested in traditional assets.

Use the following information for Questions 1 through 6.

Rob Baker, an investment manager at Welker Auto Parts, is responsible for managing his company's defined-benefit pension plan. The plan has been underfunded for several months and Baker is meeting today with Gary Thompson, the company's CFO, to discuss possible ways to erase this liability funding shortfall.

During the meeting, Baker proposes that the plan should increase the value of its pension assets by investing in riskier securities. Currently, the plan invests a majority of its funds in investment grade corporate bonds and large-cap equities. Baker is confident that investments in small-cap equities will help bring the fund back to fully funded status. Thompson, however, is not as confident that investing in riskier securities will guarantee an increase in pension asset values. He points to the company's high debt ratio as an indication of a need to take a more risk-averse stance.

Baker is skeptical of Thompson's risk-averse stance so he notifies Thompson of the high correlation of pension asset returns with the firm's operations. Baker states that the high correlation implies a high tolerance for risk. Thompson disagrees with this statement, suggesting that a firm's high ratio of active to retired lives does not grant the ability to take on more risk.

Baker and Thompson then turn to a list of additional discussion items:

Item 1: Add an option to the plan that will allow participants to retire five years earlier than currently permitted at a 5% reduction in benefit payout.

Item 2: Adopt a liability mimicking approach to the plan's asset allocation instead of the current asset-only approach.

Item 3: Freeze the plan. All new employees will participate in a new defined contribution plan where employees can select from a list of investment alternatives that will range from more conservative to more aggressive than the defined benefit plan.

Each item is independent and is to be considered in isolation, as if it is adopted and no other changes are made.

As they are leaving the meeting Thompson mentions to Baker that the company founder is starting a perpetual foundation to fund technical studies at a local community college. Thompson has been asked to serve on the foundation's board.

1. Regarding Baker's view on investing more funds in small-cap equities and Thompson's view on implementing a risk-averse stance:

Baker	Thompson
A. Inappropriate	Appropriate
B. Appropriate	Inappropriate
C. Inappropriate	Inappropriate

2. Regarding Baker's statement about the correlation between pension assets and firm operations and Thompson's statement about the ratio of active to retired lives:

Baker	Thompson
A. Incorrect	Correct
B. Correct	Incorrect
C. Incorrect	Incorrect

3. If the plan adopts the early retirement provision in Item 1, what is the *most likely* immediate effect on the plan's liquidity needs and surplus?

Liquidity Needs	Surplus
A. Increase	Increase
B. Increase	Decrease
C. Decrease	No change

4. The most typical result in a pension plan of adopting the liability mimicking approach in Item 2 is to increase the allocation to:
    A. equity and real rate bonds.
    B. nominal and real rate bonds.
    C. equity and alternative investments.

5. Assuming Item 3 is adopted and that most plan participants choose more aggressive assets than those in the pension plan portfolio, risk for the sponsor (Welker Auto Parts) will *most likely*:
    A. increase.
    B. decrease.
    C. be unchanged.

6. In contrast to a typical defined benefit plan, a foundation's risk and return objectives are likely to be:

Risk Tolerance	Return Objective
A. Higher	Higher
B. Lower	Higher
C. Lower	Lower

SELF-TEST ANSWERS: PORTFOLIO MANAGEMENT FOR INSTITUTIONAL INVESTORS

1. **A**   Baker's views are inappropriate. Despite the willingness to take greater risk by investing in small-cap equities, the plan's underfunded status has decreased the ability to take risk. Therefore, taking greater risk is inappropriate. Thompson's views are appropriate. A higher debt ratio would indicate a decreased capability of meeting the plan's liabilities and, thus, would suggest a more risk-averse stance.

2. **C**   Baker's statement is incorrect. A high correlation of pension asset returns with a firm's operations indicates a low risk tolerance. For example, the ability of the firm to make contributions will be low at the same time that the plan is underfunded. Thompson's statement is also incorrect. A high ratio of active to retired lives usually indicates an increased ability to take risk.

3. **A**   The early retirement option will increase liquidity needs. While the payments made to a given individual will be discounted by 5%, that individual can start taking money sooner, and disbursements from the plan will increase immediately. Liquidity refers to disbursement needs now, not the final amount of total payments made over time. The drop in total disbursements likely to be created by the option will reduce estimated total future plan liabilities and therefore improve the surplus (i.e., surplus being the market value of the plan assets minus the estimated present value of those future liabilities).

4. **B**   The asset-only approach tends to emphasize return and have a higher allocation to higher return assets such as equity and alternative investments. In contrast, liability mimicking will emphasize assets with a stronger positive correlation to plan liabilities and hold more nominal and real rate (real return) bonds in most cases.

5. **B**   The risk of the plan for the plan sponsor will decrease regardless of the investment choices made by each participant. In a defined contribution plan, each participant bears the investment risk, not the sponsor.

6. **A**   While specific situations can vary, a perpetual foundation may be very aggressive in their risk and return objectives in order to meet the intergenerational needs of the foundation.

Capital Market Expectations

Exam Focus

Capital market expectations are key components of the portfolio management process. When combined with the client's objectives and constraints from the investment policy statement, they lead to the strategic asset allocation. Essentially, capital market expectations consist of expected return, correlation, and standard deviation for each asset class. This Topic Review covers a variety of techniques that may be used to form capital market expectations. While many techniques should be familiar from other levels of the exam, others may be new. Any can appear on the exam. Understand and be able to discuss the issues covered in this section as well as the calculations presented.

Formulating Capital Market Expectations

LOS 17.a: Discuss the role of, and a framework for, capital market expectations in the portfolio management process.

CFA® Program Curriculum, Volume 3, page 7

Capital market expectations can be referred to as **macro expectations** (expectations regarding classes of assets) or **micro expectations** (expectations regarding individual assets). Micro expectations are most directly used in individual security selection. In other assignments, macro expectations are referred to as top-down while micro expectations are referred to as bottom-up.

Using a disciplined approach leads to more effective asset allocations and risk management. Formulating capital market expectations is referred to as **beta research** because it is related to systematic risk. It can be used in the valuation of both equities and fixed-income securities. **Alpha research**, on the other hand, is concerned with earning excess returns through the use of specific strategies within specific asset groups.

To formulate capital market expectations, the analyst should use the following 7-step process.

Step 1: Determine the specific capital market expectations needed according to the investor's tax status, allowable asset classes, and time horizon. Time horizon is particularly important in determining the set of capital market expectations that are needed.

Step 2: Investigate assets' historical performance to determine the drivers that have affected past performance and to establish some range for plausible future performance. With the drivers of past performance established, the analyst can use these to forecast expected future performance as well as compare the forecast to past results to see if the forecast appears reasonable.

Step 3: Identify the valuation model used and its requirements. For example, a comparables-based, relative value approach used in the United States may be difficult to apply in an emerging market analysis.

Step 4: Collect the best data possible. The use of faulty data will lead to faulty conclusions. The following issues should be considered when evaluating data for possible use:
- Calculation methodologies.
- Data collection techniques.
- Data definitions.
- Error rates.
- Investability and correction for free float.
- Turnover in index components.
- Potential biases.

Step 5: Use experience and judgment to interpret current investment conditions and decide what values to assign to the required inputs. Verify that the inputs used for the various asset classes are consistent across classes.

Step 6: Formulate capital market expectations. Any assumptions and rationales used in the analysis should be recorded. Determine that what was specified in Step 1 has been provided.

Step 7: Monitor performance and use it to refine the process. If actual performance varies significantly from forecasts, the process and model should be refined.

PROBLEMS IN FORECASTING

LOS 17.b: Discuss challenges in developing capital market forecasts.

CFA® Program Curriculum, Volume 3, page 13

As mentioned earlier, poor forecasts can result in inappropriate asset allocations. The analyst should be aware of the potential problems in data, models, and the resulting capital market expectations. Nine problems encountered in producing forecasts are (1) limitations to using economic data, (2) data measurement error and bias, (3) limitations of historical estimates, (4) the use of ex post risk and return measures, (5) non-repeating data patterns, (6) failing to account for conditioning information, (7) misinterpretation of correlations, (8) psychological traps, and (9) model and input uncertainty.

1. There are several **limitations to using economic data**. First, the time lag between collection and distribution is often quite long. The International Monetary Fund, for example, reports data with a lag of as much as two years. Second, data are often revised and the revisions are not made at the same time as the publication. Third, data definitions and methodology change over time. For example, the basket of goods in the Consumer Price Index changes over time. Last, data indices are often rebased over time (i.e., the base upon which they are calculated is changed). Although a rebasing is not a substantial change in the data itself, the unaware analyst could calculate changes in the value of the indices incorrectly if she does not make an appropriate adjustment.

2. The formation of capital market expectations can also be adversely affected by several forms of **data measurement errors and biases**. The first problem is *transcription errors*, which are simply recording information incorrectly and are more serious if they are biased in a certain direction. A second problem arises from *survivorship bias*. As an example, a return series based on a stock index will be biased upwards if the return calculation does not include firms that have been dropped from the index due to delistings. Third, the use of *appraisal (smoothed) data*, instead of actual returns, results in correlations and standard deviations that are biased downwards. The reason is that actual price fluctuations are masked by the use of appraised data. One potential solution is to rescale the data so that the mean return is unaffected, but the variance is increased based on the underlying economic fundamentals.

3. The **limitations of historical estimates** can also hamper the formation of capital market expectations. The values from historical data must often be adjusted going forward as economic, political, regulatory, and technological environments change. This is particularly true for volatile assets such as equity. These changes are known as *regime changes* and result in *nonstationary* data. For example, the bursting of the technology bubble in 2000 resulted in returns data that were markedly different than that from the previous five years. Nonstationarity would mean different periods in the time series have different statistical properties and create problems with standard statistical testing methods.

   Historical data is the starting point for estimating the following capital market expectations: expected return, standard deviation, and correlations. However, it is not obvious how to select the time period of historical data. A long time period is preferable for several reasons.

   - It may be statistically required. To calculate historical covariance (and correlation), the number of data points must exceed the number of covariances to be calculated.
   - A larger data set (time period) provides more precise statistical estimates with smaller variance to the estimates.
   - As a related issue, if the time period is longer for a larger data set, the calculated statistics are generally less sensitive to the starting and ending points selected for the time period.

However, long time periods also create potential problems.

- A longer time period is more likely to include *regime changes*, which are shifts in underlying fundamentals. Each regime change creates a subperiod with distinctly different characteristics. For example, the behavior of real estate and virtually every financial asset was different before and after the Financial Market Meltdown of 2008. 1) This creates *nonstationarity*, which invalidates many statistics calculated from time periods starting before and ending after the meltdown. 2) It forces the analyst to use judgment to decide whether the subperiod before or after the meltdown will be more relevant going forward.
- It may mean the relevant time period is too short to be statistically significant.
- It creates a temptation to use more frequent data, such as weekly data, rather than monthly data points in order to have a larger sample size. Unfortunately, more frequent data points are often more likely to have missing or outdated values (this is called *asynchronism*) and can result in lower, distorted correlation calculations.

Two questions can be used to help resolve the issue of time period to select:

1. Is there a reason to believe the entire (longer) time period is not appropriate?

2. If the answer to the first question is yes, does a statistical test confirm there is a regime change and the point in the time series where it occurs?

If both answers are yes, the analyst must use judgment to select the relevant sub period.

> *Professor's Note: I hope most candidates recognize the discussions above have been referring to many of the statistical testing issues covered at Level I and II. The focus here is not on performing such tests or even knowing which specific tests to use, but on recognizing times and ways testing can be relevant. Think of a senior portfolio manager who understands the larger issues and when to ask others with relevant technical skills to do further analysis. That has often been the perspective of Level III exam questions.*

4. Using **ex post data** (after the fact) to determine **ex ante** (before the fact) risk and return can be problematic. For example, suppose that several years ago investors were fearful that the Federal Reserve was going to have to raise interest rates to combat inflation. This situation would cause depressed stock prices. If inflation abated without the Fed's intervention, then stock returns would increase once the inflation scenario passes. Looking back on this situation, the researcher would conclude that stock returns were high while being blind to the prior risk that investors had faced. The analyst would then conclude that future (ex ante) returns for stocks will be high. In sum, the analyst would underestimate the risks that equity investors face and overestimate their potential returns.

5. Using historical data, analysts can also uncover **patterns** in security returns that are unlikely to occur in the future and can produce biases in the data. One such bias is *data mining*. Just by random chance, some variables will appear to have a relationship with security returns, when, in fact, these relationships are unlikely to persist. For example, if the analyst uses a 5% significance level and examines the relationship between stock returns and 40 randomly selected variables, two (5%) of the variables are expected to show a statistically significant relationship with stock returns just by random chance. Another potential bias results from the time span of data chosen (*time period bias*). For example, small-cap U.S. stocks are widely thought to outperform large-cap stocks, but their advantage disappears when data from the 1970s and 1980s is excluded.

> *Professor's Note: You can think of data mining as "beating the data into submission." That is, using different models, the analyst tests the data until some relationship (even a spurious relationship) is discovered.*

To avoid these biases, the analyst should first ask himself if there is any economic basis for the variables found to be related to stock returns. Second, he should scrutinize the modeling process for susceptibility to bias. Third, the analyst should test the discovered relationship with out-of-sample data to determine if the relationship is persistent. This would be done by estimating the relationship with one portion of the historical data and then reexamining it with another portion.

6. Analysts' forecasts may also fail to account for **conditioning information**. The relationship between security returns and economic variables is not constant over time. Historical data reflects performance over many different business cycles and economic conditions. Thus, analysts should account for current conditions in their forecasts. As an example, suppose a firm's beta is estimated at 1.2 using historical data. If, however, the original data are separated into two ranges by economic expansion or recession, the beta might be 1.0 in expansions and 1.4 in recessions. Going forward, the analyst's estimate of the firm's beta should reflect whether an expansion is expected (i.e., the expected beta is 1.0) or a recession is expected (i.e., the expected beta is 1.4). The beta used should be the beta consistent with the analyst's expectations for economic conditions.

7. Another problem in forming capital market expectations is the **misinterpretation of correlations** (i.e., causality). Suppose the analyst finds that corn prices were correlated with rainfall in the Midwestern United States during the previous quarter. It would be reasonable to conclude that rainfall influences corn prices. It would not be reasonable to conclude that corn prices influence rainfall, although the correlation statistic would not tell us that. Rainfall is an exogenous variable (i.e., it arises outside the model), whereas the price of corn is an endogenous variable (i.e., it arises within the model).

It is also possible that a third variable influences both variables. Or it is possible that there is a nonlinear relationship between the two variables that is missed by the correlation statistic, which measures linear relationships.

These scenarios illustrate the problem with the simple correlation statistic. An alternative to correlation for uncovering predictive relationships is a multiple regression. In a multiple regression, lagged terms, control variables, and nonlinear terms can all be included as independent variables to better specify the relationship. Controlling for other effects, the regression coefficient on the variable of interest is referred to as the *partial correlation* and would be used for the desired analysis.

8. Analysts are also susceptible to **psychological traps**. We discuss six possible traps in the following: (1) the anchoring trap, (2) the status quo trap, (3) the confirming evidence trap, (4) the overconfidence trap, (5) the prudence trap, and (6) the recallability trap.

If an analyst is susceptible to the **anchoring trap**, he puts too much weight on the first set of information received. For example, if during a debate on the future of the economy, the first economist to speak states that there will be a recession while the second economist states that there will be an expansion, the analyst may use the recession scenario as an anchor and put less credence on the expansion scenario.

In the **status quo trap**, the analyst's predictions are highly influenced by the recent past. If inflation is currently 4%, for example, it is easier for the analyst to forecast a value close to 4% rather than risk a forecast that differs much from past values.

The **confirming evidence trap** occurs when analysts give too much credence to evidence that supports their existing or favored beliefs. This trap may also cause analysts to look for information that supports their perspective and ignore information that does not support their view. To counter these tendencies, analysts should give all evidence equal scrutiny, seek out opposing opinions, and be forthcoming in their motives.

In the fourth trap, the **overconfidence trap**, analysts ignore their past mistakes and overestimate the accuracy of their forecasts. Analysts may mistakenly believe that others share their views. This trap leads analysts to overly limit the scenarios and range of outcomes that are considered. To prevent this trap, analysts should enlarge their spread of potential future values.

In the **prudence trap**, analysts tend to be overly conservative in their forecasts because they want to avoid the *regret* from making extreme forecasts that could end up being incorrect. To counter this fifth trap, the analyst should again widen the range of his forecasted values.

 Professor's Note: Nothing to dwell on here. Just one more discussion of behavioral biases.

Lastly, analysts fall into the **recallability trap** when they let past disasters or dramatic events weigh too heavily in their forecasts. Many believe that the U.S. stock market crash of 1929 may have depressed equity values in the subsequent 30 years. To limit the influence of this trap, the analyst should be careful to base predictions on objective data rather than emotions or recollections of the past.

9. Our last problem regarding forecasts of capital market expectations is **model and input uncertainty**. Model uncertainty refers to the inability to be sure that his predictive model is the correct one to use. For example, the analyst may be unsure whether to use a discounted cash flow (DCF) model or a relative value approach to valuing stocks. Input uncertainty refers to knowing with certainty the correct input values for the mode. For example, even if the analyst knew that the DCF model was appropriate, the correct growth and discount rates cannot be ascertained with certainty.

Tests of market efficiency usually depend on the use of a model. For example, many researchers use the market model, which uses a single independent variable (returns on the market) and beta as the relevant measure of risk. If beta is not the correct measure of risk, then the conclusions regarding market efficiency will be invalid. Some believe that market anomalies, which have been explained by behavioral finance, are in fact due to the actions of investors who are rational but use different valuation models.

Forecasting Tools

LOS 17.c: Demonstrate the application of formal tools for setting capital market expectations, including statistical tools, discounted cash flow models, the risk premium approach, and financial equilibrium models.

CFA® Program Curriculum, Volume 3, page 23

The use of formal tools helps the analyst set capital market expectations. Formal tools are those that are accepted within the investment community. When applied to reputable data, formal tools provide forecasts replicable by other analysts. The formal tools we examine are statistical tools, discounted cash flow models, the risk premium approach, and financial equilibrium models.

Statistical Tools

The various statistical tools for setting capital market expectations include projecting historical data, shrinkage estimators, time series analysis, and multifactor models. **Projecting historical data** is the most straightforward statistical tool. Here, the analyst projects the historical mean return, standard deviation, and correlations for a data set into the future. The arithmetic mean is used in estimating standard deviation and is also considered the best estimate of return in any single period. However, the geometric mean is a more accurate projection of growth over multiple periods as it includes the effects of compounding. For risky assets the geometric mean is always lower. The choice of arithmetic or geometric mean will also affect the calculation of market risk premium (MRP). With arithmetic mean, the calculation of MRP is simply market return minus the risk-free rate. With geometric mean, the more precise MRP calculation is (1 plus market return divided by 1 plus risk-free rate) – 1.

Shrinkage estimators are weighted averages of historical data and some other estimate, where the weights and other estimates are defined by the analyst. Shrinkage estimators reduce (shrink) the influence of historical outliers through the weighting process. The mean return and covariance are the parameters most often adjusted with shrinkage estimators. This tool is most useful when the data set is so small that historical values are not reliable estimates of future parameters.

For example, suppose the historical covariance between two assets is 180. Perhaps the analyst has modeled the covariance matrix between several assets using a factor model that indicates the covariance matrix (a.k.a. the **target covariance matrix**) values will increase in the future. If the estimated covariance is 220 and the analyst weights the historical covariance by 60% and the target by 40%, the shrinkage estimate would be 196 (180 × 0.60 + 220 × 0.40). It has been shown that shrinkage estimate covariances are more accurate forecasts of covariance, especially when the chosen target covariance and weights are appropriate.

Mean returns can also be forecasted with shrinkage estimators. One method weights the historical return of the subject asset the highest with the rest of the weight coming from the returns for other historical assets. For example, if the historical return for equity was 10% and the average return for all other assets was 8%, the analyst might use an 80/20 weighting and project a return of 9.6% (10% × 0.80 + 8% × 0.20) for equities.

Time series analysis forecasts a variable using previous values of itself and sometimes previous values of other variables. These models can be used to forecast means as well as variances. Empirical evidence suggests some assets, such as foreign exchange, stocks, and futures, exhibit **volatility clustering**. This is when high volatility tends to be followed by high volatility, or when low volatility persists. A model developed by JP Morgan states that volatility in the current period, σ_t^2, is a weighted average of the previous period volatility, σ_{t-1}^2, and a random error, ε_t^2 :

$$\sigma_t^2 = \theta\sigma_{t-1}^2 + (1-\theta)\varepsilon_t^2$$

The term θ measures the relationship, or rate of decay, between volatility in one period to the next. The higher θ is, the greater the persistence of volatility and the greater the tendency for volatility clustering. For example, suppose θ is 0.80 and the standard deviation in returns is 15% in period t – 1. If the random error is 0.04, then the forecasted variance for period t is:

$$\sigma_t^2 = 0.80(0.15^2) + 0.20(0.04^2) = 0.01832$$
$$\sigma_t = \sqrt{0.01832} = 0.1354 = 13.54\%$$

The forecasted standard deviation of 13.54% is close to the historical standard deviation of 15% because the historical standard deviation is weighted so heavily.

Multifactor models are used to forecast returns and can also be used to forecast covariances. The advantage of using them to forecast covariances is that the model can simplify the forecasting procedure by reducing the forecast to a common set of factors. This modeling also eliminates the noise present in a sample of data and ensures consistent forecasts given a consistent covariance matrix.

For example, suppose there are two factors driving the returns for all assets—a global equity factor and a global bond factor. If the variance for the global equity factor is

0.0211, the variance for the global bond factor is 0.0019, and the covariance between them is 0.0015, then the *factor covariance matrix* is (note that the covariance of an asset with itself is its variance):

Figure 1: Factor Covariance Matrix for Global Assets

	Global Equity Factor	*Global Bond Factor*
Global equity factor	0.0211	0.0015
Global bond factor	0.0015	0.0019

Using this factor covariance matrix, a covariance matrix for markets can be derived if we know the sensitivities (the factor sensitivities or factor loadings) of the markets to these driving factors.

A 2-factor multifactor model is specified as:

$$R_i = \alpha_i + \beta_{i,1}F_1 + \beta_{i,2}F_2 + \varepsilon_i$$

In this 2-factor model, returns for an asset i, R_i, are a function of factor sensitivities, β, and factors, F. A random error, ε_i, has a mean of zero and is uncorrelated with the factors.

Using the factor model, we can formulate the variance of Market i, σ_i^2, given the covariance, $\text{Cov}(F_1, F_2)$, of factor returns:

$$\sigma_i^2 = \beta_{i,1}^2\sigma_{F_1}^2 + \beta_{i,2}^2\sigma_{F_2}^2 + 2\beta_{i,1}\beta_{i,2}\text{Cov}(F_1,F_2) + \sigma_{\varepsilon,i}^2$$

The covariance between Markets i and j, $\text{Cov}(i,j)$, can be calculated using:

$$\text{Cov}(i,j) = \beta_{i,1}\beta_{j,1}\sigma_{F_1}^2 + \beta_{i,2}\beta_{j,2}\sigma_{F_2}^2 + (\beta_{i,1}\beta_{j,2}+\beta_{i,2}\beta_{j,1})\text{Cov}(F_1,F_2)$$

For the Exam: A calculation such as this has not been common on the exam. It would not be on my high priority list.

If a candidate chooses to study them, he will find the calculations in the CFA® text are inconsistent with regards to the scale used. In the discussion of shrinkage estimators, standard deviations are expressed as whole numbers such as 14% and covariance was 220. Then in the time series discussion, standard deviation was expressed as a decimal such as .15 (for 15%) with variance .0225 and covariance .0211. Data and solutions can be expressed in either whole number (14) or decimal fashion (.14); it is a matter of scale.

For example, suppose the factor sensitivity to the global equity factor for Market i is 0.90 and 0.80 for Market j. If the sensitivities for both markets to the global bond market are zero, then we can deduce that these two markets are equity markets. Note that this does not mean the pairwise correlation between each market and the global bond market is zero. It means that, once the effect of the equity market is controlled for, the *partial correlation* of each market and the global bond factor is zero.

The covariance in this example would be:

Cov(i,j) = (0.90)(0.80)(0.0211) + (0)(0)(0.0019) + [(0.90)(0) + (0)(0.80)]0.0015 = 0.0152

The advantage of this approach is that the consistency of the global factor covariance matrix in Figure 1 is readily established because it only has four elements. Given its consistency, the variance and covariance estimates for the markets will then be consistent.

In this example, a 2-layered approach was used; that is, the driving factors were one level and the market parameters were another. In other markets, there may be many layers of factors. For example, perhaps the equity markets in Southeast Asia are highly correlated with each other but less correlated with the rest of the world. The first layer would be the individual markets (China, Hong Kong, Indonesia, Malaysia, Philippines, Singapore, South Korea, Taiwan, and Thailand), and the second layer would be the Southeast Asian equity market as a whole. Other layers would be composed of other markets that are correlated with the Southeast Asian equity market.

Discounted Cash Flow Models

A second tool for setting capital market expectations is **discounted cash flow models**. These models say that the intrinsic value of an asset is the present value of future cash flows. The advantage of these models is their correct emphasis on the future cash flows of an asset and the ability to back out a required return. Their disadvantage is that they do not account for current market conditions such as supply and demand, so these models are viewed as being more suitable for long-term valuation.

Applied to equity markets, the most common application of discounted cash flow models is the Gordon growth model or constant growth model. It is most commonly used to back out the expected return on equity, resulting in the following:

$$P_0 = \frac{Div_1}{\hat{R}_i - g} \Rightarrow \hat{R}_i = \frac{Div_1}{P_0} + g$$

where:
$\hat{R}_i$ = expected return on stock i
Div_1 = dividend next period
P_0 = current stock price
g = growth rate in dividends and long-term earnings

This formulation can be applied to entire markets as well. In this case, the growth rate is proxied by the nominal growth in GDP, which is the sum of the real growth rate in GDP plus the rate of inflation. The growth rate can be adjusted for any differences between the economy's growth rate and that of the equity index. This adjustment is referred to as the *excess corporate growth rate*. For example, the analyst may project the U.S. real growth in GDP at 2%. If the analyst thinks that the constituents of the Wilshire 5000 index will grow at a rate 1% faster than the economy as a whole, the projected growth for the Wilshire 5000 would be 3%.

Grinold and Kroner (2002)[1] take this model one step further by including a variable that adjusts for stock repurchases and changes in market valuations as represented by the price-earnings (P/E) ratio. The model states that the expected return on a stock is its dividend yield plus the inflation rate plus the real earnings growth rate minus the change in stock outstanding plus changes in the P/E ratio:

$$\hat{R}_i = \frac{D_1}{P_0} + i + g - \Delta S + \Delta\left(\frac{P}{E}\right)$$

where:

$\hat{R}_i$ = expected return on stock i; referred to as *compound annual growth rate* on a Level III exam

$\dfrac{D_1}{P_0}$ = expected dividend yield

i = expected inflation

g = real growth rate

ΔS = percentage change in shares outstanding (positive or negative)

$\Delta\left(\dfrac{P}{E}\right)$ = percentage change in the P/E ratio (repricing term)

The variables of the Grinold-Kroner model can be grouped into three components: the expected income return, the expected nominal growth in earnings, and the expected repricing return.

1.   The **expected income return** is the current yield in percent that stockholders can expect to receive from the stock:

$$\text{expected income return} = \left(\frac{D_1}{P_0} - \Delta S\right)$$

D_1 / P_0 is current yield as seen in the constant growth dividend discount model. It is the expected dividend expressed as a percentage of the current price. The Grinold-Kroner model goes a step further in expressing the expected current yield by considering any repurchases or new issues of stock. To help understand the relationship between ΔS and the income return, consider the following:

- If the firm repurchases shares, it pays cash to the stockholders. This increases the cash return stockholders receive from the firm, a *positive repurchase yield*. Add the forecasted repurchase to the dividend yield to calculate expected income return. This would be a $-\Delta S$. In the formula, subtract $-\Delta S$ to increase the income return.

- If the firm issues new shares, it collects cash from its stockholders. This effectively decreases the net cash stockholders receive from the firm, a *negative repurchase yield*. Subtract the issuance from the dividend yield to calculate expected income return. This would be a $+\Delta S$. In the formula subtract ΔS to decrease the income return.

---

1.   Richard Grinold and Kenneth Kroner, "The Equity Risk Premium," *Investment Insights* (Barclay's Global Investors, July 2002).

2. The **expected nominal earnings growth** is the real growth in the stock price plus expected inflation (think of a nominal interest rate that includes the real rate plus inflation):

$$\text{expected nominal earnings growth} = (i + g)$$

3. The **repricing return** is captured by the expected change in the P/E ratio:

$$\text{expected repricing return} = \Delta\left(\frac{P}{E}\right)$$

It is helpful to view the Grinold-Kroner model as the sum of the expected income return, the expected nominal growth, and the expected repricing return.

$$\hat{R}_i = \exp(\text{income return}) + \exp(\text{nominal earnings growth}) + \exp(\text{repricing return})$$

$$\hat{R}_i = \left(\frac{D_1}{P_0} - \Delta S\right) + (i + g) + \left(\Delta\frac{P}{E}\right)$$

Suppose an analyst estimates a 2.1% dividend yield, real earnings growth of 4.0%, long-term inflation of 3.1%, a repurchase yield of –0.5%, and P/E re-pricing of 0.3%:

expected *current yield* (income return) = dividend yield + repurchase yield
$$= 2.1\% - 0.5\% = 1.6\%$$

expected *capital gains yield*   = real growth + inflation + re-pricing
$$= 4.0\% + 3.1\% + 0.3\% = 7.4\%$$

The total expected return on the stock market is 1.6% + 7.4% = 9.0%.

> *Professor's Note: Many candidates have had difficulty with the repurchase yield and ΔS terminology and concept. In Grinold-Kroner, they are the same number but with opposite sign. I hope the following diagram for the income return of 1.6% we just calculated will help. The terminology is a bit tricky.*

Figure 2: Grinold-Kroner Income Return

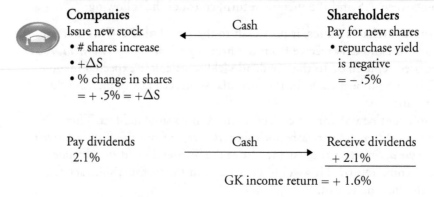

©2013 Kaplan, Inc.

Estimating Fixed Income Returns

Discounted cash flow analysis is also applied to bond markets, where the yield to maturity on the reference bond in a segment is used as the expected return for that segment. A drawback to this approach is that the yield to maturity assumes intermediate cash flows are reinvested at the yield to maturity. The analyst might adjust the YTM up or down based on an assumed reinvestment rate or use the YTM of a zero-coupon bond. A zero-coupon bond has no coupon cash flows and is not subject to reinvestment risk if held to maturity.

Risk Premium Approach

A third method to setting capital market expectations is the risk premium approach, sometimes referred to as the *build-up approach*. To determine the expected return for equities, the analyst would build up a bond yield add an equity risk premium. This approach is referred to as the *bond yield plus risk premium* approach. Alternatively the analyst could start with a bond yield and add the appropriate risk premiums.

To determine the expected return for bonds, $\hat{R}_B$, using this approach, the analyst uses the real risk-free rate and risk premiums as follows:

$$\hat{R}_B = \text{real risk-free rate} + \text{inflation risk premium} + \text{default risk premium} + \\ \text{liquidity risk premium} + \text{maturity risk premium} + \text{tax premium}$$

- The inflation premium compensates the bond investor for a loss in purchasing power over time. It can be measured by comparing the yields for inflation-indexed government bonds to non-inflation-indexed bonds of the same maturity.
- The default risk premium compensates the investor for the likelihood of non-payment and can be estimated by examining the yields for bonds of differing credit risk.
- The liquidity premium compensates the investor for holding illiquid bonds.
- The maturity risk premium reflects the yield differences of bonds of different maturities.
- The tax premium accounts for different tax treatments of bonds.

To calculate an expected equity return, an equity risk premium would be added to the bond yield.

Financial Equilibrium Models

The financial equilibrium approach assumes that supply and demand in global asset markets are in balance. In turn, financial models will value securities correctly. One such model is the International Capital Asset Pricing Model (ICAPM). The Singer and Terhaar approach begins with the ICAPM.

The equation for the ICAPM is:

$$\hat{R}_i = R_F + \beta_i \left(\hat{R}_M - R_F \right)$$

where:
$\hat{R}_i$ = expected return on asset i
R_F = risk-free rate of return
β_i = sensitivity (systematic risk) of asset i returns to the global investable market
$\hat{R}_M$ = expected return on the *global* investable market

Think of the global investable market as consisting of all investable assets, traditional and alternative.

We can manipulate this formula to solve for the risk premium on a debt or equity security using the following steps:

Step 1: The relationship between the covariance and correlation is:

$$\rho_{i,M} = \frac{\text{Cov}(i,m)}{\sigma_i \sigma_M} \Rightarrow \text{Cov}(i,m) = \rho_{i,M} \sigma_i \sigma_M$$

where:
$\rho_{i,M}$ = correlation between the returns on asset i and the global market portfolio
σ_i = standard deviation of the returns on asset i
σ_M = standard deviation of the returns on the global market portfolio

Step 2: Recall that:

$$\beta_i = \frac{\text{Cov}(i,m)}{\sigma_M^2}$$

where:
$\text{Cov}(i,m)$ = covariance of asset i with the global market portfolio
σ_M^2 = variance of the returns on the global market portfolio

Step 3: Combining the two previous equations and simplifying:

$$\beta_i = \frac{\rho_{i,M} \sigma_i \sigma_M}{\sigma_M^2} = \frac{\rho_{i,M} \sigma_i}{\sigma_M}$$

Step 4: Rearranging the ICAPM, we arrive at the expression for the risk premium for asset *i*, RP_i:

$$\hat{R}_i = R_F + \beta_i\left(\hat{R}_M - R_F\right)$$

$$\hat{R}_i - R_F = \beta_i\left(\hat{R}_M - R_F\right)$$

denoting $\hat{R}_i - R_F$ as RP_i

$$RP_i = \beta_i\left(\hat{R}_M - R_F\right); \text{ and since } \beta_i = \rho_{i,M}\frac{\sigma_i}{\sigma_M}$$

$$RP_i = \rho_{i,M}\frac{\sigma_i}{\sigma_M}\left(\hat{R}_M - R_F\right), \text{ or}$$

$$RP_i = \rho_{i,M}\sigma_i\left(\frac{\hat{R}_M - R_F}{\sigma_M}\right)$$

Note that $\left(\dfrac{\hat{R}_M - R_F}{\sigma_M}\right) =$ market Sharpe ratio

and that $\hat{R}_M - R_F$ is the market risk premium.

The final expression states that the risk premium for an asset is equal to its correlation with the global market portfolio multiplied by the standard deviation of the asset multiplied by the Sharpe ratio for the global portfolio (in parentheses). From this formula, we forecast the risk premium and expected return for a market.

Example: Calculating an equity risk premium and a debt risk premium

Given the following data, **calculate** the equity and debt risk premiums for Country X:

	Expected Standard Deviation	*Correlation With Global Investable Market*
Country X bonds	10%	0.40
Country X equities	15%	0.70
Market Sharpe ratio = 0.35		

$$RP_{bonds} = 10\% \times 0.40 \times 0.35 = 1.40\%$$

$$RP_{equities} = 15\% \times 0.70 \times 0.35 = 3.68\%$$

The Singer and Terhaar analysis then adjusts the ICAPM for market imperfections, such as illiquidity and segmentation. The more illiquid an asset is, the greater the liquidity risk premium should be. Liquidity is not typically a concern for developed world capital markets, but it can be a concern for assets such as direct real estate and private equity funds. In the case of private equity, an investment is usually subject to a lock-up period.

To estimate the size of the liquidity risk premium, one could estimate the *multi-period Sharpe ratio* for the investment over the time until it is liquid and compare it to the estimated multi-period Sharpe ratio for the market. The Sharpe ratio for the illiquid asset must be at least as high as that for the market. For example, suppose a venture capital investment has a lock-up period of five years and its multi-period Sharpe ratio is below that of the market's. If its expected return from the ICAPM is 16%, and the return necessary to equate its Sharpe ratio to that of the market's was 25%, then the liquidity premium would be 9%.

When markets are segmented, capital does not flow freely across borders. The opposite of segmented markets is integrated markets, where capital flows freely. Government restrictions on investing are a frequent cause of market segmentation. If markets are segmented, two assets with the same risk can have different expected returns because capital cannot flow to the higher return asset. The presence of investment barriers increases the risk premium for securities in segmented markets.

In reality, most markets are not fully segmented or integrated. For example, investors have a preference for their own country's equity markets (the *home country bias*). This prevents them from fully exploiting investment opportunities overseas. Developed world equity markets have been estimated as 80% integrated, whereas emerging market equities have been estimated as 65% integrated. In the example to follow, we will adjust for partial market segmentation by estimating an equity risk premium assuming full integration and an equity risk premium assuming full segmentation, and then taking a weighted average of the two. Under the full segmentation assumption, the relevant global portfolio is the individual market so that the correlation between the market and the global portfolio in the formula is 1. In that case, the equation for the market's risk premium reduces to:

$$\text{if } \rho_{i,M} = 1 \Rightarrow \text{ERP}_i = \sigma_i \left(\frac{\text{ERP}_M}{\sigma_M} \right)$$

In the following example, we will calculate the equity risk premium for the two markets, their expected returns, and the covariance between them. Before we start, recall from our discussion of factor models that the covariance between two markets given two factors is:

$$\text{Cov}(i,j) = \beta_{i,1}\beta_{j,1}\sigma_{F_1}^2 + \beta_{i,2}\beta_{j,2}\sigma_{F_2}^2 + \left(\beta_{i,1}\beta_{j,2} + \beta_{i,2}\beta_{j,1} \right)\text{Cov}(F_1, F_2)$$

If there is only one factor driving returns (i.e., the global portfolio), then the equation reduces to:

$$\text{Cov}(i,j) = \beta_i \, \beta_j \, \sigma_M^2$$

Example: Using market risk premiums to calculate expected returns, betas, and covariances

Suppose an analyst is valuing two equity markets. Market A is a developed market, and Market B is an emerging market. The investor's time horizon is five years. The other pertinent facts are:

Sharpe ratio of the global investable portfolio	0.29
Standard deviation of the global investable portfolio	9%
Risk-free rate of return	5%
Degree of market integration for Market A	80%
Degree of market integration for Market B	65%
Standard deviation of Market A	17%
Standard deviation of Market B	28%
Correlation of Market A with global investable portfolio	0.82
Correlation of Market B with global investable portfolio	0.63
Estimated illiquidity premium for A	0.0%
Estimated illiquidity premium for B	2.3%

Calculate the assets' expected returns, betas, and covariance.

Answer:

First, we calculate the equity risk premium for both markets assuming full integration. Note that for the emerging market, the illiquidity risk premium is included:

$$\text{ERP}_i = \rho_{i,M}\sigma_i(\text{market Sharpe ratio})$$
$$\text{ERP}_A = (0.82)(0.17)(0.29) = 4.04\%$$
$$\text{ERP}_B = (0.63)(0.28)(0.29) + 0.0230 = 7.42\%$$

Next, we calculate the equity risk premium for both markets assuming full segmentation:

$$\text{ERP}_i = \sigma_i(\text{market Sharpe ratio})$$
$$\text{ERP}_A = (0.17)(0.29) = 4.93\%$$
$$\text{ERP}_B = (0.28)(0.29) + 0.0230 = 10.42\%$$

Note that when we calculate the risk premium under full segmentation, we use the local market as the reference market instead of the global market, so the correlation between the local market and itself is 1.0.

We then weight the integrated and segmented risk premiums by the degree of integration and segmentation in each market to arrive at the weighted average equity risk premium:

$$ERP_i = \text{(degree of integration of } i)(\text{ERP assuming full integration}) +$$
$$\text{(degree of segmentation of } i)(\text{ERP assuming full segmentation})$$
$$ERP_A = (0.80)(0.0404) + (1 - 0.80)(0.0493) = 4.22\%$$
$$ERP_B = (0.65)(0.0742) + (1 - 0.65)(0.1042) = 8.47\%$$

The expected return in each market figures in the risk-free rate:

$$\hat{R}_A = 5\% + 4.22\% = 9.22\%$$
$$\hat{R}_B = 5\% + 8.47\% = 13.47\%$$

The betas in each market, which will be needed for the covariance, are calculated as:

$$\beta_i = \frac{\rho_{i,M}\sigma_i}{\sigma_M}$$

$$\beta_A = \frac{(0.82)(17)}{9} = 1.55$$

$$\beta_B = \frac{(0.63)(28)}{9} = 1.96$$

Lastly, we calculate the covariance of the two equity markets:

$$Cov(i,j) = \beta_i\,\beta_j\,\sigma_M^2$$
$$Cov(A,B) = (1.55)(1.96)(9.0)^2 = 246.08$$

THE USE OF SURVEYS AND JUDGMENT FOR CAPITAL MARKET EXPECTATIONS

LOS 17.d: Explain the use of survey and panel methods and judgment in setting capital market expectations.

CFA® Program Curriculum, Volume 3, page 48

Capital market expectations can also be formed using **surveys**. In this method, a poll is taken of market participants, such as economists and analysts, as to what their expectations are regarding the economy or capital market. If the group polled is fairly constant over time, this method is referred to as a **panel method**. For example, the U.S. Federal Reserve Bank of Philadelphia conducts an ongoing survey regarding the U.S. consumer price index, GDP, and so forth.[2]

---

2. Accessible at *www.philadelphiafed.org;* accessed July, 2013.

Judgment can also be applied to project capital market expectations. Although quantitative models provide objective numerical forecasts, there are times when an analyst must adjust those expectations using their experience and insight to improve upon those forecasts.

Economic Analysis

LOS 17.e: Discuss the inventory and business cycles, the impact of consumer and business spending, and monetary and fiscal policy on the business cycle.

CFA® Program Curriculum, Volume 3, page 50

The Inventory and Business Cycle

Understanding the business cycle can help the analyst identify *inflection points* (i.e., when the economy changes direction), where the risk and the opportunities for higher return may be heightened. To identify inflection points, the analyst should understand what is driving the current economy and what may cause the end of the current economy.

In general, economic growth can be partitioned into two components: (1) cyclical and (2) trend-growth components. The former is more short-term whereas the latter is more relevant for determining long-term return expectations. We will discuss the cyclical component first.

Within cyclical analysis, there are two components: (1) the inventory cycle and (2) the business cycle. The former typically lasts two to four years whereas the latter has a typical duration of nine to eleven years. These cycles vary in duration and are hard to predict because wars and other events can disrupt them.

Changes in economic activity delineate cyclical activity. The measures of economic activity are GDP, the output gap, and a recession. GDP is usually measured in real terms because true economic growth should be adjusted for inflationary components. The **output gap** is the difference between GDP based on a long-term trend line (i.e., potential GDP) and the current level of GDP. When the trend line is higher than the current GDP, the economy has slowed and inflationary pressures have weakened. When it is lower, economic activity is strong, as are inflationary pressures. This relationship is used by policy makers to form expectations regarding the appropriate level of growth and inflation. The relationship is affected by changes in technology and demographics. The third measure of economic activity, a **recession**, is defined as decreases (i.e., negative growth) in GDP over two consecutive quarters.

The **inventory cycle** is thought to be 2 to 4 years in length. It is often measured using the inventory to sales ratio. The measure increases when businesses gain confidence in the future of the economy and add to their inventories in anticipation of increasing demand for their output. As a result, employment increases with subsequent increases in economic growth. This continues until some precipitating factor, such as a tightening in the growth of the money supply, intervenes. At this point, inventories decrease and employment declines, which causes economic growth to slow.

When the inventory measure has peaked in an economy, as in the United States in 2000, subsequent periods exhibit slow growth as businesses sell out of their inventory. When it bottoms out, as in 2004, subsequent periods have higher growth as businesses restock their inventory. The long-term trend in this measure has been downward due to more effective inventory management techniques such as just-in-time inventory management.

The longer-term **business cycle** is thought to be 9 to 11 years in length. It is characterized by five phases: (1) the initial recovery, (2) early upswing, (3) late upswing, (4) slowdown, and (5) recession. We discuss the business cycle in greater detail later when we examine its effect on asset returns.

LOS 17.f: <u>Discuss</u> the impact that the phases of the business cycle have on short-term/long-term capital market returns.

CFA® Program Curriculum, Volume 3, page 52

> **For the Exam:** Be able to discuss the inventory and business cycles, as well as their relationship to one another. Have a working knowledge of, and be able to explain, the general relationships between interest rates, inflation, stock and bond prices, inventory levels, et cetera, as you progress over the cycle. For example, as the peak of the business cycle approaches, everything is humming along. Confidence and employment are high, but inflation is starting to have an impact on markets. As inflation increases, bond yields increase and both bond and stock prices start to fall.

The Business Cycle and Asset Returns

The relationship between the business cycle and assets returns is well-documented. Assets with higher returns during business cycle lows (e.g., bonds and defensive stocks) should be favored by investors because the returns supplement their income during recessionary periods. These assets should have lower risk premiums. Assets with lower returns during recessions should have higher risk premiums. Understanding the relationship between an asset's return and the business cycle can help the analyst provide better valuations.

As mentioned before, inflation varies over the business cycle, which has five phases: (1) initial recovery, (2) early expansion, (3) late expansion, (4) slowdown, and (5) recession. Inflation rises in the latter stages of an expansion and falls during a recession and the initial recovery. The phases have the following characteristics:

Initial Recovery

- Duration of a few months.
- Business confidence is rising.
- Government stimulation is provided by low interest rates and/or budget deficits.

- Falling inflation.
- Large output gap
- Low or falling short-term interest rates.
- Bond yields are bottoming out.
- Rising stock prices.
- Cyclical, riskier assets such as small-cap stocks and high yield bonds do well.

Early Upswing

- Duration of a year to several years.
- Increasing growth with low inflation.
- Increasing confidence.
- Increasing inventories.
- Rising short-term interest rates.
- Output gap is narrowing.
- Flat or rising bond yields.
- Rising stock prices.

Late Upswing

- Confidence and employment are high.
- Output gap eliminated and economy at risk of overheating.
- Inflation increases.
- Central bank limits the growth of the money supply.
- Rising short-term interest rates.
- Rising bond yields.
- Rising stock prices, but increased risk and volatility.

Slowdown

- Duration of a few months to a year or longer.
- Declining confidence.
- Inflation is still rising.
- Falling inventory levels.
- Short-term interest rates are at a peak.
- Bond yields have peaked and may be falling, resulting in rising bond prices.
- Yield curve may invert.
- Falling stock prices.

Recession

- Duration of six months to a year.
- Large declines in inventory.
- Declining confidence and profits.
- Increase in unemployment and bankruptcies.
- Inflation tops out.
- Falling short-term interest rates.
- Falling bond yields, rising prices.
- Stock prices increase during the latter stages anticipating the end of the recession.

Although it is straightforward to describe the characteristics of the various phases of the business cycle, it is not so easy to predict when they will occur. Furthermore, even if the start of a recession could be predicted, the length and severity of a recession is unpredictable.

Inflation

Aggregate inflation is measured most frequently by consumer price indices. Inflation rises in the latter stages of economic expansion and falls during a recession and the initial recovery. When forecasting, the analyst should adjust the inflation figure for long-term changes in inflation. Historically, inflation had been low because monetary growth was limited by the gold standard. Inflation rose in the developed world in the 1970s but has been tamed more recently.

Deflation, or periods of decreasing prices, reduces the ability of the central bank to stimulate the economy. Deflation results in interest rates near zero, so the central bank cannot lower rates any further to stimulate the economy. For this reason, central banks prefer a low level of inflation to the prospect of deflation.

INFLATION AND ASSET RETURNS

LOS 17.g: Explain the relationship of inflation to the business cycle and the implications of inflation for cash, bonds, equity, and real estate returns.

CFA® Program Curriculum, Volume 3, page 58

The link between asset prices and inflation is inextricably tied to the business cycle. As noted previously, inflation increases as the economy expands and the output gap shrinks, and then declines when the economy slows and the output gap widens. Inflation is negative for bonds. Hence, in a strong expansion, bonds tend to decline in price as inflationary expectations and interest rates rise. Bond prices will rise during a recession when inflation and interest rates are declining. This is also true during deflationary times. The exception here is when credit risk for a particular issue or sector increases during a recession.

Low inflation can be positive for equities, given that there are prospects for economic growth free of central bank interference. Equities provide an inflation hedge when inflation is moderate and when price increases can be passed along to the consumer. Inflation rates above 3% can be problematic, though, because of increased likelihood that the central bank will restrict economic growth. Declining inflation or deflation is also problematic because this usually results in declining economic growth and asset prices. The firms most affected are those that are highly levered and thus most sensitive to changing interest rates. They would face declining profits yet would still be obligated to pay back the same amount of interest and principal.

Deflation also reduces the value of real assets financed with debt. In the case of real estate, if the property is levered with debt, declines in the property's value lead to steeper declines in the equity position. As a result, investors flee in an attempt to preserve their

©2013 Kaplan, Inc.

equity. Fortunately, with central banks no longer tied to the gold standard, they are free to pursue the measures necessary to avoid deflation, so its occurrences are quite rare. When inflation is at or below expectations, the cash flows for real estate and other real assets rise slowly, and returns are near their long-run average. When inflation is high, the cash flows and returns for real assets are higher. In the case of many properties, rents often increase as inflation increases. Thus, real estate provides a good inflation hedge.

Low inflation does not affect the return on cash instruments. Higher inflation is a positive for cash because the returns on cash instruments increase as inflation increases. Deflation is negative for cash because the return falls to almost zero.

Consumer and Business Spending

As a percentage of GDP, consumer spending is much larger than business spending. Consumer spending is usually gauged through the use of store sales data, retail sales, and consumer consumption data. The data has a seasonal pattern, with sales increasing near holidays. In turn, the primary driver of consumer spending is consumer after-tax income, which in the United States is gauged using non-farm payroll data and new unemployment claims. Employment data is important to markets because it is usually quite timely.

Given that spending is income net of savings, savings data are also important for predicting consumer spending. Saving rates are influenced by consumer confidence and changes in the investment environment. Specifically, consumer confidence increases as the economy begins to recover from a recession, and consumers begin to spend more. At the same time, stock prices start to rise and momentum begins to build. Consumers continue spending until the economy shows definite signs that it has peaked (i.e., top of the business cycle) and reversed. At this point, consumers begin saving more and more until the economy "turns the corner," and the cycle starts over.

Business spending is more volatile than consumer spending. Spending by businesses on inventory and investments is quite volatile over the business cycle. As mentioned before, the peak of inventory spending is often a bearish signal for the economy. It may indicate that businesses have overspent relative to the amount they are selling. This portends a slowdown in business spending and economic growth.

Monetary Policy

Central banks often use monetary policy as a counter-cyclical force to optimize the economy's performance. Most central banks strive to balance price stability against economic growth. The ultimate goal is to keep growth near its long-run sustainable rate, because growth faster than the long-run rate usually results in increased inflation. As discussed previously, the latter stages of an economic expansion are often characterized by increased inflation. As a result, central banks usually resort to restrictive policies towards the latter part of an expansion.

To spur growth, a central bank can take actions to reduce short-term interest rates. This results in greater consumer spending, greater business spending, higher stock prices, and higher bond prices. Lower interest rates also usually result in a lower value of the domestic currency, which is thought to increase exports. In addition to the direction of a change in interest rates being important, it is also the level of interest rates that is important. If, for example, rates are increased to 4% to combat inflation but this is still low compared to the average of 6% in a country, then this absolute rate may still be low enough to allow growth while the rise in rates may begin to dampen inflation. The equilibrium interest rate in a country (the rate at which a balance between growth and inflation is achieved) is referred to as the neutral rate. It is generally thought that the neutral rate is composed of an inflation component and a real growth component. If, for example, inflation is targeted at 3% and the economy is expected to grow by 2%, then the neutral rate would be 5%.

THE TAYLOR RULE

LOS 17.h: Demonstrate the use of the Taylor rule to predict central bank behavior.

CFA® Program Curriculum, Volume 3, page 63

The neutral rate is the rate that most central banks strive to achieve as they attempt to balance the risks of inflation and recession. If inflation is too high, the central bank should increase short-term interest rates. If economic growth is too low, it should cut interest rates. The **Taylor rule** embodies this concept. Thus, it is used as a prescriptive tool (i.e., it states what the central bank should do). It also is fairly accurate at predicting central bank action.

For the Exam: Be able to discuss and apply the Taylor rule. It has been covered at all levels of the exam.

The Taylor rule determines the target interest rate using the neutral rate, expected GDP relative to its long-term trend, and expected inflation relative to its targeted amount. It can be formalized as follows:

$$r_{target} = r_{neutral} + \left[0.5 \left(GDP_{expected} - GDP_{trend} \right) + 0.5 \left(i_{expected} - i_{target} \right) \right]$$

where:

r_{target} = short-term interest rate target

$r_{neutral}$ = neutral short-term interest rate

$GDP_{expected}$ = expected GDP growth rate

GDP_{trend} = long-term trend in the GDP growth rate

$i_{expected}$ = expected inflation rate

i_{target} = target inflation rate

Example: Calculating the short-term interest rate target

Given the following information, **calculate** the short-term interest rate target.

Neutral rate	4%
Inflation target	3%
Expected inflation	7%
GDP long-term trend	2%
Expected GDP growth	0%

Answer:

$$r_{target} = 4\% + \left[0.5(0\% - 2\%) + 0.5(7\% - 3\%)\right]$$
$$= 4\% + (-1\% + 2\%) = 5\%$$

In this example, the weak projected economic growth calls for cutting interest rates. If inflation were not a consideration, the target interest rate would be 1% lower than the neutral rate. However, the higher projected inflation overrides the growth concern because projected inflation is 4% greater than the target inflation rate. In net, the target rate is 5% because the concern over high inflation overrides the weak growth concern.

Fiscal Policy

Another tool at the government's disposal for managing the economy is fiscal policy. If the government wants to stimulate the economy, it can implement loose fiscal policy by decreasing taxes and/or increasing spending, thereby increasing the budget deficit. If they want to rein in growth, the government does the opposite to implement fiscal tightening.

There are two important aspects to fiscal policy. First, it is not the level of the budget deficit that matters—it is the change in the deficit. For example, a deficit by itself does not stimulate the economy, but increases in the deficit are required to stimulate the economy. Second, changes in the deficit that occur naturally over the course of the business cycle are not stimulative or restrictive. In an expanding economy, deficits will decline because tax receipts increase and disbursements to the unemployed decrease. The opposite occurs during a recession. Only changes in the deficit directed by government policy will influence growth.

THE YIELD CURVE

LOS 17.i: Evaluate 1) the shape of the yield curve as an economic predictor and 2) the relationship between the yield curve and fiscal and monetary policy.

CFA® Program Curriculum, Volume 3, page 66

The yield curve demonstrates the relationship between interest rates and the maturity of the debt security and is sensitive to actions of the federal government as well as current and expected economic conditions. When both fiscal and monetary policies are expansive, for example, the yield curve is sharply upward sloping (i.e., short-term rates are lower than long-term rates), and the economy is likely to expand in the future. When fiscal and monetary policies are restrictive, the yield curve is downward sloping (i.e., it is *inverted*, as short-term rates are higher than long-term rates), and the economy is likely to contract in the future.

Fiscal and monetary policies may reinforce or conflict each other. If the policies reinforce each other, the implications for the economy are clear. In all cases, there are likely implications for the yield curve:

- If both are stimulative, the yield curve is steep and the economy is likely to grow.
- If both are restrictive, the yield curve is inverted and the economy is likely to contract.
- If monetary is restrictive and fiscal is stimulative, the yield curve is flat and the economy is unclear.
- If monetary is stimulative and fiscal is restrictive, the yield curve is moderately steep and the economy is unclear.

ECONOMIC GROWTH TRENDS

LOS 17.j: Identify and interpret the components of economic growth trends and demonstrate the application of economic growth trend analysis to the formulation of capital market expectations.

CFA® Program Curriculum, Volume 3, page 67

Economic growth can be partitioned into cyclical and trend components. Economic trends determine long-term economic growth whereas as cyclical components are shorter term. Trends are determined in part by demographics, productivity, and structural changes in governmental policies.

In forecasting a country's long-term economic growth trend, the trend growth rate can be decomposed into two main components: (1) **changes in employment levels** and (2) **changes in productivity**. Essentially, the two together measure how many people are working and what each person's output is. The former component can be further broken down into **population growth** and the **rate of labor force participation**.

For example, employment levels may increase in the United States both due to an influx of immigrants and due to senior citizens staying in the workforce longer. Some developed countries tend to have an older population that limits their growth (e.g., Japan). Government policies that encourage workforce participation increase the labor force participation growth rate.

The productivity component can be broken down into subcomponents as well: **spending on new capital inputs** and **total factor productivity growth**. The latter results from more efficient use of inputs and better technology. The former component accounts for much of the fast growth in Asia, as much has been spent there on new equipment. Note that as an investment grows, the earnings derived from it must grow faster for higher stock prices to result. This may explain why some fast growing, high investment economies have unimpressive stock returns (i.e., their fast growth is not fast enough).

Some developed countries have laws that limit increases in productivity. For example, in Germany, labor regulations are fairly rigid and limit increases in worker productivity.

Example: Forecasting the long-term economic growth rate

Assume that the population is expected to grow by 2% and that labor force participation is expected to grow by 0.25%. If spending on new capital inputs is projected to grow at 2.5% and total factor productivity will grow by 0.5%, what is the long-term projected growth rate?

Answer:

The sum of the components equals 2% + 0.25% + 2.5% + 0.5% = 5.25%, so the economy is projected to grow by this amount.

Higher long-term growth rate trends benefit the equity investor through a higher growth rate, usually without excessive inflation. The trend growth rates for developed countries are fairly stable over time, while emerging countries are expected to have higher trending growth rates. Eventually, though, emerging countries grow into developed countries, and their growth slows.

As mentioned before, consumer spending is the largest component of GDP and is fairly stable over the business cycle. The reason is that individuals tend to consume an amount that is fairly constant over time and related to their expected long-run income. This is the essence of Milton Friedman's permanent income hypothesis. As applied to the formulation of capital market expectations, it means that economic slowdowns will not affect consumer consumption much. In a recession, individuals will save less and decrease their consumption by only a small amount. In an expansion, individuals consume more, but less than their income increases. In sum, when events occur that consumers perceive as temporary, their consumption and aggregate consumer spending will not change a great deal.

A more important component of changes in the long-term growth rate in an economy is governmental structural policies, which are policies designed to enhance or regulate growth. The question, however, is the types of policies that enhance growth, and there are four general guidelines.

First, although the government should provide the infrastructure needed for growth (e.g., roads, the internet, educational systems), the government should interfere with the economy as little as possible. It is generally agreed that the private sector provides the most efficient allocation of resources. Although most governments are trending towards privatization of formerly owned government businesses, there is still a good deal of government regulation.

Second, a government should have a responsible *fiscal policy*. Although budget deficits may be used to stimulate the economy, consistently high budget deficits often lead to inflation when the central bank accommodates the deficit with higher growth in the money supply. Budget deficits are also often accompanied by trade deficits, which may result in an eventual devaluation of the home currency. In addition, public borrowing may *crowd out* more productive private borrowing.

Third, a government should have tax policies that are transparent, consistently applied, pulled from a wide base, and not overly burdensome. Although some inefficiency is expected from the redistribution of wealth, tax policies should promote growth as much as possible.

Lastly, the government should promote competition in the marketplace, thereby increasing the efficiency of the economy. Technological advances and openness to foreign competition through the reduction of tariffs are important factors for growth.

LOS 17.k: Explain how exogenous shocks may affect economic growth trends.

CFA® Program Curriculum, Volume 3, page 72

In addition to being influenced by governmental policies, trends are still subject to unexpected surprises or shocks that are exogenous to the economy, and many shocks and the degree of their impact on capital markets cannot be forecasted. For example, turmoil in the Middle East may change the long-term trend for oil prices, inflation, and economic growth in the developed world. Shocks may also arise through the banking system. An extreme example is the U.S. banking crisis of the 1930s, when a severe slowdown in bank lending paralyzed the economy.

Exogenous shocks are unanticipated events that occur outside the normal course of an economy. Since the events are unanticipated, they are not already built into current market prices, whereas normal trends in an economy, which would be considered endogenous, are built into market prices. Exogenous shocks can be caused by different factors, such as natural disasters, political events, or changes in government policies.

Although positive shocks are not unknown, exogenous shocks usually produce a negative impact on an economy and oftentimes spread to other countries in a process referred to as *contagion*. Two common shocks relate to changes in oil supplies and crises in financial markets. Oil shocks have historically involved increasing prices caused by a reduction in oil production. The increased oil prices can lead to increased inflation and a subsequent slowdown of the economy from decreased consumer spending and increased unemployment. Conversely, a decline in oil prices, as was the case in 1986 and 1999, can produce lower inflation, which boosts the economy. A significant decline in oil prices, however, can lead to an overheated economy and increasing inflation.

Financial crises are also not uncommon. Consider the Latin America debt crisis in the early 1980s, the devaluation of the Mexican peso in 1994, the Asian and Russian financial crises of the late 1990s, and most recently, the worldwide decline in property values. Banks are usually vulnerable in a financial crisis, so the central bank steps in to provide financial support by increasing the amount of money in circulation to reduce interest rates. This is difficult to do, however, in an already low inflation, low interest rate environment and especially in a deflationary environment.

Links Between Economies

LOS 17.l: <u>Identify</u> and <u>interpret</u> macroeconomic, interest rate, and exchange rate linkages between economies.

CFA® Program Curriculum, Volume 3, page 74

Economic links between countries have become increasingly important through time, especially for small countries with undiversified economies. Larger countries with diverse economies, such as the United States, are less affected but are still influenced by globalization.

Macroeconomic links refer to similarities in business cycles across countries. Economies are linked by both international trade and capital flows so that a recession in one country dampens exports and investment in a second country, thereby creating a slowdown in the second country. Note, though, that even among developed countries, economies are not perfectly integrated. For example, the Federal Reserve in the United States and the European Central Bank will respond to local effects in their economies, which creates differences in U.S. and European economic growth.

Another link between economies results from **exchange rates**. As an extreme case, Ecuador has adopted the U.S. dollar as its currency. More commonly, many countries peg their currency to others. For example, until 2005, China pegged their currency to the U.S. dollar. The benefit of a peg is that currency volatility is reduced and inflation can be brought under control. Countries are not always successful in maintaining a peg, however, because the weaker country in the peg usually abandons it, devaluing their currency. For this reason, interest rates between the two countries will often reflect a risk premium, with the weaker country having higher interest rates.

> *Professor's Note: When a currency is pegged, its value is set at a fixed exchange rate with another currency (or to a basket of currencies or another measure of value, such as gold). As the value of the other currency rises and falls, so does the value of the currency pegged to it. The opposite of a fixed exchange rate is a floating exchange rate, which is often preferred because it allows the currency to respond directly to foreign exchange markets. In addition, pegged exchange rates deprive federal governments the use of monetary policy to help control economic growth.*

Interest rate differentials between countries can also reflect differences in economic growth, monetary policy, and fiscal policy. For example, in the early 1980s, the United States had a robust economy, an increasing budget deficit, and high real and nominal interest rates due to a tight monetary policy. It is theorized that real interest rate differentials between countries should not exist, and over time, exchange rates will equalize differences. Countries with high *real interest rates* should see the value of their currency increase.

Professor's Note: Don't be confused with the relationships in Study Session 10, in which the currency of the country with the higher relative nominal interest rate will sell at a forward discount (i.e., is expected to depreciate). In Study Session 10, we assume real rates are equal, so forward discounts or premiums are based upon inflation expectations.

EMERGING MARKET ECONOMIES

LOS 17.m: <u>Discuss</u> the risks faced by investors in emerging-market securities and the country risk analysis techniques used to evaluate emerging market economies.

CFA® Program Curriculum, Volume 3, page 75

Emerging markets offer the investor high returns at the expense of higher risk. Many emerging markets require a heavy investment in physical and human (e.g., education) infrastructure. To finance this infrastructure, many emerging countries are dependent on foreign borrowing, which can later create crisis situations in their economy, currency, and financial markets.

Many emerging countries also have unstable political and social systems. The lack of a middle class in these countries does not provide the constituency for needed structural reforms. These small economies are often heavily dependent on the sale of commodities, and their undiversified nature makes them susceptible to volatile capital flows and economic crises.

The investor must carefully analyze the risk in these countries. For the bond investor, the primary risk is credit risk—does the country have the capacity and willingness to pay back its debt? For equity investors, the focus is on growth prospects and risk. There are six questions potential investors should ask themselves before committing funds to these markets.

1. **Does the country have responsible fiscal and monetary policies?** To gauge fiscal policy, most analysts examine the deficit to GDP ratio. Ratios greater than 4% indicate substantial credit risk. Most emerging counties borrow short term and must refinance on a periodic basis. A buildup of debt increases the likelihood that the country will not be able to make its payments. Debt levels of 70 to 80% of GDP have been troublesome for developing countries.

2. **What is the expected growth?** To compensate for the higher risk in these countries, investors should expect a growth rate of at least 4%. Growth rates less than that may indicate that the economy is growing slower than the population, which can be problematic in these underdeveloped countries. The structure of an economy and government regulation is important for growth. Tariffs, tax policies, and regulation of foreign investment are all important factors for growth.

3. **Does the country have reasonable currency values and current account deficits?** A volatile currency discourages needed foreign investment, and an overvalued currency may encourage excessive borrowing by the emerging market government. Current account deficits (roughly speaking, imports are greater than exports) greater than 4% of GDP can be problematic because the deficit must be financed through external borrowing.

4. **Is the country too highly levered?** Although emerging countries are dependent on foreign financing for growth, too much debt can eventually lead to a financial crisis if foreign capital flees the country. These financial crises are accompanied by currency devaluations and declines in emerging market asset values. Foreign debt levels greater than 50% of GDP indicate that the country may be overlevered. Debt levels greater than 200% of the current account receipts also indicate high risk.

5. **What is the level of foreign exchange reserves relative to short-term debt?** Foreign exchange is important because many emerging country loans must be paid back in a foreign currency. The investor should be wary of countries where the foreign exchange reserves are less than the foreign debt that must be paid off within one year.

6. **What is the government's stance regarding structural reform?** If the government is supportive of structural reforms necessary for growth, then the investment environment is more hospitable. When the government is committed to responsible fiscal policies, competition, and the privatization of state-owned businesses, there are better prospects for growth.

ECONOMIC FORECASTING

LOS 17.n: Compare the major approaches to economic forecasting.

CFA® Program Curriculum, Volume 3, page 78

To determine capital market expectations, analysts use a variety of approaches. We examine three of the most common methods: (1) econometrics, (2) economic indicators, and (3) a checklist approach. After a brief introduction to each, we describe each method's advantages and disadvantages.

Econometric analysis utilizes economic theory to formulate the forecasting model. The models can be quite simple to very complex, involving several data items of various time period lags to predict the future. For example, the analyst may want to forecast GDP using current and lagged consumption and investment. The analyst may even input forecasts of consumption and investment to forecast GDP. Ordinary least squares regression is most often used, but other statistical methods are also available.

Advantages:
- Once established, can be reused.
- Can be quite complex and may accurately model real world conditions.
- Can provide precise quantitative forecasts of economic conditions.

Disadvantages:

- May be difficult and time intensive (expensive) to create.
- Proposed model may not be applicable in future time periods.
- Better at forecasting expansions than recessions.
- Requires scrutiny of output to verify validity.

Economic indicators are available from governments, international organizations (e.g., the Organization of Economic Cooperation and Development), and private organizations (e.g., the Conference Board in the United States). They attempt to characterize an economy's phase in the business cycle and are separated into lagging indicators, coincident indicators, and leading indicators.

Using their own indicators or those provided by an outside source, analysts prefer leading indicators because they help predict the future path of the economy. The leading indicators can be used individually or as a composite. As an example of the latter, the Conference Board provides ten leading indicators. Some analysts would use these in an index, where if the majority of the indicators predict expansion, the analyst forecasts an economic expansion. Traditionally, three consecutive months of increase (decrease) for the index are expected to signal the start of an economic expansion (contraction) within a few months.

Advantages:

- Available from outside parties.
- Easy to understand and interpret.
- Can be adapted for specific purposes.
- Effectiveness has been verified by academic research.

Disadvantages:

- Not consistently accurate as economic relationships change through time.
- Forecasts from leading indicators can be misleading by giving false signals.

In a **checklist approach**, the analyst checks off a list of questions that should indicate the future growth of the economy. For example, to forecast GDP the analyst may want to ask himself, "What was the latest employment report? What is most likely the central bank's next move, given the latest information released? What is the latest report on business investment?"

Given the answers to these questions, the analyst can then use his judgment to formulate a forecast or derive a more formal model using statistics. In either case, subjective assessments must be made as to what variables are important for the forecasts.

Advantages:

- Simple.
- Allows changes in the model over time.

Disadvantages:

- Requires subjective judgment.
- May be time intensive to create.
- May not be able to model complex relationships.

> **For the Exam:** This forecasting material could easily be put into the framework of two analysts arguing about forecasting techniques, and you would have to critique statements they make.

ECONOMIC CONDITIONS AND ASSET CLASS RETURNS

LOS 17.o: <u>Demonstrate</u> the use of economic information in forecasting asset class returns.

CFA® Program Curriculum, Volume 3, page 87

LOS 17.p: <u>Evaluate</u> how economic and competitive factors affect investment markets, sectors, and specific securities.

CFA® Program Curriculum, Volume 3, page 91

Investors ultimately use capital market expectations to form their beliefs about the attractiveness of different investments. This is one of the primary steps in top-down analysis. We next examine how economic information can be used in forecasting asset class returns. We start with cash.

> **For the Exam:** Now we get to allocating assets according to our capital market expectations and how we expect assets to react to them. I would expect this to show up on the exam in determining a tactical allocation for an active manager.

Cash Instruments

Cash typically refers to short-term debt (e.g., commercial paper) with a maturity of one year or less. Cash managers adjust the maturity and creditworthiness of their cash investments depending on their forecasts for interest rates and the economy. If, for example, a manager thinks interest rates are set to rise, he will shift from 9-month cash instruments down to 3-month cash instruments. If he thinks the economy is going to improve, so that less creditworthy instruments have less chance of default, he will shift more assets into lower-rated cash instruments. Longer maturity and less creditworthy instruments have higher expected return but also more risk.

The interest rate for overnight loans among U.S. banks is the Federal Funds rate and is set by the Federal Reserve through its purchases and sales of government debt. This rate is fairly stable except during periods of unusual market volatility. In the European Union, the European Central Bank targets the repo rate.

The yield for debt securities of various maturities reflects the market's anticipation of yields over future periods. To earn excess returns, the manager must be able to forecast future rates better than other managers, and this in part requires anticipation of what the central bank will do in the future.

Credit Risk-Free Bonds

The most common type of credit risk-free bonds are those issued by governments in developed countries. The yield on these bonds is composed of a real yield and the expected inflation over the investment horizon. If, for example, the investor thinks that inflation will be 2% over the life of the bond and the investor requires a real return of 4%, then the investor would only purchase the bond if its yield were 6% or more. Based on historical data, the real yield on an ex ante basis should be roughly 2–4%.

The investor with a short time horizon will focus on cyclical changes in the economy and changes in short-term interest rates. Higher expected economic growth results in higher yields because of anticipated greater demand for loanable funds and possibly higher inflation. A change in short-term rates, however, has less predictable effects. Usually an increase in short-term rates increases the yields on medium- and long-term bonds. Medium- and long-term bond yields may actually fall, though, if the interest rate increase is gauged sufficient to slow the economy.

Over the past 40 years, the inflation premium embedded in bonds has varied quite a bit in developed countries. In the 1960s, it was quite low but rose in the late 1970s as investors became accustomed to higher inflation. More recently, it has dropped as inflation has been low.

Credit Risky Bonds

The most common type of credit risky bonds are corporate bonds. To estimate the credit risk premium assigned to individual bonds, the analyst could subtract the yield of Treasuries from that of corporate bonds of the same maturity to calculate the spread. During a recession, the credit risk premium, or spread, increases because default becomes more likely. At the same time, the credit offered by banks and the commercial paper market also dries up so that corporations have to offer higher yields to attract investors. More favorable economic conditions result in lower credit risk premiums.

Emerging Market Government Bonds

The key difference between developed country government bonds and emerging market government bonds is that most emerging debt is denominated in a non-domestic currency. Emerging market bonds are usually denominated in a hard currency (e.g., dollars, euros); thus, the emerging market government must obtain the hard currency to pay back the principal and interest. The default risk for emerging market debt is appropriately higher. To assess this risk, analysts use country risk analysis, which focuses on the economic and political environment in a country (as discussed previously for emerging markets).

Inflation-Indexed Bonds

Several governments issue bonds that adjust for inflation so that the investor is protected against it. An example is U.S. Treasury Inflation Protected Securities (TIPS). These bonds are both credit risk and inflation risk free. But they are not free of price risk. Their prices and yields still vary as economic conditions change and as the supply and demand for these instruments vary. The yield on these bonds has been correlated with three economic factors. Their yield:

- Rises (falls) as the real economy expands (contracts). This is primarily because their yield is tracking short-term interest rates, which also move with the economy.
- Falls as inflation accelerates and more investors seek to buy the inflation-index bonds. The increase in demand leads to higher prices and lower yields.
- Changes with supply and demand. These markets are somewhat small, making supply and demand changes more important.

Common Stock

To understand how economic conditions affect stock values, recall that the value of an asset is the present value of its future cash flows. For stocks, both the cash flows (earnings) and discount rate (risk-adjusted required return) are important. Earnings are commonly used to value the stock market because they should be reflected in both the cash paid out as dividends and as capital gains. Aggregate earnings depend primarily on the trended rate of growth in an economy, which in turn depends on labor force growth, new capital inputs, and total factor productivity growth.

As discussed earlier, when the government promotes competition in the marketplace, this increases the efficiency of the economy and should lead to higher long-term growth in the economy and the stock market. Of course, an investor would prefer an individual stock to have a monopolistic, noncompetitive position in their product market. This, however, would not be healthy for the growth of the overall stock market.

Shorter-term growth is affected by the business cycle. In a recession, sales and earnings decrease. Noncyclical or defensive stocks (e.g., utilities) are less affected by the business cycle and will have lower risk premiums and higher valuations than cyclical stocks (e.g., technology firms). Cyclical stocks are characterized by high business risk (sensitivity to the business cycle) and/or high fixed costs (operating leverage).

Recall that in the early expansion phase of the business cycle, stock prices are generally increasing. This is because sales are increasing, but input costs are fairly stable. For example, labor does not ask for wage increases because unemployment is still high, and idle plant and equipment can be pushed into service at little cost. Furthermore, firms usually emerge from a recession leaner because they have shed their wasteful projects and excessive spending. Later on in the expansion, earnings growth slows because input costs start to increase. As mentioned earlier, interest rates will also increase during late expansion, which is a further negative for stock valuation.

A stock's valuation in the market is reflected in its price-earnings (P/E) ratio. P/E ratios are higher in an early expansion period when interest rates are low and earnings prospects are high. They decline as earnings prospects decline. Note that for cyclical stocks, P/E ratios may be quite high in a recession, if investors are anticipating that the economy will soon recover. P/E ratios are also affected by long-term trends. For example, the 1990s was thought to be a new era of productivity, earnings growth, low inflation, and low interest rates. P/E ratios were abnormally high during this time period. Low inflation results in high P/E ratios because earnings are more *real* and less subject to interpretation.

Emerging Market Stocks

Historical returns for emerging market stocks are higher and more variable than those in the developed world and seem to be positively correlated with business cycles in the developed world. This correlation is due to trade flows and capital flows. In addition, emerging countries share many of the same sectors as those in the developed world. The analyst should have a good understanding of country and sector patterns when valuing emerging market stocks.

Real Estate

Real estate assets are affected by interest rates, inflation, the shape of the yield curve, and consumption. Interest rates affect both the supply of, and demand for, properties through mortgage financing rates. They also determine the capitalization rate (i.e., discount rate) used to value cash flows.

FORECASTING EXCHANGE RATES

LOS 17.q: Discuss the relative advantages and limitations of the major approaches to forecasting exchange rates.

CFA® Program Curriculum, Volume 3, page 98

The value of a currency is determined by its supply and demand, which in turn is affected by trade flows and capital flows. For example, if the United States has a trade deficit with Japan (i.e., it imports more from Japan than it exports to Japan), the value of the dollar should decline against the yen. The reason is that to obtain the foreign good, U.S. consumers are essentially selling their dollars to obtain yen.

In regard to capital flows, if U.S. Treasury bonds are in high demand due to their safety and attractive return, foreign investors will sell their currency in order to obtain dollars. The value of the foreign currency will fall while the value of the dollar will rise. Capital will flow into a country when capital restrictions are reduced, when an economy's strong growth attracts new capital, or when interest rates are attractive. Higher interest rates generally attract capital and increase the domestic currency value. At some level, though, higher interest rates will result in lower currency values because the high rates may stifle an economy and make it less attractive to invest there.

The emphasis on international diversification has increased capital flows. Capital flows can be volatile but are less so if the capital is invested in real assets through foreign direct investment. Currency values can also become volatile when a country is forced to abandon a pegged value targeted by its government.

The volatility in currency values makes them difficult to forecast but presents both risks and rewards for portfolio managers. We examine four methods of forecasting exchange rates: (1) relative purchasing power parity, (2) relative economic strength, (3) capital flows, and (4) savings and investment imbalances.

The first method is the relative form of **purchasing power parity** (PPP). PPP states that differences in inflation between two countries will be reflected in changes in the exchange rate between them. Specifically, the country with higher inflation will see its currency value decline. For example, assume Japanese inflation is projected to be a cumulative 8.2% over the next five years, while U.S. inflation is 13.2% over the same period. U.S. inflation is thus projected to be 5% higher. If the current exchange rate is ¥100/$, then the projected exchange rate is approximately ¥100/$ × (1 − 0.05) = ¥95/$ (note that the dollar has depreciated here because it buys five less yen).

PPP does not hold in the short term or medium term but holds approximately in the long term (five years or more). PPP is given attention by governments and forecasters, but its influence on exchange rates may be swamped by other factors, such as trade deficits.

The second method of forecasting currency values is the **relative economic strength approach**. The idea behind this approach is that a favorable investment climate will attract investors, which will increase the demand for the domestic currency and increase the currency's value. Investors would be attracted by strong economic growth in a country. Alternatively, high short-term interest rates may also attract investors. High short-term interest rates will attract investors who buy the currency in order to invest the currency at those high short-term rates. Interestingly, even if the general consensus is the currency is overvalued based on fundamentals, high rates may still attract attention and keep the currency overvalued or cause further appreciation in the short-run. The relative economic strength approach may be better suited to forecasting short-run changes in currency value.

The third approach to forecasting exchange rates is the **capital flows approach**. This approach focuses primarily on long-term capital flows, such as those into equity investments or foreign direct investments. For example, the strength of the U.S. dollar in the later 1990s was thought to be due to the strength of the U.S. stock market.

The flow of long-term funds complicates the relationship between short-term rates and currency values as discussed in the relative strength approach. For example, a cut in U.S. short-term rates may actually strengthen the dollar because the cut might promote U.S. growth and the attractiveness of U.S. stocks. This makes the central bank's job more difficult. If the Federal Reserve wanted to boost short-term rates to increase the value of the dollar and tame inflation, their action may actually result in a decline in the value of the dollar as investors find U.S. capital assets less attractive.

The last approach is the **savings-investment imbalances approach**. This approach is not readily implemented for forecasting but explains why currencies may diverge from equilibrium values for extended periods. This approach starts with the concept that an economy must fund investment through savings. If investment is greater than domestic savings, then capital must flow into the country from abroad to finance the investment. A savings deficit can be attributable to both the government and private sector.

In order to attract and keep the capital necessary to compensate for the savings deficit, the domestic currency must increase in value and stay strong (perhaps as a result of high interest rates or economic growth). At the same time, the country will have a current account deficit where exports are less than imports. Although a current account deficit would normally indicate that the currency will weaken, the currency must stay strong to attract foreign capital.

The aforementioned scenario typically occurs during an economic expansion when businesses are optimistic and use their savings to make investments. Eventually, though, the economy slows, investment slows, and domestic savings increase. It is at this point that the currency will decline in value.

In addition to the four approaches described previously, one could also examine government intervention to determine the future path of exchange rates. This approach is not very fruitful, though, because most observers don't think governments can exert much control over exchange rates. The reason is that government trading is too small in volume to affect the massive currency markets. Furthermore, currencies are more influenced by economic fundamentals than by periodic trading by governments.

REALLOCATING A GLOBAL PORTFOLIO

LOS 17.r: Recommend and justify changes in the component weights of a global investment portfolio based on trends and expected changes in macroeconomic factors.

CFA® Program Curriculum, Volume 3, page 91

For the Exam: This LOS asks you to use much of what you have learned here and apply it to portfolio management. Given that the emphasis of the Level III exam is portfolio management, you need to be able to pull all this material together.

Example: Applying capital market expectations

A portfolio manager has a global portfolio invested in several countries and is considering other countries as well. The decisions the manager faces and the economic conditions in the countries are described in the following. In each case, the portfolio manager must reallocate assets based on economic conditions.

Decision #1: Reallocation to Country A

The portfolio manager has noticed that the yield curve is downward sloping in this country. The current portfolio in this country is 60% stocks and 40% bonds. Suggest changes to the portfolio based on this information.

Decision #2: Allocation to Country B

Country B has experienced declining prices and this trend is expected to continue. The manager has no funds invested in this country yet but is considering investments in bonds, equity, and real estate. In which assets should the manager invest?

Decision #3: Allocations to Emerging Country C or Country D

The manager is considering the purchase of government bonds in either emerging Country C or D.

The countries have the following characteristics:

Characteristics of Countries C and D

	Country C	Country D
Foreign exchange/Short-term debt	147%	78%
Debt to GDP	42%	84%

Decision #4: Country, Asset, and Currency Allocations

The manager will make a long-term investment in either Country E or F, based on projections of each economy's trended growth rate. Given that decision, the manager will then decide whether to invest in stocks or bonds. Lastly, the manager will use the savings-investment imbalances approach to gauge the strength of the currencies. The countries have the following characteristics:

Characteristics of Countries E and F

	Country E	Country F
Population growth	2.5%	2.0%
Labor force participation growth	0.2%	0.9%
Growth in spending on new capital inputs	1.5%	2.2%
Growth in total factor productivity	0.4%	0.8%
Expected savings relative to investment	Surplus	Deficit

Answers:

Decision #1: Reallocation to Country A

The downward sloping yield curve indicates that the economy is likely to contract in the future. In recessions, bonds outperform stocks because inflation and interest rates decrease and economic growth is slow. Assuming the accuracy of the yield curve forecast and that interest rates will fall further, the portfolio manager should consider reallocating from stocks into bonds.

Decision #2: Allocation to Country B

The manager should invest in bonds. In periods of declining prices or deflation, bonds perform well because there is no inflation and interest rates are declining. Stocks usually perform poorly during deflationary periods because economic growth is slowing. Real estate also performs poorly during deflationary times, particularly when the investment is financed with debt.

Decision #3: Allocations to Emerging Country C or Country D

The manager should purchase the bonds of Country C. Many emerging market bonds are denominated in a hard currency, so less risky countries have greater foreign currency reserves. Low levels of leverage are also preferred. One measure of leverage is the debt to GDP ratio.

Decision #4: Country, Asset, and Currency Allocations

To forecast the long-term economic growth rate, we sum population growth, labor force participation growth, growth in spending on new capital inputs, and growth in total factor productivity.

In Country E, it is 2.5% + 0.2% + 1.5% + 0.4% = 4.6%.

In Country F, it is 2.0% + 0.9% + 2.2% + 0.8% = 5.9%.

Country F has the higher trended growth rate, so the manager should invest there. The growth rate of 5.9% is quite attractive, and given that the manager is investing for the long term, the investment should be made in equities because equities will benefit the most from this high growth rate. Bond returns are based more on expectations of interest rates and inflation. A high growth economy may experience higher inflation and interest rates at some point that would be negative for bonds.

In the absence of other information, we would surmise from the savings-investment imbalances approach that Country E's currency will depreciate because the country has a savings surplus. Foreign capital will not be needed and, hence, Country E does not require a high currency value. Country F's currency will appreciate because the savings deficit will require a strong currency to attract foreign capital.

For the Exam: In sum, you need to be able to determine the relevant inputs to economic forecasts and what the forecasted economic conditions mean for asset values. Also, be ready to use the forecasting tools discussed earlier and identify problems in forecasting.

KEY CONCEPTS

LOS 17.a

Capital market expectations (macro expectations) help in formulating the strategic asset allocation. They can also assist in detecting short-term asset mispricing exploitable through tactical asset allocation. Formulating capital market expectations is referred to as beta research because it is related to systematic risk.

To formulate capital market expectations, use the following process:
- Determine the relevant capital market expectations given the investor's tax status, allowable asset classes, and time horizon.
- Investigate assets' historical performance as well as the determinants of their performance.
- Identify the valuation model used and its requirements.
- Collect the best data possible.
- Use experience and judgment to interpret current investment conditions.
- Formulate capital market expectations.
- Monitor performance and use it to refine the process.

LOS 17.b

High-quality forecasts are consistent, unbiased, objective, well supported, and have a minimum amount of forecast error.

There are several limitations to using economic data associated with data timeliness, data revisions, changes in index composition, and rebasing of the index.

Forecasts can be adversely affected by transcription errors, survivorship bias, and the use of appraisal (smoothed) data.

The use of historical estimates for forecasts is less relevant if there has been a regime change that results in nonstationary data. The arguments for using a short time span of data are the presence of regime change, the data may not be available, and there may be asynchronous data. The arguments for using a long time span of data are statistics often require it, it increases the precision of population parameter estimates, and the parameter estimates will be less sensitive to the time span chosen.

Using ex post data may cause the analyst to underestimate ex ante risk and overestimate ex ante return if the analyst is unaware of risk faced by investors in the past.

Using historical data, analysts can *uncover* patterns in security returns that are due to data mining and time period bias. To avoid these biases, the analyst should examine the economic basis for the variables, scrutinize their modeling process for susceptibility to these biases, and test the discovered relationship with out-of-sample data.

Analysts' forecasts may also fail to account for conditioning information. Their forecasts should reflect current economic conditions.

The simple correlation statistic may be misleading for evaluating predictive relationships. An alternative to the correlation statistic is a multiple regression.

Analysts are susceptible to the following psychological traps:

- Anchoring trap—an analyst puts too much weight on the first set of information he receives.
- Status quo trap—an analyst bases predictions on the recent past.
- Confirming evidence trap—an analyst gives too much credence to evidence that supports her existing or favored beliefs.
- Overconfidence trap—an analyst ignores his shortcomings and forecasts too narrow a range of possibilities.
- Prudence trap—an analyst tends to be overly conservative in her forecasts.
- Recallability trap—an analyst lets past disasters or dramatic events weigh too heavily in his forecasts.

When forecasting, an analyst cannot be sure that her predictive model is correct and/or whether the data are correct.

LOS 17.c

The statistical tools for setting capital market expectations include projecting historical data, shrinkage estimators, time series analysis, and multifactor models.

When using historical data, the arithmetic mean is the best when projecting for a single year, whereas the geometric mean is best for projecting over several years.

Shrinkage estimators are weighted averages of historical data and another analyst-determined estimate.

Using time series analysis, an analyst can forecast means as well as variances, which is useful when assets exhibit volatility clustering.

Multifactor models can be used to forecast returns, variances, and covariances. Their advantage is that they simplify the forecasting procedure by reducing the forecast to a common set of factors. This modeling also eliminates the noise present in a sample of data and ensures consistent forecasts given a consistent covariance matrix.

Using a modified discounted cash flow analysis for an equity market, the expected return is the dividend yield plus the inflation rate plus the real earnings growth rate minus the change in stock outstanding plus changes in the P/E ratio.

The yield to maturity on a reference bond is used as the expected return for a bond segment. The drawback to this approach is that the yield to maturity assumes that intermediate cash flows are reinvested at the yield to maturity.

A risk premium approach estimates the expected return on equity as a long-term government bond yield plus an equity risk premium. For bonds, the expected return is determined using the real risk-free rate plus an inflation premium, a default risk premium, a liquidity premium, a maturity risk premium, and a tax premium.

Using a financial equilibrium approach, the equity risk premium for a market is equal to its correlation with the global portfolio, multiplied by the standard deviation of the asset, multiplied by the Sharpe ratio for the global portfolio.

LOS 17.d

Capital market expectations can also be formed using surveys. In this method, a poll is taken of market participants (e.g., economists and analysts) to determine what their expectations are regarding the economy or capital market. If the group polled is constant over time, this method is referred to as a panel method.

Surveys have been taken regarding the equity risk premium, with investors expecting a premium in the range of 2% to 3.9%. Other studies have found that the expectations of practitioners are consistently more optimistic than that of academics.

Judgment can also be applied to project capital market expectations. Although quantitative models provide objective numerical forecasts, there are times when an analyst must adjust those expectations using her experience and insight to improve upon those forecasts.

LOS 17.e

Understanding the business cycle can help the analyst identify inflection points where the risk and opportunities for higher return may be heightened. To identify inflection points, the analyst should understand what is driving the current economy and what may cause the end of the current economy.

The inventory cycle is often measured using the inventory to sales ratio. The measure increases when businesses gain confidence in the future of the economy and add to their inventories in anticipation of increasing demand for their output. As a result, employment increases with subsequent increases in economic growth. This continues until some precipitating factor, such as a tightening in the growth of the money supply, intervenes. At this point, inventories decrease, employment declines, and economic growth slows.

LOS 17.f

The relationship between the business cycle and assets returns is well documented. Assets with higher returns during business cycle lows (e.g., bonds and defensive stocks) should be favored by investors because the return supplements their income during recessionary periods—these assets should have lower risk premiums. Assets with lower returns during recessions should have higher risk premiums. Understanding the relationship between an asset's return and the business cycle can help the analyst provide better valuations.

LOS 17.g

Inflation varies over the business cycle, rising in the latter stages of an expansion and falling during a recession and the initial recovery.

Deflation reduces the value of investments financed with debt (e.g., real estate) because leverage magnifies losses.

Bond prices will rise during a recession when inflation and interest rates are declining. In a strong expansion, bonds tend to decline in price as inflationary expectations and interest rates rise.

Equities provide an inflation hedge when inflation is moderate. High inflation can be problematic because slow growth may result from central bank action. Declining inflation or deflation is harmful because this can result in declining economic growth.

Increasing inflation is positive for cash instruments because the returns on cash instruments increase as inflation increases. Deflation is negative for cash because the return falls to zero.

LOS 17.h

The Taylor rule can be formalized as follows:

$$r_{target} = r_{neutral} + \left[0.5\left(GDP_{expected} - GDP_{trend}\right) + 0.5\left(i_{expected} - i_{target}\right)\right]$$

Example:
Given the following information, calculate the short-term interest rate target.

Neutral rate	4%
Inflation target	3%
Expected Inflation	7%
GDP long-term trend	2%
Expected GDP growth	0%

Answer:

$$r_{target} = 4\% + \left[0.5\left(0\% - 2\%\right) + 0.5\left(7\% - 3\%\right)\right] = 5\%$$

LOS 17.i

The yield curve demonstrates the relationship between interest rates and the maturity of the debt security and is sensitive to actions of the federal government as well as current and expected economic conditions. For example, when both fiscal and monetary policies are expansive, the yield curve is sharply upward sloping, which indicates that the economy is likely to expand in the future. When fiscal and monetary policies are restrictive, the yield curve is downward sloping, indicating that the economy is likely to contract in the future.

When fiscal and monetary policies are in disagreement, the shape of the yield curve is less definitively shaped. Recall that monetary policy controls primarily short-term interest rates. If monetary policy is expansive while fiscal policy is restrictive, the yield curve will be upward sloping, though it will be less steep than when both policies are expansive. If monetary policy is restrictive while fiscal policy is expansive, the yield curve will be more or less flat.

LOS 17.j

In forecasting a country's long-term economic growth trend, the trend growth rate can be decomposed into two main components and their respective subcomponents:
1. Changes in employment levels.
   - Population growth.
   - Rate of labor force participation.

2. Changes in productivity.
   - Spending on new capital inputs.
   - Total factor productivity growth.

Example:
Assume that expected population growth is 2% and expected labor force participation growth is 0.25%. If spending on new capital inputs is projected to grow at 2.5% and total factor productivity will grow by 0.5%, what is the long-term projected growth rate?

Answer:
The sum of the components equals 2% + 0.25% + 2.5% + 0.5% = 5.25%, so the economy is projected to grow by this amount.

LOS 17.k

Exogenous shocks are unanticipated events that occur outside the normal course of an economy and have a negative impact upon it. They can be caused by different factors, such as natural disasters, political events, or changes in government policies. Typically, two types of shocks have occurred, which are oil shocks and financial crises. Oil shocks are usually caused by crises in the Middle East followed by decreased oil production, leading to increasing prices, inflation, reduced consumer spending, higher unemployment, and a slowed economy. The opposite shock would be a decline in oil prices, leading to lower inflation and boosting the economy. Financial crises have occurred when countries can't meet their debt payments, currencies are devalued, and property values have declined. In a financial crisis, banks usually become vulnerable, forcing the central bank to provide stability to the economy by reducing interest rates, which is difficult to do in an already low interest rate environment.

LOS 17.l

Macroeconomic links refer to similarities in business cycles across countries. Economies are linked by both international trade and capital flows so that a recession in one country dampens exports and investment in a second country, thereby creating a slowdown in the second country.

Exchange rate links are found when countries peg their currency to others. The benefit of a peg is that currency volatility is reduced and inflation can be brought under control. Interest rates between the countries will often reflect a risk premium, with the weaker country having higher interest rates.

Interest rate differentials between countries can also reflect differences in economic growth, monetary policy, and fiscal policy. It is theorized that real interest rate differentials between countries should not exist, and over time exchange rates will equalize differences.

LOS 17.m

Emerging market risks stem from unstable political and social systems and heavy infrastructure investments financed by foreign borrowing. Investors should answer six questions before investing in these markets:

1. Does the country have responsible fiscal and monetary policies? This is determined by examining the deficit to GDP ratio.

2. What is the expected growth? Should be at least 4%.

3. Does the country have reasonable currency values and current account deficits? A volatile currency discourages needed foreign investment, and an overvalued currency encourages excessive government borrowing.

4. Is the country too highly levered? Too much debt can lead to a financial crisis if foreign capital flees the country.

5. What is the level of foreign exchange reserves relative to short-term debt? Many emerging country loans must be paid back in a foreign currency.

6. What is the government's stance regarding structural reform? A supportive government makes the investment environment more hospitable.

LOS 17.n

Econometric analysis utilizes economic theory to formulate the forecasting model. The models range from being quite simple to very complex, involving several data items of various time period lags to predict the future.

Economic indicators attempt to characterize an economy's phase in the business cycle and are separated into lagging indicators, coincident indicators, and leading indicators. Analysts prefer leading indicators because they help predict the future path of the economy.

In a checklist approach, the analyst checks off a list of questions that should indicate the future growth of the economy. Given the answers to these questions, the analyst can then use his judgment to formulate a forecast or derive a more formal model using statistics.

LOS 17.o

Investors ultimately use capital market expectations to form their beliefs about the attractiveness of different investments. Following are examples of how specific information can be used to forecast asset class returns.

*   If a cash manager thought that interest rates were set to rise, she would shift to short-term cash instruments.
*   A change in short-term rates has unpredictable effects for the yields on long-term bonds.
*   During a recession, the risk premium on credit risky bonds increases.
*   Most emerging market debt is denominated in a non-domestic currency, which increases its default risk.
*   The yields for inflation-indexed bonds will fall if inflation increases.
*   In the early expansion phase of the business cycle, stock prices are increasing. Later in the expansion, earnings growth and stock returns slow.
*   The returns for emerging market stocks are affected by business cycles in the developed world.
*   Interest rates affect real estate returns through both the supply and demand as well as the capitalization rate used to discount cash flows.

LOS 17.p

When the government promotes competition in the marketplace, the efficiency of the economy increases, likely leading to higher long-term growth in the economy and the stock market.

Shorter-term growth is affected by the business cycle. In a recession, sales and earnings decrease. Non-cyclical or defensive stocks are less affected by the business cycle and thus will have lower risk premiums and higher valuations than cyclical stocks. Cyclical stocks are characterized by high business risk and/or high fixed costs.

LOS 17.q

- The relative form of purchasing power parity (PPP) states that differences in inflation between two countries will be reflected in changes in the exchange rate between them. Specifically, the country with higher inflation will see its currency value decline.
- The relative economic strength approach: The idea behind this approach is that a favorable investment climate will attract investors, which will increase the demand for the domestic currency, therefore increasing its value.
- The capital flows approach focuses primarily on long-term capital flows such as those into equity investments or foreign direct investments.
- The savings-investment imbalances approach starts with the concept that an economy must fund investment through savings. If investment is greater than domestic savings, then capital must flow into the country from abroad to finance the investment.

LOS 17.r

This LOS effectively asks you to apply LOS 17.a through LOS 17.q in determining the optimal reallocation for a global portfolio. For the exam, you should be able to interpret forecasts as well as develop forecasts for market returns using the Grinold-Kroner model. You could be asked to assess the valuation of a stock market using the H-model, Fed model, Yardeni model, Tobin's q, or the equity q. Using the Taylor model, you should be able to determine the proper level of short-term interest rates. You should be able to calculate the risk premium for integrated and segmented markets to determine whether expected returns are appropriate.

Know the effects of stages in the economic business cycle on different types of investments and be able to determine which investments are best given the current stage of the cycle and government fiscal and monetary policies. You should be able to discuss the relative strengths of currencies given current interest rates and investment opportunities. The bottom line is the necessity of using a thorough economic analysis to determine which of several global investments is most appropriate for the investor.

CONCEPT CHECKERS

1. Suppose an analyst values stocks using discount rates based on projected risk-free rate ranges of 3% to 5%. The same analyst uses risk-free rate projections of 4% to 6% to determine the allocation to fixed income. **Discuss** the likely effect on the investor's asset allocation.

2. It is now January 2007. An analyst would like to forecast U.S. equity returns. She is considering using either 15 years of historical annual returns or 50 years of historical annual returns. **Provide** the arguments for and against each selection of data length.

3. An analyst realizes that the variance for an exchange rate tends to persist over a period of time, where high volatility is followed by more high volatility. What statistical tool would the analyst *most likely* use to forecast the variance of the exchange rate?

4. Suppose an analyst is valuing two markets, A and B. What is the equity risk premium for the two markets, their expected returns, and the covariance between them, given the following?

Sharpe ratio of the global portfolio	0.29
Standard deviation of the global portfolio	8.0%
Risk-free rate of return	4.5%
Degree of market integration for Market A	80%
Degree of market integration for Market B	65%
Standard deviation of Market A	18%
Standard deviation of Market B	26%
Correlation of Market A with global portfolio	0.87
Correlation of Market B with global portfolio	0.63
Estimated illiquidity premium for Market A	0.0%
Estimated illiquidity premium for Market B	2.4%

5. Are there any attractive investments during deflationary periods?

6. During an economic expansion, an analyst notices that the budget deficit has been declining. She concludes that the government's fiscal policy has shifted to a more restrictive posture. **Comment** on her conclusion.

7.   **Calculate** the short-term interest rate target given the following information.

Neutral rate	5%
Inflation target	3%
Expected Inflation	6%
GDP long-term trend	3%
Expected GDP	5%

8.   A forecaster notes that the yield curve is steeply upwardly sloping. **Comment** on the likely monetary and fiscal policies in effect and the future of the economy.

9.   An analyst would like to project the long-term growth of the economy. Which of the following would you recommend he focus on: changes in consumer spending or potential changes in tax policy due to a new government coming into office?

10. An analyst is evaluating an emerging market for potential investment. She notices that the country's current account deficit has been growing. Is this a sign of increasing risk? If so, **explain** why.

11. An analyst is evaluating two countries. Maldavia has a GDP of $60 billion and has an economy that is dominated by the mining industry. Oceania has a GDP of $1.2 trillion and has an economy that sells a variety of items. He is predicting a global economic slowdown. Which country is at greater risk?

12. An analyst believes that GDP is best forecast using a system of equations that can capture the fact that GDP is a function of many variables, both current and lagged values. Which economic forecasting method is she *most likely* to use?

13. At a conference, Larry Timmons states that the relationship between short-term interest rates and long-term bond yields is not uniform. He also states that the relationship between a domestic currency value and interest rates is not uniform. **Explain** what Timmons is talking about.

14. At the beginning of the fiscal year, Tel-Pal, Inc., stock sells for $75 per share. There are 2,000,000 shares outstanding. An analyst predicts that the annual dividend to be paid in one year will be $3 per share. The expected inflation rate is 3.5%. The firm plans to issue 40,000 new shares over the year. The price-to-earnings ratio is expected to stay the same, and nominal earnings will increase by 6.8%. Based upon these figures, what is the expected return on a share of Tel-Pal, Inc., stock in the next year?

15. An analyst forecasts the historical covariance of the returns between Tel-Pal, Inc., stock and Int-Pal, Inc., stock to be 1,024. A newly forecasted covariance matrix predicts the covariance will be 784. The analyst weights the historical covariance at 30% and the forecast at 70%. **Calculate** the shrinkage estimate of the covariance.

16.   **List** and **explain** three psychological traps that would encourage an analyst to place too much weight on past information and less weight on new information.

17.   An analyst notices that the growth of the national inventory-to-sales ratio has slowed after increasing for several years. **Identify** what this implies for stage of the business cycle and for economic growth. **Explain** how a recent phenomenon has affected the ratio, independent of the business cycle.

18.   The phase of the business cycle where we *most likely* expect to observe rising short-term interest rates and flat bond yields is:
       A. late expansion.
       B. initial recovery.
       C. early expansion.

19.   **Describe** three characteristics each for an oil shock and a financial crisis.

ANSWERS – CONCEPT CHECKERS

1. It is likely that the investor's asset allocation will be too heavily weighted towards equity, given that the discount rates used to determine the equity allocation will be lower than that used for fixed income. This example illustrates that high-quality forecasts using capital market expectations should be consistent. They also should be objectively formed, unbiased, well supported, and have a minimum amount of forecast error.

2. If the analyst uses 15 years of historical data, then her sample may be unduly influenced by the time span chosen. In this case, the U.S. equity returns for the past 15 years are likely quite high relative to probable future returns. Using 15 years of historical data would also not provide enough data points for statistical calculations if annual returns are used. A longer time span of data would increase the precision of population parameter estimates.

    Using 50 years of data may also be problematic if there has been regime change. For example, changes in Federal Reserve policy may render stock return data from 50 years ago irrelevant. Although data availability and asynchronous data can sometimes be a problem when using long time spans of data, this is unlikely the case for historical U.S. equity data.

3. The analyst would most likely forecast the variance using time series analysis. In time series analysis, forecasts are generated using previous values of a variable and previous values of other variables. If an exchange rate exhibits volatility clustering, then its variance will persist for periods of time and can be forecasted using a time series model.

4. First, we calculate the equity risk premium for both markets assuming full integration. Note that for Market B, the illiquidity risk premium is added in:

$$\text{ERP}_i = \rho_{i,M}\sigma_i\left(\frac{\text{ERP}_M}{\sigma_M}\right)$$

$$\text{ERP}_A = 0.87(0.18)0.29 = 4.54\%$$

$$\text{ERP}_B = 0.63(0.26)0.29 + 0.0240 = 7.15\%$$

The equity risk premium for both markets assuming full segmentation is:

$$\text{ERP}_i = \sigma_i\left(\frac{\text{ERP}_M}{\sigma_M}\right)$$

$$\text{ERP}_A = (0.18)0.29 = 5.22\%$$

$$\text{ERP}_B = (0.26)0.29 + 0.0240 = 9.94\%$$

Weighting the integrated and segmented risk premiums by the degree of integration and segmentation in each market:

$$\text{ERP}_A = (0.80 \times 0.0454) + [(1-0.80) \times 0.0522] = 4.68\%$$

$$\text{ERP}_B = (0.65 \times 0.0715) + [(1-0.65) \times 0.0994] = 8.13\%$$

The expected return in each market is then:

$$\hat{R}_A = 4.5\% + 4.68\% = 9.18\%$$

$$\hat{R}_B = 4.5\% + 8.13\% = 12.63\%$$

The betas in each market are:

$$\beta_i = \rho_{i,M}\sigma_i / \sigma_M$$

$$\beta_A = (0.87)(18)/8 = 1.96$$

$$\beta_B = (0.63)(26)/8 = 2.05$$

The covariance is then:

$$cov_{i,j} = \beta_i\beta_j\sigma_M^2$$

$$cov_{A,B} = (1.96)(2.05)(8.0)^2 = 257.15$$

5. Bonds actually perform well during periods of falling inflation or deflation because interest rates are declining. This holds true as long as credit risk does not increase. Equities do poorly in periods of declining inflation or deflation due to declining economic growth and asset prices. Deflation also reduces the value of investments financed with debt, such as real estate, because leverage magnifies losses. Deflation is negative for cash because the return on cash declines to near zero.

6. Her conclusion may not be warranted. In an economic expansion, the budget deficit will decline naturally because tax receipts increase and disbursements to the unemployed decrease. The changes she is observing may be independent of the government's fiscal policy.

   Note that only government-directed changes in fiscal policy influence the growth of the economy. Changes in the deficit that occur naturally over the course of the business cycle are not stimulative or restrictive.

7. $$r_{target} = 5.0\% + [0.5 \times (5\% - 3\%) + 0.5 \times (6\% - 3\%)]$$

   $$= 5.0\% + [1.0\% + 1.5\%] = 7.5\%$$

   In this example, the higher than targeted growth rate and higher than targeted inflation rate argue for a targeted interest rate of 7.5%. This rate hike is intended to slow down the economy and inflation.

8. If the yield curve is steeply upwardly sloping, then it is likely that both fiscal and monetary policies are expansive. The economy is likely to expand in the future.

9. Although consumer spending is the largest component of GDP, it is fairly stable over the business cycle. The reason is that consumers tend to spend a fairly constant amount over time. Thus, it is likely that the analyst should focus on the potential changes in tax policy. This governmental structural policy has a potentially large impact on the long-run growth rate of an economy.

10. When exports are less than imports, a current account deficit results. This can be problematic because the deficit must be financed through external borrowing. If the emerging country becomes overlevered, it may not be able to pay back its foreign debt. A financial crisis may ensue where foreign investors quickly withdraw their capital. These financial crises are accompanied by currency devaluations and declines in emerging market asset values.

11. A global economic slowdown would affect smaller countries with undiversified economies more because economic links are more important for these types of countries. Larger countries with diverse economies are less affected by events in other countries.

12.   Econometric analysis would be the best approach to use. It can model the complexities of reality using both current and lagged values. Ordinary least squares regression is most often used, but other statistical methods are also available.

13.   The relationship between short-term interest rates and long-term bond yields is not uniform because although bond yields usually increase when short-term rates increase, this is not always the case. If short-term rates increase enough such that a recession becomes more likely, the yields on bonds will fall as investors anticipate that the demand for loanable funds will fall.

       The relationship between a domestic currency value and interest rates is not uniform because although the currency value will increase as interest rates increase, this is not the case if interest rates increase high enough to slow down the economy. In this case, foreign investors shy away from the country because the country becomes a less attractive place to invest.

14.   The equation for expected return on Tel-Pal, Inc., using these inputs is:

$$\hat{R}_T = \frac{\text{Div}_1}{P_0} + \text{inflation} + \text{real growth in earnings} - \%\Delta \text{ shares} + \Delta\left(\frac{P}{E}\right)$$

$$\hat{R}_T = \left(\frac{\$3}{\$75} \times 100\right) + 3.5\% + 3.3\% - 2\% + 0$$

$$\hat{R}_T = 8.8\%$$

       The expected return is 8.8%. The expected dividend return is 4%, and the expected percentage increase in the number of shares is 2%. Expected inflation is 3.5%, which should be subtracted from the nominal earnings forecast to get the forecast of real earnings growth.

15.   The shrinkage estimate is simply the weighted average of the historical value and the forecasted value. The shrinkage estimate is:

       856 = 30% × 1,024 + 70% × 784

16.   *Anchoring Trap*: The analyst places too much weight on the first information received. Once having formed an opinion, the analyst will not want to deviate too far from the first opinion as new information arrives.

       Status Quo Trap: The analyst will not want to deviate too far from the recent past.

       The Prudence Trap: The analyst will tend to ignore information that will lead to extreme forecasts.

       The Recallability Trap: The analyst lets past disasters and dramatic events weigh too heavily in the forecast and ignores newer information.

17.   A slowing in the growth of the aggregate inventory-to-sales ratio in an economy is associated with later stages of the business cycle, perhaps late upswing or slowdown. It is likely caused by less business optimism with reductions in production and employment, hence a lower rate of economic growth.

       Business has adopted just-in-time inventory approaches and generally reduced the amount of inventory they hold. As a result, inventory-to-sales ratios have declined in general and are independent of the stage of the business cycle.

18. **C** *Early Expansion*: In this period of the business cycle, we expect to observe rising short-term interest rates and flat or rising bond yields.

The expectations of short-term and long-term yields for the other phases are listed as follows:

Late Expansion: Both short-term and long-term rates increasing.

Initial Recovery: Low or falling short-term rates, and bond yields have bottomed out.

19. Oil shocks and financial crises are two types of exogenous shocks that have been repeatedly observed over time and tend to spread to other countries. Oil shocks are usually characterized as (1) a reduction in oil production as a result of turmoil in the Middle East, (2) leading to higher oil prices and inflation, (3) reduced consumer spending, (4) increased unemployment, and (5) a slowed economy. (6) An oil shock could also be a reduction in oil prices resulting in the opposite effects.

A financial crisis is usually characterized by (1) a country not being able to meet its debt payment, (2) a currency devaluation, or (3) a significant reduction in asset prices. (4) Banks usually become vulnerable in a financial crisis. To stabilize the economy, the country's central bank intervenes to increase liquidity by reducing or maintaining low interest rates.

The following is a review of the Economic Concepts for Asset Valuation in Portfolio Management principles designed to address the learning outcome statements set forth by CFA Institute. This topic is also covered in:

Equity Market Valuation[1]

Exam Focus

Any of the calculations and approaches in this Topic Assignment are fair game for the exam. Some may be familiar from other levels of the exam and some will be new. The focus will be on formulating capital market expectations for the equity asset class and not on individual security valuation. Also be prepared for conceptual questions regarding implications or drawing conclusions when there is insufficient data for a calculation but sufficient data for a conclusion.

Cobb-Douglas Production Function

LOS 18.a: Explain the terms of the Cobb-Douglas production function and demonstrate how the function can be used to model growth in real output under the assumption of constant returns to scale.

CFA® Program Curriculum, Volume 3, page 128

The **Cobb-Douglas production function (CD)** uses the country's labor input and capital stock to estimate the total real economic output. The general form of the function is:

$$Y = AK^{\alpha} L^{\beta}$$

where:
Y = total real economic output
A = total factor productivity (TFP)
K = capital stock
L = labor input
α = output elasticity of K ($0 < \alpha < 1$)
β = output elasticity of L ($\alpha + \beta = 1$)

Applying natural logs, assuming that $\beta = (1 - \alpha)$, and making a few other assumptions, we see the form of the CD that is used to estimate *expected changes* in real economic

---

1. Terminology used throughout this topic review is industry convention as presented in Reading 18 of the 2014 CFA Level III exam curriculum.

output. Each of the inputs, as well as the output, is now stated in terms of growth (i.e., percentage change), a simple linear equation:

$$\frac{\Delta Y}{Y} \cong \frac{\Delta A}{A} + \alpha \frac{\Delta K}{K} + (1-\alpha)\frac{\Delta L}{L}$$

where:

$\dfrac{\Delta Y}{Y}$ = % change in real output $(\%\Delta Y)$

$\dfrac{\Delta A}{A}$ = % change in total factor productivity $(\%\Delta TFP)$

$\dfrac{\Delta K}{K}$ = % change in capital stock $(\%\Delta K)$

$\dfrac{\Delta L}{L}$ = % change in labor $(\%\Delta L)$

Empirical studies also suggest it is reasonable to assume *constant returns to scale*, any given change in capital or labor (for example, from 2% to 3% or 5% to 6%) has a linear effect on output. Constant returns to scale also means TFP can be assumed to be a constant. This is an elaborate way of saying the linear version of Cobb-Douglas produces reasonable results.

Assume both capital and labor increase by 4%, and TFP is 2%. The resulting expected change in real GDP is 6%.

$$\%\Delta Y = \%\Delta TFP + \alpha(\%\Delta K) + (1-\alpha)\%\Delta L$$
$$= 2\% + \alpha(4\%) + (1-\alpha)4\% = 6\%$$

More realistic assumptions might have capital and labor grow by different rates. Suppose TFP, capital, and labor increase by 1.7%, –0.5%, and 2.1% respectively, with $\alpha = 0.35$:

$$\%\Delta Y = 1.7\% + 0.35(-0.5\%) + 0.65(2.1\%)$$
$$= 1.7\% + -0.175\% + 1.365\% = 2.89\%$$

Estimating TFP

Percentage changes in capital and labor can be obtained from national accounts, and α and β, the output elasticities of capital and labor, vary from country to country. The change in TFP (i.e., $\%\Delta A$) is the **Solow residual** and can be determined by rearranging the equation:

$$\text{Solow residual} = \%\Delta TFP = \%\Delta Y - \alpha(\%\Delta K) - (1-\alpha)\%\Delta L$$

An economy's TFP can change over time due to the following:

- Changing technology.
- Changing restrictions on capital flows and labor mobility.
- Changing trade restrictions.

- Changing laws.
- Changing division of labor.
- Depleting/discovering natural resources.

LOS 18.b: Evaluate the relative importance of growth in total factor productivity, in capital stock, and in labor input given relevant historical data.

CFA® Program Curriculum, Volume 3, page 132

Once we have estimated the growth equation, $\%\Delta Y = \%\Delta A + \alpha\ \%\Delta K + (1 - \alpha)\ \%\Delta L$, we can use the historical growth of capital and labor, along with the estimates of output elasticities for labor and capital, to decompose the growth of GDP in order to evaluate the relative effects of labor growth, capital accumulation, and increases in factor productivity on economic growth.

For the Exam: Questions on economic growth could take either a qualitative or quantitative format as illustrated in the two following examples.

Example: Effects of changing factors on economic growth

In the template provided, **state** and **explain** the probable effect on total economic output associated with an *increase* in each of the factors, holding the other factors constant:

Factor Increased	Probable Effect on Economic Growth	Explanation
Savings rate	Increase	More capital available at reduced interest rates. Increased investment in capital stock.
Labor force	Increase	Increase in labor force growth rate.
Production efficiency	Increase	Increase in TFP.
Environmental and pollution controls	Decrease	Retooling and other costs; possibly reduced and/or more expensive output.
Children per household	Increase	Increase in labor force growth rate.
Number of two-wage-earner households	Increase	Increase in labor force growth rate.
Retirement age	Increase	Increase in labor force growth rate.
Import taxes/restrictions	Decrease	Increased costs; possibly reduced and/or more expensive output.

For the Exam: When asked to state the effect that changing factors can have on economic output ($\Delta Y/Y$), consider the factors' possible impacts on production efficiency, the labor force, and/or capital stock. Always think in terms of partial derivatives. Consider the impact of each factor individually while holding the others constant. Resist considering the impact that a change in one factor will have on another factor.

Also, some factors might have only a short-term effect on economic output, while others can have longer-lasting effects. For example, one-time costs incurred to meet increased environmental restrictions by replacing outdated equipment will have a short-term dampening effect. Once the retooling is completed, the economy would be expected to return to its long-term average growth rate. Factors, such as import restrictions, however, could have a longer-lasting impact on economic growth, depending on how quickly (and if) domestic replacements can be established.

Example: Estimating the change in economic output

While performing an analysis of three economies, an analyst compiled the growth and elasticity data in the following table.

10-Year Forecast (Growth Figures Are Annual Averages)

Country	% Growth in Total Factor Productivity	% Growth in Capital Stock	% Growth in Labor Input	Output Elasticity of Capital (α)
A	1.0	2.0	1.0	0.5
B	2.0	2.5	4.5	0.3
C	3.0	8.0	2.5	0.7

i. For each economy, **determine** the expected 10-year average annual GDP growth rate.

ii. **Comment** on the three economies.

Answer:

i. Expected growth in GDP:

$$\%\Delta Y \cong \%\Delta A + \alpha(\%\Delta K) + (1-\alpha)(\%\Delta L)$$

A: $\%\Delta Y = 1.0 + 0.5(2.0) + 0.5(1.0) = 2.50\%$
B: $\%\Delta Y = 2.0 + 0.3(2.5) + 0.7(4.5) = 5.90\%$
C: $\%\Delta Y = 3.0 + 0.7(8.0) + 0.3(2.5) = 9.35\%$

ii. Over the next ten years, economies A, B, and C are expected to experience average annual GDP growth rates of 2.50%, 5.90%, and 9.35%, respectively. The population of Economy A would appear to be close to equilibrium, as it is expected to grow at an average annual rate of only 1%. Together, the lower growth rates in capital, labor, TFP, and output for Economy A suggest it is a large, developed economy.

The workforce growth rate of 4.5% for Country B is relatively high, and Country B gains significantly from growth in the workforce. Increases in the capital stock, on the other hand, have less of an effect on output. The impressive workforce growth rate combined with a modest expected growth in capital stock could indicate a relatively small economy in the early stages of development.

Growth in the workforce of Economy C has slowed. Capital stock, however, is expected to increase significantly over the next ten years. Relative to Economy B, rapidly growing capital stock combined with an ability to translate capital growth into increased economic output (i.e., $\alpha = 0.7$) indicates an economy that is larger, more developed, and faster growing.

LOS 18.c: Demonstrate the use of the Cobb-Douglas production function in obtaining a discounted dividend model estimate of the intrinsic value of an equity market.

LOS 18.d: Critique the use of discounted dividend models and macroeconomic forecasts to estimate the intrinsic value of an equity market.

CFA® Program Curriculum, Volume 3, page 133

When we use a dividend discount model to estimate the value of an equity market index, we implicitly assume that the growth rate in corporate earnings and dividends is the same as the growth rate in gross domestic product (GDP). Even though these growth rates can differ in the short run, over longer periods, this assumption is reasonably accurate.

If an economy is expected to grow at a relatively high rate currently that will decline to a sustainable rate of growth over a period of years, we can apply a form of the dividend discount model—the **H-model**. The H-model assumes that the current "super-normal" growth rate (g_S) of dividends will decline linearly to the long-term sustainable growth rate (g_L). For a stock index, we can use the annual dividend at time zero (D_0), the number of years to reach the sustainable growth rate (N), and the required rate of return on equity securities (r) to calculate the current index value based on economic fundamentals (V_0) as:

$$P_0 = \frac{D_0}{r - g_L}\left[\left(1 + g_L\right) + \frac{N}{2}\left(g_S - g_L\right)\right]$$

where:
P_0 = current price (value)
D_0 = current dividend
r = real equity discount rate
g_S = short-term real rate of growth expected to decline linearly over N years to the real, long-term sustainable growth rate, g_L

Compare the H-model to the *constant growth dividend discount model*, which assumes the stock or stock index has already reached the period of long-term, sustainable growth:

$$P_0 = \frac{D_1}{r - \bar{g}} = \frac{D_0\left(1 + \bar{g}\right)}{r - \bar{g}}$$

where:
D_0 = current dividend
P_0 = current price (value)
D_1 = next expected dividend
r = real required return on equity
$\bar{g}$ = real, long-term sustainable (constant) growth rate; compare to g_L in the H-model

When we utilize the H-model, we use real (inflation-adjusted) discount rates and growth rates[2], and the discount rate depends on the expected volatility of the market. High volatility in a developing market can be caused by significant structural and regulatory changes as well as behavioral factors. Also, in a developing market, the government can own considerable proportions of the publicly available stocks. The uncertainty (i.e., risk) associated with the ultimate disposition of government-owned equities (e.g., whether the government will exert its ownership interests or divest of the equities) can have a dampening effect on P/E ratios.

Professor's Note: As you saw in Topic Review 18, Capital Market Expectations, and will see in Topic Review 30, Emerging Markets Finance, the degree to which the developing country's economy (GDP) is correlated with the developed world can affect the discount rate applied to its equity. If the developing economy is not highly correlated with the developed world, for example, the diversification benefit from including its equities in a global portfolio can reduce the return required by global investors.

---

2. In valuing an index, we can use either nominal or real rates, but real rates are preferred because they are more stable and easier to predict.

©2013 Kaplan, Inc.

> **Example: Estimating the intrinsic value and justified P/E ratio of a developing equity market**
>
> To estimate the intrinsic value of a developing market index using the H-Model, we need the real required return, r, the current dividend, D_0, the supernormal rate of growth, g_s, the long-term sustainable rate of growth, g_L, and the period of time, N, over which the growth rate will decline linearly.
>
> **Answer:**
>
> The market's forecasted EPS is 20.30. Assuming a required real return on equity of 10%, a current dividend of 12, current supernormal growth of 10.5%, a long-term sustainable rate of growth of 3.0%, and a 30-year period of linear growth decline, the estimated intrinsic value of the index is 369.43, and with forecasted earnings per share of 20.30, the justified P/E ratio is 18.2:
>
> $$V_0 = \frac{D_0}{r - g_L}\left[(1 + g_L) + \frac{N}{2}(g_S - g_L)\right]$$
>
> $$= \frac{12}{0.10 - 0.03}\left[(1.03) + \frac{30}{2}(0.105 - 0.03)\right] = 369.43$$
>
> $$\frac{P}{E}(\text{justified}) = \frac{369.43}{20.30} = 18.199 = 18.20$$

Estimating intrinsic value is difficult enough in developed markets. The problems multiply for developing markets or markets for economies undergoing fundamental change such as those of the former Eastern (Europe) Bloc.

1. Economic data can be scarce or unreliable. Even if available, fundamental economic change could make past data no longer relevant to current conditions and valuation.

2. Stock or market earnings growth rates will not track economic growth for countries undergoing structural economic change with extended periods of rising or falling corporate profits as a share of GDP.

3. The model used here is based on real inputs with inflation removed. (For economies with stable inflation, real or nominal inputs should produce similar results.) However, developing economies can and do experience long periods of erratic monetary policy, inflation, and even hyperinflation. The accuracy of the inputs or outputs of any model in such conditions is questionable.

Figures 1 through 4 show the sensitivity of intrinsic value to changes in each of the input variables in the H-model.[3] Each input variable is increased and decreased by 10% and 20% from its value in the example while holding the others constant. (The shaded rows in the tables indicate the base values in the example.) The third column in each table shows the resulting intrinsic value, and the last column shows the percentage change in

---

3. Because the goal is showing the sensitivity of calculated intrinsic value to changes in estimates of the inputs, the current dividend, D_0, which is not an estimate, is held constant in each of the tables.

intrinsic value from the base case. The sign and magnitude of the relationship between the input variable and intrinsic value is indicated in the title of each table. For example, in Figure 1, we see that the relationship between intrinsic value and N is positive and less than 1.0. That means the change in intrinsic value is in the same direction as the change in N but is smaller in percentage terms. Required return is the only input variable that exhibits a negative relationship with intrinsic value, and the relationship is greater than -1.0. The change in intrinsic value is opposite the change in required return and is greater in percentage terms.

Figure 1: Sensitivity of Intrinsic Value to Length of Period of Growth Decline, N (Positive Relationship < 1.0)

Period of Growth Decline (N) in Years	% Change	Intrinsic Value	% Change
24	–20%	330.86	–10.44
27	–10%	350.15	–5.22
30	—	369.43	—
33	+10%	388.72	+5.22
36	+20%	408.00	+10.44

Forecasted EPS 20.30; real return on equity of 10%; current dividend 12; g_s = 10.5%; g_L = 3.0%.

Figure 2: Sensitivity of Intrinsic Value to Sustainable Growth Rate, g_L (Positive Relationship < 1.0)

Sustainable Growth Rate (g_L) in Percent	% Change	Intrinsic Value	% Change
2.4	–20%	353.52	–4.31
2.7	–10%	361.14	–2.24
3.0	—	369.43	—
3.3	+10%	378.44	+2.44
3.6	+20%	388.31	+5.11

Forecasted EPS 20.30; real return on equity of 10%; current dividend 12; g_s = 10.5%; N = 30 years.

Figure 3: Sensitivity of Intrinsic Value to Supernormal Growth Rate, g_S (Positive Relationship < 1.0)

Supernormal Growth Rate (g_S) in Percent	% Change	Intrinsic Value	% Change
8.40	–20%	315.43	–14.62
9.45	–10%	342.43	–7.31
10.50	—	369.43	—
11.55	+10%	396.43	+7.31
12.60	+20%	423.43	+14.62

Forecasted EPS 20.30; real return on equity of 10%; current dividend 12; g_L = 3.0%; N = 30 years.

Figure 4: Sensitivity of Intrinsic Value to Required Real Return on Equity (Negative Relationship > –1.0)

Required Real Return (r) in Percent	% Change	Intrinsic Value	% Change
8.0	–20%	517.20	+40.00
9.0	–10%	431.00	+16.67
10.0	—	369.43	—
11.0	+10%	323.25	–12.50
12.0	+20%	287.33	–22.22

Forecasted EPS 20.30; current dividend 12; g_s = 10.5%; g_L = 3.0%; N = 30 years.

Example: Estimating the sustainable rate of growth, required return, and intrinsic value of a developed equity market

An analyst has gathered the data in the following table for a large, mature developed market index. The current level of the index is 3,250, and the current dividend is $150.

Long-Term Economic Growth Factors

% Growth in Total Factor Productivity	% Growth in Capital Stock	% Growth in Labor Input	Output Elasticity of Capital (α)	Output Elasticity of Labor $(1 - \alpha)$
1.5	1.5	0.5	0.6	0.4

i.   **Determine** the implied sustainable rate of growth in GDP.
ii. Using the growth rate calculated in *i*, **calculate** the required market return.
iii. The analyst believes a required return of 7.0% is appropriate for this market. Based on the analyst's required return, **calculate** the intrinsic value of the index.

Answer:

i.   Based on the expected long-term rates of change in capital, labor, and total factor productivity, the long-term sustainable growth in GDP is estimated at 2.6%:

$$\%\Delta Y \cong \%\Delta A + \alpha(\%\Delta K) + (1-\alpha)(\%\Delta L) = 1.5 + 0.6(1.5) + 0.4(0.5) = 2.6\%$$

ii. Because this is a mature, developed market, we can use the constant growth dividend discount model, rearranged to solve for *r*, to estimate the market required return:

$$P_0 = \frac{D_1}{r-g} = \frac{D_0(1+g)}{r-g} \Rightarrow r = \frac{D_0(1+g)}{P_0} + g$$

$$r = \frac{150(1+0.026)}{3,250} + 0.026 = \frac{153.90}{3,250} + 0.026 = 0.07335 = 7.3\%$$

iii. Using the current dividend of $150, the long-term sustainable rate of growth of 2.6%, and the analyst's required return of 7.0%, the analyst would estimate the intrinsic value of the index at 3,498:

$$P_0 = \frac{D_1}{r-g} \Rightarrow \frac{153.90}{0.07-0.026} \cong 3,498$$

Based on the analyst's estimated required return, the index is undervalued by 3,498 − 3,250 = 248 points or 7.1% below fair value.

Professor's Note: The long-term average sustainable rate of growth in GDP is fairly stable for a large, mature economy. Any significant differences between analysts' estimated intrinsic values and the actual values of a mature market index would, therefore, likely be due to disagreement in the market's required return.

Changes in Required Return, r

Using data from the previous example, Figure 5 shows the sensitivity of the value of the market to changes in the estimated required return. In each calculation, the assumed long-term growth in GDP is 2.6%, and the current dividend is $150:

Figure 5: Intrinsic Values With Changing Rates of Return

$g_L = 2.6\%; D_0 = \$150$	
Market Required Return, r	$V_0 \ (or \ P_0) = D_1 \, / \, (r - g_L)$
6.4%	153.90 / (0.064 − 0.026) = 4,050
6.7%	153.90 / (0.067 − 0.026) = 3,754
7.0%	153.90 / (0.070 − 0.026) = 3,498
7.3%	153.90 / (0.073 − 0.026) = 3,274
7.6%	153.90 / (0.076 − 0.026) = 3,078
7.9%	153.90 / (0.079 − 0.026) = 2,904

LOS 18.e: <u>Contrast</u> top-down and bottom-up approaches to forecasting the earnings per share of an equity market index.

CFA® Program Curriculum, Volume 3, page 142

In a **top-down forecast**, the analyst utilizes macroeconomic factors (e.g., interest rate expectations, expected growth in GDP) to estimate the performance of market-wide indicators, such as the S&P 500. Successive steps include identifying sectors in the market that will perform best, given market expectations.

The analyst could start by comparing the relative values of various market composites to their historical patterns to identify any that appear to be under- or over-priced. Next, the analyst could attempt to identify any momentum in the indices. In the final macro-analysis, the analyst compares the expected performance of the indices to general asset classes, such as equities, bonds, and alternatives to identify which class of assets will be expected to under- or out-perform. After selecting asset classes to over- or under-weight, the analyst could move down to sector and security selection if desired.

In a **bottom-up forecast**, the analyst first takes a microeconomic perspective by focusing on the fundamentals of individual firms. The analyst starts the bottom-up analysis by looking at an individual firm's product or service development relative to the rest of the industry. The analyst should assess the firm's management and its willingness and ability to adopt the technology necessary to grow or even maintain its standing in the industry. Given the analyst's expectations for the firm, the analyst uses some form of cash flow analysis to determine the firm's investment potential (i.e., expected return). If desired, the individual security analysis could be aggregated up into sector and asset class returns that could be compared to the top-down estimates.

Which to Use

The method used depends on the analyst's strategy, as well as any portfolio constraints. For example, a manager who focuses on a long-short, market-neutral strategy would probably pursue a purely bottom-up analysis. The manager has little need for aggregating the forecasts for individual securities into industry or market forecasts. Another manager's strategy could focus on allocating among markets or industries. In these cases, there is little need for the top-down manager to go any lower, or the bottom-up manager to go any higher, than the first step.

For the Exam: To determine which approach is better for the manager, you will have to determine the manager's focus. For example, if you encounter a macro hedge fund manager who focuses on optimal allocations of global markets or currencies, a purely top-down approach would be indicated. An active manager who buys and sells individual securities to capture short-term pricing inefficiency should utilize a bottom-up approach.

Estimating Market Earnings Per Share (EPS)

Analysts are sometimes encouraged to confirm market EPS estimates by using both the top-down and bottom-up methods. If the methods yield significantly different estimates, the analyst should analyze both estimates to determine the source(s) of discrepancy. There are two primary reasons why forecasting earnings per share with the two methods can yield different results:

1. *The models used in a top-down analysis.* Econometric models use historical values and variables adjusted to varying degrees by the user, and they suffer from the same weaknesses as all such models. For example, they may be slow in capturing structural changes (i.e., changes in the sensitivities of the individual factors). The model might have worked well in the past, but recent structural changes might have altered the relationships between the independent and dependent variables.

   The models can also be specified incorrectly. Variables in the model that explained behavioral and financial relationships in the past might no longer be appropriate, and/or other variables might be more appropriate.

2. *Manager bias.* A bottom-up analysis is usually based, to a degree, on manager expectations. Because most managers expect their firms to out-perform the industry average, aggregating individual manager expectations can lead to significantly over-estimated industry expectations.

   Also, believing they can hold on longer than other firms as the economy sinks into a recession, individual managers tend to be more optimistic than would be warranted by a top-down model. On the other hand, they will tend to be more pessimistic as the market begins to recover. The potential for these biases must be assessed when the economy is entering or leaving a recession. If there is evidence of significant manager bias, the top-down method might be more appropriate.

> **For the Exam:** The bottom line is that both top-down analysis and bottom-up analysis have strengths and weaknesses. Top-down analysis doesn't incorporate the input of individual managers, while individual managers tend to be overly optimistic about their firm's future. Be able to recognize the deficiencies of each method and discuss the implications.

RELATIVE EQUITY MARKET VALUATION

LOS 18.f: <u>Discuss</u> the strengths and limitations of relative valuation models.

LOS 18.g: <u>Judge</u> whether an equity market is under-, fairly, or over-valued using a relative equity valuation model.

CFA® Program Curriculum, Volume 3, page 149

Relative value models use the relative values of assets and markets to identify investment opportunities. In the following material, we will discuss three relative value models: (1) the Fed model, (2) the Yardeni model, and (3) the 10-year Moving Average Price/Earnings model. These models are used to assess the relative attractiveness of stocks versus bonds.

The **Fed model** assumes that the expected operating earnings yield on the S&P 500 (i.e., expected aggregate operating earnings divided by the current index level) should be the same as the yield on long-term U.S. Treasuries:

$$\text{Fed model ratio} = \frac{\text{S\&P earnings yield}}{\text{10-year Treasury yield}}$$

If the S&P 500 earnings yield is higher than the Treasury yield, the interpretation is that the index value is too low relative to earnings. Equities are undervalued and should increase in value. Likewise, if the earnings yield is lower than the Treasury yield, the index is considered too high for the level of earnings. Equities are over-valued and should fall.

There are three basic criticisms of the Fed model, based on implied assumptions regarding risk, growth, and inflation.

The Fed model does the following:

1. *Ignores the equity risk premium.* Assuming the yield on treasuries is the same as the earnings yield on the S&P ignores the inherent risk of equities.

2. *Ignores earnings growth.* Growth expectations affect earnings, but Treasury yields have no growth components. By assuming the yield on a Treasury should be the same as corporate earnings yield, the model implicitly assumes zero growth in earnings.

3. *Compares a real variable to a nominal variable.* The yield on a Treasury is adjusted to incorporate changes in inflation and is thus considered nominal. The earnings yield will not automatically adjust to incorporate changes in inflation and could be considered real.

Although flawed, the Fed model is used by analysts in a type of spread analysis. Rather than assume the two yields should be equal, as in the model, analysts watch the *ratio* of the earnings and Treasury yields. When the ratio is above its long-term average, the difference between the earnings yield and Treasury yield (the spread) is historically high. Equity prices would be expected to increase, lowering the earnings yield and, thus, the ratio of the two yields (i.e., the yield spread would narrow).

For the Exam: If asked to list criticisms of the Fed model, mention that it:
- Does not consider the equity risk premium.
- Ignores growth in earnings.
- Compares a real variable (index level) to a nominal variable (Treasury yield).

The Yardeni Model

The **Yardeni model** for estimating the equilibrium earnings yield (i.e., the fair earnings yield) is based on a variation of the constant growth dividend discount model (CGM), in which investors value total earnings rather than dividends:

$$P_0 = \frac{E_1}{r - g}$$

We can restate the CGM to show that the earnings yield must be the difference between the required return on equity and expected long-term growth. This is logical, because we assume the total return on equity, r, must be the sum of the earnings yield, E_1 / P_0, and growth (i.e., capital gains), g:

$$P_0 = \frac{E_1}{r-g} \Rightarrow r = \frac{E_1}{P_0} + g \Rightarrow \frac{E_1}{P_0} = r - g$$

Yardeni incorporates risk into his model by using the yield on A-rated corporate bonds, Y_B, as the required return on equity, r. The difference between the yields on A-rated corporates and risk-free treasuries serves as a proxy, although most likely understated, for the equity risk premium. Also, instead of the long-term growth assumed in the CGM, Yardeni uses a 5-year growth forecast, LTEG,[4] for the S&P 500. The model becomes:

$$\frac{E_1}{P_0} = Y_B - d(LTEG)$$

where:

$\dfrac{E_1}{P_0}$ = expected market $(e.g., S\&P)$ earnings yield

Y_B = yield on A-rated corporate bonds

d = weighting factor for the importance of earnings growth; historically around 0.10

$Y_B - d(LTEG)$ = Yardeni earnings yield

Professor's Note: Yardeni uses the yield on A-rated corporates. Viewed from the perspective of a build up model, this would include the risk-free rate plus a default premium. Effectively, the default premium is approximating the equity risk premium. Then, to account for the fact that the earnings yield on the left-hand side of the equation ignores growth, he subtracts a growth factor.

The earnings yield from the Yardeni model is compared to the market earnings yield. If the market yield is high compared to the Yardeni earnings yield, equities are underpriced. Equities would be expected to rise in value, reducing the market earnings yield.

$$\text{if } \frac{E_1}{P_0} - \left[Y_B - d(LTEG)\right] > 0 \Rightarrow \text{market is undervalued}$$

$$\text{if } \frac{E_1}{P_0} - \left[Y_B - d(LTEG)\right] < 0 \Rightarrow \text{market is overvalued}$$

---

4.   LTEG is the 5-year consensus growth forecast provided by Thomson Financial.

Like the Fed model, the Yardeni model can be applied as a ratio:

$$\text{if } \frac{E_1}{P_0} - \left[Y_B - d(LTEG)\right] > 0 \Rightarrow \frac{\text{earnings yield}}{Y_B - d(LTEG)} > 1.0 \Rightarrow \text{market is undervalued}$$

$$\text{if } \frac{E_1}{P_0} - \left[Y_B - d(LTEG)\right] < 0 \Rightarrow \frac{\text{earnings yield}}{Y_B - d(LTEG)} < 1.0 \Rightarrow \text{market is overvalued}$$

The Yardeni model can also be used to estimate a fair value for the equity market. If we rearrange the model to solve for P_0, it starts to look like the traditional CGM with Y_B in place of the required return and $d(LTEG)$ in place of g:

$$\frac{E_1}{P_0} = Y_B - d(LTEG) \Rightarrow P_0 = \frac{E_1}{Y_B - d(LTEG)}$$

Example: Using the Yardeni Model

i. Assume the long-term (5-year) growth forecast is 9.85% and d = 0.10. If A-rated corporate bonds yield 6%, **determine** the fair earnings yield.

ii. If the current earnings yield implied by the equity index and projected forward earnings is 5.5%, **determine** whether equities are over- or undervalued.

iii. Using the Yardeni model, **calculate** a fair value of the market P/E ratio.

Answer:

i.
$$\frac{E_1}{P_0} = Y_B - d(LTEG)$$
$$= 0.06 - 0.10(0.0985) = 0.05015 = 5.015\%$$

ii. The fair earnings yield predicted by the Yardeni model is about 5%. If the current market earnings yield is 5.5%, this would imply that the value of the index is too low compared to projected earnings. According to the Yardeni model the market is *undervalued*.

iii. The Yardeni model calculates the fair earnings ratio, which is the ratio of earnings to price. To convert the earnings ratio to a P/E ratio, we simply invert it:

$$\frac{E_1}{P_0} = 0.05015 \Rightarrow \frac{P_0}{E_1} = \frac{1}{0.05015} = 19.94$$

For the Exam: When answering questions about the Yardeni model, important considerations include the following:

- It incorporates a proxy for the equity market risk premium (the yield on A-rated corporate debt).
- The risk premium used is actually a measure of default risk, not a true measure of equity risk.
- It relies on an estimate of the value investors place on earnings growth (d), which is assumed to be constant over time.
- The growth rate used in the model (LTEG) might not be an accurate estimate of long-term sustainable growth.

10-Year Moving Average Price/Earnings Ratio, P/10-Year MA(E)

The numerator of the **P/10-year MA(E)** is the market price of the S&P 500 price index, and the denominator is the average of the previous ten years' reported real earnings. Both the numerator and denominator are adjusted for inflation using the consumer price index. Similar to a trailing P/E ratio, the P/10-year MA(E) compares the inflation adjusted price of the market at a point in time to the market's average real earnings over the previous ten years.

To use the P/10-year MA(E) the analyst compares its current value to its historical average to determine whether the market is over- or underpriced. If the ratio currently stands at 18.0, and the historical average is 16.0, for example, the current price (i.e., level of the index) is high relative to earnings. The index would be considered over-priced and would be expected to revert to its historical mean of 16.

Professor's Note: Real simply means restating the price or earnings in today's dollars. For example, you could restate earnings from past years in real terms by multiplying the earnings figure by the ratio of today's CPI to the relevant year CPI. Assume earnings per share for 2008 were $3.00, and you wish to restate them as of June 2010 (i.e., restate them in June 2010 dollars). You would multiply December 2008 EPS by the ratio of 217.965 to 210.228, the CPIs for June 2010 and December 2008, respectively.

$$\textit{restated 2008 earnings} = \textit{nominal 2008 earnings} \times \textit{inflation adjustment factor}$$

$$= \textit{nominal 2008 earnings} \times \left(\frac{CPI_{6/2010}}{CPI_{12/2008}} \right)$$

$$= \$3.00 \times \left(\frac{217.965}{210.228} \right) = \$3.00 \times 1.036803 = \$3.11$$

When you restate values at a later date (bring them forward in time), the ratio of CPIs will be greater than 1.0 so that the value increases. To restate them in a previous year (take them back in time), the ratio of the CPIs will be less than 1.0, and the value decreases.

For the Exam: When answering questions about the P/10-year MA(E), important considerations include:

- By restating earnings and prices according to CPI, it considers the effects of inflation.
- By using 10-year average earnings, it captures the effects of business cycles, but by its nature it is backward-looking—current or expected earnings could provide more useful information.
- It does not consider the effects of changes in accounting rules or methods.
- Empirical studies have found that very high or low P/10-year MA(E) ratios have persisted, limiting its usefulness in forming short-run expectations.

Asset-Based Models

Tobin's q compares the current market value of a company to the replacement cost of its assets. The theoretical value of Tobin's q is 1.0. If the current Tobin's q is above (below) 1.0 the firm's stock is presumed to be overpriced (underpriced).

The **equity q** focuses directly on equity values. It compares the aggregate market value of the firm's equity to the replacement value of the firm's net worth (i.e., net assets). Again, the neutral value of the ratio is 1.0.

Both ratios are considered *mean-reverting*. A q value for either above 1.0 would be expected to fall as the overvalued stock price declines. Using the opposite argument, a value less than 1.0 suggests the undervalued stock should rise.

$$\text{Tobin's q} = \frac{\text{asset market value}}{\text{asset replacement cost}} = \frac{\text{market value of debt + equity}}{\text{asset replacement cost}}$$

$$\text{equity q} = \frac{\text{market value of equity}}{\text{replacement value of net worth}} = \frac{\#\text{ outstanding shares} \times \text{price per share}}{\text{replacement value of assets} - \text{liabilities}}$$

Both ratios have some long term value as indicators. However, it is difficult to estimate replacement values and high or low q ratios can persist for long periods of time; in other words, the expected stock price correction may not quickly occur.

KEY CONCEPTS

LOS 18.a

The Cobb-Douglas function (CD) relates real economic output to capital stock and labor as well as factor productivity:

$$Y = AK^{\alpha} L^{\beta}$$

By applying natural logs and making other assumptions, it can be restated to predict changes in output:

$$\frac{\Delta Y}{Y} \cong \frac{\Delta A}{A} + \alpha \frac{\Delta K}{K} + (1-\alpha)\frac{\Delta L}{L}$$

$$\text{Solow residual} = \Delta TFP = \frac{\Delta A}{A} \cong \frac{\Delta Y}{Y} - \alpha \frac{\Delta K}{K} - (1-\alpha)\frac{\Delta L}{L}$$

where:
A = total factor productivity (TFP)
K = capital stock
L = labor input
α = output elasticity of K; the change in Y for a 1-unit change in K $(0 < \alpha < 1)$
β = output elasticity of L; the change in Y for a 1-unit change in L $(\alpha + \beta = 1)$

LOS 18.b

Once we have estimated the growth equation, $\%\Delta Y = \%\Delta A + \alpha \, \%\Delta K + (1 - \alpha) \, \%\Delta L$, we can use the historical growth of capital and labor, along with the estimates of output elasticities for labor and capital, to decompose the growth of GDP in order to evaluate the relative effects of labor growth, capital accumulation, and increases in factor productivity on economic growth.

LOS 18.c,d

We assume the growth rate in corporate earnings and dividends is the same as the growth rate in gross domestic product (GDP). If an economy is expected to grow at a particularly high rate of growth for a number of years and then revert to a sustainable growth rate, we apply the H-model:

$$P_0 = \frac{D_0}{r - g_L}\left[(1 + g_L) + \frac{N}{2}(g_S - g_L)\right]$$

When growth is assumed constant, we can use the constant growth dividend discount model:

$$P_0 = \frac{D_1}{r - \bar{g}} = \frac{D_0\left(1 + \bar{g}\right)}{r - \bar{g}}$$

LOS 18.e

In a top-down forecast, the analyst utilizes macroeconomic factors to estimate the performance of market-wide indicators. Successive steps include identifying sectors in the market and then individual securities that will perform best, given market expectations.

In a bottom-up forecast, the analyst first takes a microeconomic perspective by focusing on the fundamentals of individual firms. For a macro forecast, the analyst can then aggregate the expected performance of individual securities.

To determine which to use, determine the manager's focus. For example, a macro hedge fund manager who focuses on optimal allocations of global markets or currencies would use a purely top-down approach. An active manager who buys and sells individual securities to capture short-term pricing inefficiency would utilize a bottom-up approach.

LOS 18.f,g

The Fed model assumes the yield on long-term U.S. Treasuries should be the same as the expected operating earnings yield on the S&P 500. When the S&P 500 earnings yield is higher (lower) than the Treasury yield, the interpretation is that the index is too low (high).

The Fed model:
- Does not consider the equity risk premium.
- Ignores growth in earnings.
- Compares a real variable (index level) to a nominal variable (Treasury yield).

The Yardeni model assumes investors value total earnings rather than dividends:

$$P_0 = \frac{E_1}{r - g} \Rightarrow \frac{E_1}{P_0} = Y_B - d(LTEG)$$

Important considerations include:
- It uses the yield on A-rated corporate debt as the equity risk premium.
- The risk premium used is actually a measure of default risk, not a true measure of equity risk.
- It relies on an estimate of the value investors place on earnings growth (*d*), which is assumed to be constant over time.
- The growth rate used in the model (LTEG) might not be a fair estimate of long-term sustainable growth.

P/10-year MA(E): The numerator is the value of the price index, and the denominator is the average of the previous ten years' reported earnings. Both are adjusted for inflation using the consumer price index.

Important considerations include:
- It considers the effects of inflation.
- It captures the effects of business cycles.
- Current or expected earnings could provide more useful information.
- It does not consider the effects of changes in accounting rules or methods.
- Very high or low P/10-year MA(E) ratios can persist, limiting its usefulness in forming short-run expectations.

$$\text{Tobin's q} = \frac{\text{market value of debt} + \text{equity}}{\text{asset replacement cost}}$$

$$\text{equity q} = \frac{\text{market value of equity}}{\text{replacement value of assets} - \text{liabilities}}$$

Important considerations include:
- Both ratios are mean-reverting.
- Both have demonstrated a negative relationship with equity returns.
- Replacement costs can be difficult to estimate.
- Very high or low ratios can persist, limiting their usefulness in forming short-run expectations.

CONCEPT CHECKERS

1. While analyzing potential global investments, Gretchen Fenledder, CFA, gathered the data in Table A on emerging Equity Market Index Y:

    Table A: Economic Data for Index Y*

Last dividend (D_0)	150
Forecast earnings per share	600
Current and sustainable long-term growth rate	2.5%
Required return	8.5%
Forward operating yield (E/P)	6.0%

    * Yield on 10-year government bond = 6%

    Based on the data in Table A:
    a. **Determine** the intrinsic price level of the index.
    b. **Determine** whether the market is over- or under-valued using the Fed model.

2. Fenledder also gathered data for Equity Market Index Z as shown in Table B:

    Table B: Economic Data for Equity Market Index Z

Expected growth in total factor productivity	1.5%
Expected growth in labor	3.0%
Expected growth in capital stock, $\alpha = 0.6$	2.2%

    a. **Explain** each of the terms in the Cobb-Douglas production function (CD).
    b. **Calculate** the implied growth (percentage change) in real economic output for Market Z using the data in Table B and the Cobb-Douglas function.
    c. **Define** and **discuss** the Solow residual.

3. **Describe** top-down and bottom-up economic analysis. **Explain** the situations that would imply either a top-down or a bottom-up analysis would be more appropriate and when the use of both would be justified.

4. **Compare** Tobin's q and the equity q for market valuation. **Provide** and **explain** one strength and one weakness of each.

5. **Explain** three weaknesses of the Fed model.

6. **Describe** the Yardeni model. Referring to specific variables in each, **explain** how the Yardeni and Fed models could arrive at different conclusions about the relative value of an equity market.

7.   In the template provided, **indicate** and **explain** the effect on the growth of an economy, given the indicated change in the following growth factors:
   i.   Slowing growth of the population.
   ii. Decrease in the government-mandated retirement age.
   iii. Relaxation of import duties and other trade restrictions.
   iv. Tax relief to encourage technological innovation.

Template for Question 7:

Factor	Effect on Economic Growth (circle one)	Explanation
i. Slowing growth of the population.	Increase Decrease	
ii. Decrease in the government-mandated retirement age.	Increase Decrease	
iii. Relaxation of import duties and other trade restrictions.	Increase Decrease	
iv. Corporate tax relief to encourage technological innovation.	Increase Decrease	

©2013 Kaplan, Inc.

8.   In the template provided, **determine** whether a top-down or bottom-up forecast would be better indicated for each scenario. **Justify** your selection.

Template for Question 8:

Scenario	Top-Down or Bottom-Up (circle one)	Justification
A global macro-hedge fund takes large positions in foreign currencies.	Top-down Bottom-up	
Portfolio manager Active A employs a market neutral strategy and adds market exposure with equity futures.	Top-down Bottom-up	
Active Investors, LLP, advertises that they earn alpha through stock selection.	Top-down Bottom-up	

ANSWERS – CONCEPT CHECKERS

1.

Last dividend (D_0)	150
Current and sustainable long-term growth rate	2.5%
Required return	8.5%
Forward operating yield (E/P)	6.0%

* Yield on 10-year government bond = 6%

a. We are provided with the long-term sustainable growth rate, the required return, and the current dividend, so we know to use the constant growth dividend discount model to determine the intrinsic value of the index:

$$P_0 = \frac{D_1}{r-g} = \frac{D_0(1+g)}{r-g} = \frac{150(1.025)}{0.085-0.025} = \frac{153.75}{0.06} = 2,562.50$$

b. The Fed model compares the operating yield on the index to the yield in the intermediate-term government bond:

Fed model ratio = earnings yield / government yield = 0.06 / 0.06 = 1.0

Based on expected earnings, the market appears to be correctly priced.

If the Fed model produces a ratio greater than 1.0, the earnings yield is considered too high (earnings are high relative to prices), indicating that the market is currently under-valued and would be expected to rise. If the ratio is less than 1.0, the earnings yield is too low, and the market is deemed to be over-valued.

2. a. The CD production function, assuming constant returns to scale, relates the economy's labor and capital inputs to its real economic output:

$Y \quad = AK^{\alpha} L^{\beta}$

where:
Y   = total real economic output
A   = total factor productivity (TFP)
K   = capital stock
L   = labor input
α = output elasticity of K ($0 < \alpha < 1$)
β = output elasticity of L ($\alpha + \beta = 1$)

We can rearrange the CD to state the percentage change in real total economic output in terms of the percentage changes in the factors:

$$\frac{\Delta Y}{Y} \cong \frac{\Delta A}{A} + \alpha \frac{\Delta K}{K} + (1-\alpha)\frac{\Delta L}{L}$$

$\frac{\Delta Y}{Y} = \%$ change in real output $(\%\Delta Y)$: growth in GDP

$\frac{\Delta A}{A} = \%$ change in total factor productivity $(\%\Delta TFP)$

$\frac{\Delta K}{K} = \%$ change in capital stock $(\%\Delta K)$

$\frac{\Delta L}{L} = \%$ change in labor $(\%\Delta L)$

The assumption of constant returns to scale implies that $\%\Delta TFP$ is zero, so that equal percentage changes in labor and capital will produce the same percentage change in real output.

b.

Expected growth in total factor productivity	1.5%
Expected growth in labor	3.0%
Expected growth in capital stock, α = 0.6	2.2%

$$\frac{\Delta Y}{Y} \cong \frac{\Delta A}{A} + \alpha \frac{\Delta K}{K} + (1-\alpha)\frac{\Delta L}{L}$$

$$\frac{\Delta Y}{Y} \cong 1.5\% + 0.6(2.2\%) + 0.4(3.0\%) = 4.02\%$$

c. The Solow residual is the percentage change in total factor productivity. Given the expected change in the real economic output, expected changes in labor and capital, and the economy's elasticities of capital and labor, we arrange the CD to solve for the Solow residual:

Solow residual $= \%\Delta TFP = \%\Delta Y - \alpha(\%\Delta K) - (1-\alpha)\%\Delta L$

An economy's TFP can change over time due to:
i.   Changing technology.
ii. Changing restrictions on capital flows and labor mobility.
iii. Changing trade restrictions.
iv. Changing laws.
v.   Changing division of labor.
vi. Depleting/discovering natural resources.

As an example of calculating the Solow residual, we use the growth of 4.02% calculated in Question 2 along with the other data provided and solve for %ΔTFP:

$$\%\Delta Y = \%\Delta TFP - \alpha(\%\Delta K) - (1-\alpha)(\%\Delta L) \Rightarrow$$

$$\%\Delta TFP(\text{Solow residual}) = \%\Delta Y - \alpha(\%\Delta K) - (1-\alpha)(\%\Delta L)$$
$$= 4.02\% - 0.6(2.2\%) - 0.4(3.0\%) = 1.5\%$$

3. In a top-down forecast, the analyst utilizes macroeconomic factors to estimate the performance of market-wide indicators, such as the S&P 500. Successive steps include identifying sectors in the market that will perform best given market expectations.

The analyst starts by comparing the relative values of various market composites to their historical patterns to identify any that appear to be under- or over-priced. Next, the analyst attempts to identify any momentum in the indices. In the final macro-analysis, the analyst compares the expected performance of the indices to general asset classes, such as equities, bonds, and alternatives to identify which class of assets will be expected to under- or out-perform.

In a bottom-up forecast, the analyst takes a microeconomic perspective by focusing on the fundamentals of individual firms. The analyst starts the bottom-up analysis by looking at an individual firm's product or service development relative to the rest of the industry. The analyst should assess the firm's management and its willingness and ability to adopt the technology necessary to grow or even maintain its standing in the industry. Given the analyst's expectations for the firm, the analyst uses some form of cash flow analysis to determine the firm's investment potential (i.e., expected return).

The method used depends on the analyst's strategy. A manager who utilizes a long-short, market neutral strategy would probably pursue a purely bottom-up analysis. Another manager's strategy could focus on allocating among markets or industries. In these cases, there is little need for the top-down manager to go any lower or the bottom-up manager to go any higher than the first step.

When approaching or leaving recessions, manager expectations can be biased. It would be wise in these situations for the bottom-up analyst to also utilize a top-down approach to confirm earnings estimates.

4. Tobin's q compares the current market value of a company to the replacement cost of its assets. The theoretical value of Tobin's q is 1.0. If the current Tobin's q is above (below) 1.0, the firm's stock is presumed to be overpriced (underpriced).

The equity q compares the current market value of the firm's equity to the replacement value of the firm's net worth (i.e., net assets). Again, the expected value of the ratio is 1.0.

Both ratios are considered *mean-reverting*. With a q value above 1.0, stock price should fall and below 1.0, stock price should rise.

$$\text{Tobin's q} = \frac{\text{asset market value}}{\text{asset replacement cost}} = \frac{\text{market value of debt + equity}}{\text{asset replacement cost}}$$

$$\text{equity q} = \frac{\text{market value of equity}}{\text{replacement value of net worth}} = \frac{\text{\# outstanding shares} \times \text{price per share}}{\text{replacement value of assets} - \text{liabilities}}$$

Strengths of both models include:
- Both are mean-reverting, so they are easy to use.
- Both have usefulness as demonstrated by a negative relationship with equity returns. Higher (lower) ratios have forecasted lower (higher) equity returns.

Weaknesses include:
- Replacement costs can be difficult to estimate.
- Empirical studies have found that very high or low ratios have persisted for both, limiting their usefulness in forming short-run expectations.

5. The Fed model does not consider the equity risk premium, it ignores growth in earnings, and it compares a real variable (index level) to a nominal variable (Treasury yield).

    Ignores growth in earnings: It compares the earnings yield on the market index (only a portion of the total return on the index) to the total expected return on the Treasury security. It does not include the growth portion of the expected index return.

    Real and nominal variables: The yield on the Treasury security includes an inflation premium while earnings are considered a real variable.

6. The Yardeni model is based on the constant growth dividend discount model (CGM), stated in terms of earnings rather than dividends:

    $$P_0 = \frac{E_1}{r - g}$$

    The earnings yield must be the difference between the required return on equity and expected long-term growth:

    $$P_0 = \frac{E_1}{r - g} \Rightarrow r = \frac{E_1}{P_0} + g \Rightarrow \frac{E_1}{P_0} = r - g$$

    The model uses the yield on A-rated corporate bonds as the required return on equity. Instead of the long-term growth assumed in the CGM, Yardeni uses a 5-year growth forecast for the S&P 500.

    $$\frac{E_1}{P_0} = Y_B - d(LTEG)$$

    where:
    Y_B = yield on A-rated corporate bonds
    d = a weighting factor for the importance of earnings growth; historically around 0.10

    If the current market earnings yield is high compared to the Yardeni earnings yield, equities are under-priced. Equities would be expected to rise in value:

    $$\text{if } \frac{E_1}{P_0} - \left[Y_B - d(LTEG)\right] > 0 \Rightarrow \text{market is under-valued}$$

    $$\text{if } \frac{E_1}{P_0} - \left[Y_B - d(LTEG)\right] < 0 \Rightarrow \text{market is over-valued}$$

The Fed model assumes the expected operating earnings yield on the S&P 500 should be same as the yield on long-term U.S. Treasuries:

$$\text{Fed model ratio} = \frac{\text{S\&P earnings yield}}{\text{Treasury yield}}$$

If the S&P 500 earnings yield is higher than the Treasury yield, the index value is low relative to earnings, and the market should increase in value. If the S&P 500 earnings yield is lower than the Treasury yield, the index value is high relative to earnings, and the market should drop in value.

In order to discuss circumstances where the two could yield different conclusions about market valuation, we reproduce them as ratios and see that both contain the expected S&P earnings yield in the numerator:

$$\text{Fed model ratio} = \frac{\text{S\&P earnings yield}}{\text{Treasury yield}}$$

$$\text{Yardeni ratio} = \frac{\text{S\&P earnings yield}}{Y_B - d(\text{LTEG})}$$

In situations where $[Y_B - d(\text{LTEG})]$ is dramatically different from the Treasury yield, the two ratios can yield conflicting conclusions. For example, Y_B might be historically high while interest rates are historically low (i.e., interest rates are low but risk aversion is high, making the risk premium on A-rated bonds high). In that case, the resulting Yardeni ratio could be less than 1.0 (indicating the market is over-valued) while the Fed model is greater than 1.0 (indicating the market is under-valued).

7.

Factor	Effect on Economic Growth (circle one)	Explanation
i. Slowing growth of the population.	Decrease	Increase in labor input slowing.
ii. Decrease in the government-mandated retirement age.	Decrease	Assuming it induces individuals to retire earlier, reduction in labor input.
iii. Relaxation of import duties and other trade restrictions.	Increase	Increased international competition; falling prices.
iv. Corporate tax relief to encourage technological innovation.	Increase	Short-term depression on growth with increased costs and retooling but increased in long-run due to technological improvements.

8.

Scenario	Top-Down or Bottom-Up (circle one)	Justification
A global macro-hedge fund takes large positions in foreign currencies.	Top-down	With their focus on the relative values of global currencies, there is no need for the hedge fund to focus on individual firms.
Portfolio manager Active A employs a market neutral strategy and adds market exposure with equity futures.	Bottom-up	Active A's primary strategy is market neutral. They generate alpha by going long and short in individual stocks expected to out- or under-perform in weights that will drive the ultimate market exposure (systematic risk) to zero. The selection of equity futures is a passive approach to adding market exposure.
Active Investors, LLP, advertises that they earn alpha through stock selection.	Bottom-up	Stock selection represents the stereotypical bottom-up approach. Because they generate alpha through stock selection, the focus is on the valuation of individual stocks, not macrowide indices or factors.

Use the following information for Questions 1 through 6.

Economist James Jones prepares economic forecasts for Global Bancorp, one of the world's largest investment banks. The markets have been volatile with 1.3% inflation, and a change in the party in power in Washington has many investors worried about the future. Jones has been tasked with projecting what will happen in the year ahead.

Jones begins by looking at interest rates in the hopes of offering some help to Global's bond department. He knows the yield curve is flat, but wants more insight on the future direction of interest rates. Jones finds the Taylor rule useful for predicting the Federal Reserve's action, so he attempts to calculate a short-term interest rate target based on the following data:

Current short-term rate target:	4.15%
Neutral rate:	3.57%
Target inflation rate:	2.00%
Expected inflation rate:	0.60%
Expected GDP growth, current year:	3.84%
Long-term estimated GDP growth rate:	3.27%
Risk-free rate:	4.11%

Jones also performs some analysis of the U.S. economy from an equity perspective. The stock market has been going up, and sales and profit growth are on the increase. P/E ratios are very high, but wage growth is very low.

While emerging markets are not Jones' area of expertise, he has also been asked to make a recommendation regarding investment in Venvakia. In his research, Jones learns the following information:

Venvakia's population is rising at a 3.2% rate, while the rate of participation in the labor force is rising at a 0.9% clip. Over the last year, GDP increased 4.5%. The world's GDP rose 3%. In an effort to boost growth, the government funds high-quality colleges to improve the versatility of the Venvakian workforce.

Venvakia's government is uncommonly steady relative to that of other countries in its part of the world. The country's tax rate is quite low, and there are very few deductions allowed for either consumers or businesses. Spending on capital inputs is expected to fall 1.5% this year, though total factor productivity is expected to rise 0.4%. The inflation rate is currently 1.3% and expected to stay at that level this year. Consumer consumption is expected to rise 4.4% this year, and an expected appreciation in Venvakian currency should boost buying power.

After collecting data on Venvakia, Jones submits his investment recommendation to Global's foreign desk.

1. What is the *most likely* current blend of fiscal and monetary policy?

Monetary policy	Fiscal policy
A. Restrictive	Expansive
B. Expansive	Restrictive
C. Restrictive	Restrictive

2. The target short-term interest rate using the Taylor rule is *closest* to:
    A. 3.15%.
    B. 2.74%.
    C. 3.73%.

3. If Jones' inflation forecast is incorrect and inflation is 2.0%, which types of accounts are *most* at risk?
    A. Defined-benefit plans.
    B. Individual investors.
    C. Property-and-casualty insurers.

4. Based on Jones' forecasts, what action should the bond portfolio managers take?
    A. Increase duration.
    B. Decrease duration.
    C. Underweight cyclicals.

5. Venvakia's long-term economic growth forecast is *closest* to:
    A. 3.0%.
    B. 3.7%.
    C. 7.1%.

6. Should Global invest in Venvakian businesses?
    A. No, because government policies are not likely to enhance growth.
    B. Yes, because economic growth is likely to remain higher than the global average.
    C. No, because economic growth is likely to fall below the global average.

SELF-TEST ANSWERS: ECONOMIC CONCEPTS

1. **A**   The key piece of data here is the fact that the yield curve is flat. When fiscal policy is expansive but monetary policy is restrictive, the yield curve is more or less flat. No other mix is likely to cause a flat yield curve.

2. **A**   To calculate the target interest rate, use the following equation. Target rate = neutral rate + 0.5 × (expected GDP − GDP trend) + 0.5 × (expected inflation − target inflation). Target rate = 3.57% + 0.5 × (3.84% − 3.27%) + 0.5 × (0.6% − 2.0%) = 3.15%.

3. **B**   Inflation has been 1.3% and Jones is forecasting 0.6%. If Jones is wrong and inflation rises to 2%, individual investors are the most susceptible. Their expenses will rise, while they often have few options for increasing their investment to compensate. Defined benefit and insurance companies have both assets and liabilities so the impact on them is less clear.

4. **A**   Jones projects a target short-term interest rate of 3.15% (see Question 2), lower than the current rate. To take advantage of the likely rate reduction, bond managers should increase duration. With a higher duration the bonds will appreciate more in price when rates fall. This assumes Jones is right. A mix of high stock valuations, a rising market, strong sales and profit growth, and modest growth in labor costs suggests the economy is in the early expansion phase, historically a good time to invest in (i.e., over-weight) cyclicals, but not very relevant to a bond manager.

5. **A**   The components of a long-term growth forecast are population growth, labor market participation, capital input spending, and total factor productivity. The sum of those four inputs is 3.0% (= 3.2 + 0.9 − 1.5 + 0.4).

6. **B**   Economic growth is higher than the global average. The political system is stable and the Venvakian government imposes modest taxation while investing in the education of the workforce. In addition, the currency is expected to appreciate, boosting the return for a foreign investor.

ASSET ALLOCATION

EXAM FOCUS

This assignment returns to the earlier topic of strategic asset allocation (SAA) and explores six approaches to SAA. Several of the approaches are highly mathematical and based on computer modeling. In such material, past testing has focused on concepts and conclusions but not math. Before moving into the discussion of the approaches to strategic asset allocation, a variety of related and often previously covered topics are discussed. The section on what constitutes an asset class, when an asset class will add value to the portfolio, and issues associated with international investments deserve some attention.

The mean-variance approach to SAA has been taught at Levels I and II; be familiar with it. The basics are reviewed again and the practical use of corner portfolios is added as a realistic way to simplify the math and construct a close approximation of the efficient frontier (EF). Know the math for corner portfolios. The last approach to SAA covered is the experience-based approach, which is just another name for the process of elimination covered in earlier sessions on the IPS. The assignment concludes with an introductory discussion of tactical asset allocation (TAA). TAA will be covered in more detail in later sessions.

Grasp the basics and the concept of the six approaches to SAA, how they differ, and the pros and cons, plus any math for mean-variance and corner portfolios. The experience-based approach has been frequently tested as part of an IPS question. Be prepared.

Note: The assigned material is quite explicit that the computer-based approaches are available through commercially available software packages. Do not try and learn details that are not covered in the material. Any personal interest beyond the scope of the exam should be pursued after the exam.

STRATEGIC ASSET ALLOCATION

LOS 19.a: Explain the function of strategic asset allocation in portfolio management and discuss its role in relation to specifying and controlling the investor's exposures to systematic risk.

CFA® Program Curriculum, Volume 3, page 181

Strategic asset allocation combines capital market expectations (expected return, standard deviation, and correlation) with the investor's risk, return, and investment constraints (from the IPS). Strategic asset allocation is long term in nature, and the weights are called *targets* and the portfolio represented by the strategic asset allocation is a *policy portfolio*, or *target portfolio or benchmark*.

Each asset class has its own quantifiable systematic risk, and strategic asset allocation is a conscious effort to gain the desired exposure to systematic risk via specific weights to individual asset classes. Each asset class represents relatively similar investments (e.g., long-term corporate bonds) with similar systematic risk factors. Exposure to specific asset classes in specific proportions enables portfolio managers to effectively monitor and control their systematic risk exposure. In other words, strategic asset allocation reflects the investor's desired systematic risk exposure.

TACTICAL ASSET ALLOCATION

LOS 19.b: Compare strategic and tactical asset allocation.

CFA® Program Curriculum, Volume 3, page 183

Tactical asset allocation is the result of active management wherein managers deviate from the strategic asset allocation to take advantage of any perceived *short-term* opportunities in the market. Hence, tactical asset allocation introduces additional risk, which should be justified by additional return, often called alpha.

LOS 19.c: Discuss the importance of asset allocation for portfolio performance.

CFA® Program Curriculum, Volume 3, page 184

Asset allocation is performed as two distinct processes: (1) strategic and (2) tactical asset allocation. The first, strategic allocation, responds to the interaction of the investor's long-term strategic (policy) needs and long-run capital market expectations. The allocation itself is typically specified in a range of percentages (e.g., a strategic allocation for domestic equity of 30% to 40%), and if the actual percentage wanders outside that range, the portfolio is rebalanced.

SAA is generally the prime determinate of performance. One empirical study showed that 94% of the variability of total portfolio returns is explained by the strategic asset allocation.[1] Other studies show similar results. In contrast, TAA is a small increment in return. Beyond its empirical importance, SAA benefits the client and manager with a clearly defined allocation based upon systematic risk factors consistent with the client's objectives and constraints.

LOS 19.d: Contrast the asset-only and asset/liability management (ALM) approaches to asset allocation and discuss the investor circumstances in which they are commonly used.

CFA® Program Curriculum, Volume 3, page 186

ALM strategic asset allocation is determined in conjunction with modeling the liabilities of the investor. For investors with specific liabilities (e.g., defined benefit pension plans or insurance companies), asset allocation is tailored to meet liabilities and to

---

1. Brinson, Gary P., L. Randolph Hood, and Gilbert L. Beebower. 1986. "Determinants of Portfolio Performance." *Financial Analysts Journal*, vol. 42, no. 4 (July/August).

maximize the surplus given an acceptable level of risk. This usually results in a relatively high allocation to fixed-income assets. Strategic asset allocation involves specifically modeling liabilities and determining the asset allocation appropriate to fund them. Even for those investors who don't have specific (contractual) liabilities, future obligations (e.g., retirement living expenses for an individual investor) can be modeled as liabilities, and an ALM approach to strategic asset allocation can be applied.

In *asset-only* strategic asset allocation, the focus is on earning the highest level of return for a given (acceptable) level of risk without any consideration for liability modeling. The liability (explicit or implied from future expected cash outflows) is indirectly taken into consideration through the required rate of return. Because the asset-only approach does not specifically model liabilities, the risk of not funding liabilities is not accurately controlled.

DYNAMIC AND STATIC ASSET ALLOCATION

LOS 19.e: Explain the advantage of dynamic over static asset allocation and discuss the trade-offs of complexity and cost.

CFA® Program Curriculum, Volume 3, page 187

Dynamic asset allocation takes a multi-period view of the investment horizon. In other words, it recognizes that asset (and liability) performance in one period affects the required rate of return and acceptable level of risk for subsequent periods. *Static asset allocation* ignores the link between optimal asset allocations across different time periods. For example, the manager using a static approach might estimate the necessary mean-variance inputs at a point in time and then construct the long-term portfolio accordingly. The manager using dynamic allocation allows for changing parameters over time using such techniques as Monte Carlo simulation. This allows the manager to build in expected changes to inputs as well as model unanticipated changes in macroeconomic factors.

Dynamic asset allocation is difficult and costly to implement. However, investors who have significant liabilities, especially those with uncertain timing and/or amount (e.g., non-life insurance companies), find the costs acceptable. Investors who undertake an asset-liability approach to strategic asset allocation typically prefer dynamic asset allocation to static asset allocation.

LOS 19.f: Explain how loss aversion, mental accounting, and fear of regret may influence asset allocation policy.

CFA® Program Curriculum, Volume 3, page 195

Recall that **loss aversion** makes investors focus on gains and losses rather than risk and return as prescribed by modern portfolio theory. Loss aversion can lead an investor to take increasingly greater risk in an attempt to recover from a loss. This *risk-seeking behavior* in turn can lead to highly concentrated or otherwise riskier portfolios.

Mental accounting is the tendency for individuals to identify and immunize individual goals rather than use a diversified portfolio to meet all goals considered together. This can be thought of as a pyramiding approach. The base of the pyramid represents the largest and most critical goals, such as retirement living expenses and children's educations. The investor focuses on immunizing these goals with very low risk investments, such as Treasuries and high-grade corporate bonds. Once the most important goals are met, the investor looks at the goals that are secondary in importance and uses somewhat riskier investments to meet them. In this fashion, the individual moves in a step-wise manner, identifying and immunizing goals of continually decreasing importance.

Regret is the feeling of disappointment or shame that investors feel from having to admit making a poor investment decision. A feeling of regret can be avoided if the investor does not have to actually recognize a loss. For example, an investor will hold an investment, even though it has fallen in value, in hopes that it will return to its previous, higher level. If the investor instead sold the investment at a loss, the investor would feel the resulting stigma of having made a bad investment.

Fear of regret can make investors avoid taking actions that could lead to regret. For example, the investor holding the losing investment will continue holding the asset rather than sell it. The result could obviously be an even greater loss. From the opposite perspective, an investor fearing regret will tend to hold a winner too long. Fearing selling a rising stock too soon and losing out on even higher returns, the investor will continue holding the stock, possibly until it begins to fall in value. Thus, fear of regret leads investors to hold both losing and winning investments too long.

Fear of regret can also lead to investing only in "comfortable" investments, such as domestic stocks and bonds. By deliberately excluding some asset classes, such as foreign investments, the investor avoids the possibility of making uninformed and possibly poor investment decisions he could later regret. Thus, fearing making a poor decision, the investor fails to hold investments that could improve the return/risk characteristics of the portfolio.

SPECIFYING RISK AND RETURN OBJECTIVES

LOS 19.g: <u>Evaluate</u> return and risk objectives in relation to strategic asset allocation.

CFA® Program Curriculum, Volume 3, page 189

> *Professor's Note: Return and risk objectives are determined in accordance with the investor's specified constraints. This portion of the IPS relating to objectives and constraints and a process of elimination SAA is better covered in the earlier study sessions devoted to those topics. Ultimately the SAA must blend the client's O&C with reasonable capital market expectations.*

For the Exam: This section takes a slightly different approach to the return calculation than the earlier assignments. Many portfolios include in the objectives a need to maintain real value or to maintain the investor's standard of living. This requires that the return include the relevant rate of inflation and possibly portfolio expenses. This assignment suggests a compounding approach to that calculation. The brief discussion of additive versus compounding found here has caused considerable confusion for candidates.

Consider a perpetual foundation needing a 5% current distribution, expenses of 0.5%, and expected general inflation of 2%. However, inflation relating to the foundations distributions is 3%. 3% would be the relevant inflation rate. The required return would be:

- Additive: 5 + 3 + 0.5 = 8.5%.
- Compounded: (1.05)(1.03)(1.005) − 1 = 8.69%.

The issues can be summarized as:

- The difference in the two approaches grows as the inputs become larger numbers.
- The earlier and primary readings on this topic generally took the additive approach. Some of the earlier process of elimination questions would not have been solvable with a compounded return number.
- This section confirms that the additive approach is more common in real-world policy statements and generally adequate in most situations.
- If the distribution and expense needs are based on beginning market value and distributed at the end of the period, the additive approach is the correct solution. It provides the return necessary to increase the amount of distribution and portfolio value with inflation in perpetuity.
- In other cases such as the distribution is made monthly during the year (not at year end), additive is not sufficient and compounded better approximates the necessary return.
- There are references in the CFA text stating compounded is better in multi-period situations. However, there is no explanation of what constitutes "multi-period." When multiple distributions occur during the year, compounded is a better approximation of the needed return.
- This section does discuss multi-period in the context of path dependency and Monte Carlo simulation. Such analysis shows that if a fixed amount is withdrawn during both up and down markets, it has a greater percentage impact on the portfolio during down periods. This suggests the return target should be set higher. Compounding does set a higher number than additive.

Bottom line: for the exam I suggest you use the additive approach unless the question or facts clearly request compounding or refer to a multi-period calculation or to path dependency issues. In those cases I would use compounding.

The investor's **risk objective** should be specified in light of the investor's risk aversion. In Study Sessions 4 and 5, we classified investors as having below-average, average, or above-average *risk tolerance*. Investors can be placed into numerical categories using this very rough approximation or through answers to questionnaires. One possible numerical rating scheme might be to score investors from 1 to 10 based upon their tolerance for risk. Those with below-average risk tolerance (highly risk-averse investors) are given a score of 7 to 10, while those who are highly tolerant of risk (low risk aversion) are given a score of 1 to 3.

Then, using a well-accepted quantitative relationship, we can determine the *utility-adjusted* return the investor will realize from the portfolio:

$$U_P = \hat{R}_P - 0.005(A)\left(\sigma_P^2\right)$$

where:
U_P = the investor's utility from investing in the portfolio
(i.e., the investor's utility-adjusted return)
$\hat{R}_P$ = the portfolio expected return
A = the investor's risk aversion score
σ_P^2 = the portfolio variance

Suppose an investor requires before-tax return of 8%, his risk aversion score is 7, and he can invest in one of two portfolio allocations, A or B, which meet his required return and risk (standard deviation) objectives:

- Allocation A (Portfolio A) has an expected return of 8.5% and a standard deviation of 9%.
- Allocation B (Portfolio B) has an expected return of 8.8% and a standard deviation of 10%.

The investor would be better off with Allocation A. Even though it has a somewhat lower expected return, its risk-adjusted return is actually higher:

$$U_A = \hat{R}_A - 0.005(A)\left(\sigma_A^2\right) = 8.5\% - 0.005(7)(9\%)^2 = 5.67\%$$
$$U_B = \hat{R}_B - 0.005(A)\left(\sigma_B^2\right) = 8.8\% - 0.005(7)(10\%)^2 = 5.30\%$$

> *Professor's Note: Be able to make the calculation if asked. In the curriculum this formula may also appear with 0.5 instead of 0.005 as a multiplier. 0.5 can be used but the inputs of expected return and risk must be entered in decimal fashion and the output will be in decimal expression. The result will be the same. For example, for Portfolio A and B:*
>
> $$U_A = \hat{R}_A - 0.5(A)\left(\sigma_A^2\right) = 0.085 - 0.5(7)(0.09)^2 = 0.0567 = 5.67\%$$
> $$U_B = \hat{R}_B - 0.5(A)\left(\sigma_B^2\right) = 0.088 - 0.5(7)(0.10)^2 = 0.0530 = 5.30\%$$

Suppose the investor's risk aversion score was 2:

$$U_A = \hat{R}_A - 0.005(A)\left(\sigma_A^2\right) = 8.5\% - 0.005(2)(9\%)^2 = 7.69\%$$
$$U_B = \hat{R}_B - 0.005(A)\left(\sigma_B^2\right) = 8.8\% - 0.005(2)(10\%)^2 = 7.80\%$$

Now Allocation B is preferred. There are at least two implications of these results:

1. When choosing from a set of efficient portfolios such as Portfolio B versus A where Portfolio B has both a higher expected return and higher standard deviation than A, the choice is driven by the investor's risk aversion.

2. As risk aversion increases (denoted with a higher risk aversion score), the deduction for (adjustment for) risk increases.

Roy's Safety-First Measure

In addition to standard deviation as a measure of risk (volatility), the acceptable level of risk can be stated in terms of *downside risk* measures such as shortfall risk, semivariance, and target semivariance. **Shortfall risk** is the risk of exceeding a maximum acceptable dollar loss. **Semivariance** is the *bottom half* of the variance (i.e., the variance calculated using only the returns below the expected return). **Target semivariance** is the semivariance using some target minimum return, such as zero.

Roy's Safety-First Measure is one of the oldest and most cited measures of downside risk. The measure is stated as a ratio of *excess return* to risk:

$$RSF = \frac{\hat{R}_P - R_{MAR}}{\sigma_P}$$

where:
$\hat{R}_P$ = portfolio expected return
R_{MAR} = the investor's minimum acceptable return
σ_P = portfolio standard deviation

The *excess return* in Roy's measure is the expected return in excess of the investor's minimum acceptable return. Dividing excess return by the portfolio standard deviation tells us how many standard deviations the minimum acceptable return lies below the portfolio expected return.

For example, we will assume our investor in the previous example also requires that the portfolio not lose any money (i.e., the minimum acceptable return is 0). Applying Roy's Safety-First Measure to Allocations A and B, we determine that Allocation A is preferred:

$$RSF_A = \frac{\hat{R}_P - R_{MAR}}{\sigma_P} = \frac{8.5 - 0}{9} = 0.94$$

$$RSF_B = \frac{\hat{R}_P - R_{MAR}}{\sigma_P} = \frac{8.8 - 0}{10} = 0.88$$

> **For the Exam:** Notice that the two measures, utility-adjusted return and Roy's Safety-First Measure, chose the same allocation for the first investor (aversion score of 7) but not the second investor (aversion score of 2). All risk-adjusted measures do not produce the same rankings. On the exam follow directions carefully as to what measure is specified.

SPECIFYING ASSET CLASSES

LOS 19.h: Evaluate whether an asset class or set of asset classes has been appropriately specified.

CFA® Program Curriculum, Volume 3, page 197

Throughout our discussion of strategic and tactical asset allocation, we have assumed that asset classes are correctly identified. We assumed that the manager has appropriately placed assets into groups according to their descriptions and characteristics such as risk and return. For example, including emerging markets equities and domestic equities in a single class labeled *equities* would be appropriate only from a general description standpoint; their risk and return characteristics are obviously significantly different. A primary factor to consider in determining whether asset classes are properly defined is whether the classes held together will produce the desired diversification.

In addition to their descriptions and characteristics, we should ensure that the classes are not highly correlated. A high correlation between classes would indicate that the classes are related from a risk and return standpoint and would defeat the purpose of holding separate classes in an allocation (lack of diversification).

Individual assets should be defined clearly within a single classification. If it can be legitimately argued that assets can be placed in more than one class, the descriptions of the classes are too vague (have not been correctly specified). Again, this defeats the purpose of placing assets into classes for allocation purposes.

In addition to the desired diversification effect, the asset classes should define the majority of all possible investable assets. This not only increases the set of investable assets, but also pushes up the efficient frontier (i.e., increases return at all levels of risk). Remember that the domestic efficient frontier for equities is shifted upward with the inclusion of international equities and that the frontier is pushed even farther up with the inclusion of other asset classes.

Depending upon the strategy employed, the manager will want to rebalance the portfolio to the original strategic allocation, whether the allocation has varied due to performance or tactical allocation. This implies that the asset classes should have sufficient liquidity.

To sum up, asset classes have been appropriately specified if:

1. Assets in the class are similar from a descriptive as well as a statistical perspective.

2. They are not highly correlated so they provide the desired diversification.

3. Individual assets cannot be classified into more than one class.

4. They cover the majority of all possible investable assets.

5. They contain a sufficiently large percentage of liquid assets.

Some well-accepted asset classes include domestic equity, domestic fixed income, global equity, global fixed income, cash and equivalents, and alternative investments, which may be further divided into classes, such as real estate, private equity, et cetera.

 Professor's Note: LOS 19.i is discussed later with LOS 19.r.

Inflation-Adjusted Securities, Global Securities, and Alternative Investments

LOS 19.j: Evaluate the theoretical and practical effects of including additional asset classes in an asset allocation.

CFA® Program Curriculum, Volume 3, page 199

The goal in selecting asset classes for strategic asset allocation is to improve the long-term portfolio risk and return. Asset classes that meet the five criteria of a well-specified asset class and accomplish this goal should be included in the SAA. On a short-term basis, asset classes that improve risk and return could be included in a tactical asset allocation.

Theoretical effects would include the effect on overall portfolio risk and return. This effect will depend on the asset class's return, stand-alone risk (standard deviation), and correlation with other portfolio assets. Practical effects would include issues such as liquidity, legal, tax, political, currency, and other factors that vary by asset class.

Inflation-protected "bond-like" securities such as Treasury Inflation Protected Securities (TIPS) are an example of a recently developed asset class that provides theoretical and practical benefits. They provide a fixed real coupon rate, but the principal and coupon payments adjust upward (or downward) with inflation (or deflation). The coupon payment on any payment date is the fixed real rate times the adjusted principal. Final principal payment is also in adjusted principal. TIPS meet the criteria of an appropriate asset class because:

1. TIPS of varying maturity are strongly correlated with each other.

2. Their correlation with traditional, nominal bonds and equities are low.

3. They respond to different economic variables than do nominal bonds. Nominal bond volatility responds to the volatility of nominal interest rates, while TIPS volatility responds to the volatility of real interest rates.

4. TIPS provide inflation protection not found in traditional fixed or floating bonds.

International investments and alternative investments (such as real estate, private equity, and hedge funds) also exhibit the characteristics of distinct asset classes and provide benefits warranting inclusion in the asset allocation process. Inclusion would mean they should be considered as an asset class for asset allocation. Their use for a specific client would also depend on that client's objectives and constraints.

Determining Whether to Add an Investment to the Portfolio

LOS 19.k: <u>Demonstrate</u> the application of mean–variance analysis to decide whether to include an additional asset class in an existing portfolio.

CFA® Program Curriculum, Volume 3, page 201

Mean-variance analysis assumes asset classes can be analyzed and described by expected return, standard deviation, and correlation. If the asset class considered for inclusion is constrained to a positive weight (no short selling), a relatively simple decision rule can be used to determine if it will be beneficial to add the asset class to the portfolio. A decision rule based on the new investment's Sharpe ratio, the current portfolio Sharpe ratio, and the correlation of the returns on the two is used.[2] If the Sharpe ratio of the new investment is greater than the current portfolio Sharpe ratio multiplied by the correlation of the new investment's returns with the portfolio's returns, adding the investment to the portfolio will improve the portfolio Sharpe ratio:

$$\text{if } S_i > S_p \times \rho_{i,p} \text{ adding the investment will improve the portfolio Sharpe ratio}$$

where:
S_i = Sharpe ratio of proposed investment
S_p = current portfolio Sharpe ratio
$\rho_{i,p}$ = correlation of the returns on the proposed investment with the portfolio returns

Sharpe Ratio is the: (expected return of the asset less the risk free rate) divided by the standard deviation of the asset.

---

2. This methodology can be applied to individual assets or asset classes.

Example 1: Will adding the asset improve the portfolio Sharpe ratio?

A manager is considering adding an investment to his diversified portfolio, but he is unsure of the correlation of the new investment with his portfolio. **Determine** the maximum correlation between the new investment and his portfolio that would make the new investment acceptable (risk-free rate = 3%).

	Portfolio	*New Investment*[1]
Expected return	12%	12%
Standard deviation	18%	30%
Sharpe ratio	(12 − 3) / 18 = 0.50	(12 − 3) / 30 = 0.30

1. Remember, the proposed investment could have been an asset class. For example, a manager might be considering adding a class of foreign investments to a domestic portfolio.

Answer 1: Calculate the correlation coefficient that makes the equation an identity.

$$S_i = S_p \times \rho_{i,p}$$

$$0.30 = 0.50 \times \rho_{i,p} \Rightarrow \rho_{i,p} = \frac{0.30}{0.50} = 0.60$$

- If the correlation of the new investment with the portfolio is 0.60, then $S_i = S_p \times \rho_{i,p}$, and adding the new investment will leave the portfolio Sharpe ratio unchanged.
- If the correlation is less than 0.60, then $S_i > S_p \times \rho_{i,p}$, and adding the investment will *increase* the portfolio Sharpe ratio.
- If the correlation is greater than 0.60, then $S_i < S_p \times \rho_{i,p}$, and adding the investment will *decrease* the portfolio Sharpe ratio.

Example 2: Selecting an asset for the portfolio

A portfolio manager is considering three investments, only one of which he will add to his portfolio. Data on the investments and his portfolio are provided in the table. Based on the data provided, determine which investment the manager should select.

	Portfolio	Investment 1	Investment 2	Investment 3
Sharpe ratio[1]	0.41	0.30	0.31	0.19
Correlation with current portfolio, ρ		0.77	0.80	0.40

1. $S_i = \dfrac{\hat{R}_i - R_F}{\sigma_i}$

Answer 2: Follow these steps:

1. If Sharpe ratios are not presented, you would be provided with expected returns, standard deviations, and the risk-free rate.

2. Multiply the portfolio Sharpe ratio by the correlation of each asset with the portfolio.

3. If the Sharpe ratio of an investment is greater than the respective product in #2, the investment is acceptable.

$$\text{if } S_i > S_p \times \rho_{i,p} \Rightarrow \text{the investment will increase the portfolio Sharpe ratio}$$
$$S_1 = 0.30; \quad S_p \times \rho_{1,p} = 0.41 \times 0.77 = 0.316; \quad S_1 < S_p \times \rho_{i,p}$$
$$S_2 = 0.31; \quad S_p \times \rho_{2,p} = 0.41 \times 0.80 = 0.328; \quad S_2 < S_p \times \rho_{i,p}$$
$$S_3 = 0.19; \quad S_p \times \rho_{3,p} = 0.41 \times 0.40 = 0.164; \quad S_3 > S_p \times \rho_{i,p}$$

We see from the calculations that only Investment 3 would increase the portfolio Sharpe ratio. Even though it has the lowest Sharpe ratio of the three investments, it also has the lowest correlation with the portfolio.

RISK IN INTERNATIONAL ASSETS

LOS 19.l: Describe risk, cost, and opportunities associated with nondomestic equities and bonds.

CFA® Program Curriculum, Volume 3, page 203

The additional risks to consider are currency risk, political risk, and home country bias.

Currency risk: Investing in a foreign-denominated security exposes the investor to changes in value of foreign asset and changes in value of the foreign currency. This has implications for the return of the asset and for its volatility.

Professor's Note: For example, a German investor could buy a U.K. stock or bond denominated in GBP. If income and price change of the asset in GBP is 5%, the total return for an investor who values her portfolio in GBP is 5%. I'll refer to this as the local market return (LMR). However the German investor is also affected by the change in value of the GBP, the foreign currency from the investor's perspective. If the GBP declines 2%, the total return for the German investor is approximately 5% – 2% = 3%. Referring to the change in value of the foreign currency (–2%) as the local currency return (LCR), the total return on the investment is approximately LMR + LCR. If the LMR and LCR are consistently either both positive or both negative, this positive correlation amplifies return volatility for the foreign investor. On the other hand, if LMR and LCR have negative correlation, this will reduce return volatility for the foreign investor.

These concepts should sound familiar from earlier levels of the CFA material. The math will be discussed further in other readings and study sessions. The rest of this section is a non-math discussion of theoretical and practical issues in adding international investments to the portfolio. Mathematical discussions of this material are found in other parts of the curriculum.

Currency should generally be a smaller concern than some naive investors may fear.

The correlation of LMR and LCR is generally less than +1.0. Therefore, the volatility of the investor's position will be less than the sum of the volatility of the LMR and LCR. The more the correlation of LMR and LCR approach –1.0, the lower the volatility of the investment for the investor. For example, suppose every time LCR is negative, LMR is positive and vice versa; total return to the investor can be quite stable.

In a global portfolio exposed to multiple currencies, some will likely have positive LCR while others have negative LCR. The correlations across all currencies would likely be less than +1.0, again creating a diversification effect. In addition, over time, a currency is unlikely to continually appreciate or depreciate; it will more likely show mean reversion. Over time currency risk tends to become a smaller consideration.

Empirical evidence suggests that the standard deviation of currency is only about half the standard deviation of stock prices. It is the less important determinant of risk. (In the bond market, the currency volatility is generally higher than bond volatility, reflecting bonds are generally less volatile than stocks, making it a more important consideration for bond investors).

Political risk: Exists when a country has (1) irresponsible fiscal and/or monetary policy, and/or (2) lacks reasonable legal and regulatory rules to support but not stifle financial markets. It could arise if a government confiscates property without compensation, unduly restricts foreign investment or suspends capital and currency movement, manipulates the currency or taxes foreign investors unfairly, is unstable or defaults on its debt, and allows or requires companies to be managed for goals inconsistent with those of the shareholders.

Home country bias: Refers to the observation that investors tend to overweigh investments in their own country, creating a suboptimal portfolio allocation. It could reflect lack of familiarity with foreign investments, financial reporting, and language. It can also reflect lack of liquidity and higher political risk in foreign markets or a need to match domestic liabilities with domestic assets.

Costs in International Assets

- Transaction costs can be higher and liquidity can be lower. Market impact transaction costs (a buy order that drives up the market price or a sell order that drives down the market price before order completion) are more significant than explicit transaction costs such as commissions or bid asked spread. Market impact cost is highest in emerging markets.
- Withholding taxes on foreign investors may not be fully offset by tax treaties. For tax exempt investors, they are a pure cost as the investor has no tax return in their own country on which to claim an offset.
- Free-float can be an issue. The stated market capitalization may include shares held by the government or other investors who will not sell.
- Inefficient market infrastructure can result in high costs for security registration, settlement, custody, management, or information.

Opportunities in International Assets

The theoretical argument for international investment is potentially higher return and lower risk with low correlation resulting in enhanced Sharpe ratios. Empirical evidence does not always support this expectation because it appears correlations of financial markets rise during financial crises. When diversification is most needed, all markets go down together. Another argument against diversification is that if an investor resides in a country with high returns, international diversification will lower the return.

The rise in correlation during financial crises can be explained by:

- Markets becoming less segmented and more integrated. In a segmented market, the economy of that country should determine return and risk characteristics. As a country integrates, its economy is more correlated with other economies, and its expected markets would become more correlated.
- Industry factors becoming more important than country factors in determining a company's risk and return. In integrated economies, companies can diversify their operations internationally, making company results more dependent on the economies where the company operates and less dependent on the economy of its home country.

The empirical evidence on country risk varies. It supports that currency and industry risk factors dominate developed market equity returns, while country factors remain important for emerging markets. Despite this, diversification across countries remains important because:

- The importance of country or industry factors is not consistent but varies by the specific industry in the specific country. Investors need to consider both factors.
- In small economies investors have few investment opportunities and must consider international investment to gain reasonable diversification.

- Investment opportunity can be better outside the investor's country.
- Currency matters and may itself provide diversification (if the LMR and LCR returns have low correlation).

In conclusion, the benefits of international diversification are:

1. Foreign markets could be undervalued and, thus, offer better expected return.

2. While the investor's home market may have had the best returns in the past, that is not a reliable indicator of future returns.

3. Even if correlations rise in the short run during crises, the long-run benefits of diversification can remain.

4. Correlations among bond markets tend to be lower than among equity markets. Adding international bonds to domestic-only portfolios can be particularly beneficial in reducing risk for risk averse investors.

Global index funds can be used to gain diversification at lower cost and without home country bias.

LOS 19.m: Explain the importance of conditional return correlations in evaluating the diversification benefits of nondomestic investments.

CFA® Program Curriculum, Volume 3, page 207

The previously discussed approach to determining whether a new asset class will benefit the portfolio compares the Sharpe ratio of the new asset class to the existing portfolio Sharpe times correlation of the new asset class to existing portfolio. This is a mean-variance based approach that assumes correlations and standard deviations are stable over time. The observation that correlations increase during financial crises is inconsistent with this assumption and indicates **conditional return correlations** (i.e., correlations that depend on market volatility and conditions). Diversification benefits fail when they are most needed.

Part (but not all) of the rising correlation can be explained away by technical issues in the way correlation is calculated; the mathematics of calculating correlation bias the statistic upward as standard deviations rise. Alternative methods exist to calculate correlation conditioned on the level of return. A portfolio could be optimized both assuming normal conditions and assuming crisis conditions.

A simpler method to determine what is happening to correlation is to plot rolling correlations between markets over time. The plot reveals:

- Correlations have been rising over time, and potential diversification benefits have decreased as markets integrate.
- Correlations did rise during crises periods and then fell back after the crises, within a generally rising upward trend.

Emerging Markets

Emerging markets are economies early in the integration process. Brazil, Russia, India, China, and other smaller markets are often classified as emerging. Emerging markets could be 25% of world equity value and a rising portion of government and corporate bond value as more debt is issued in such markets. The traditional thinking is they offer higher return and stand-alone risk but low correlation with other markets. As these economies mature, their return characteristics are converging with developed markets. However, as they attract more capital, their asset and currency values can appreciate. The special considerations of emerging market investing include:

- Investability. Liquidity and free-float can be limited with adverse market impact, which drives up the price paid to execute purchase orders. Governments of emerging market economies may impose capital and currency restrictions or discriminatory taxes.
- Non-normal return distributions inconsistent with mean-variance assumptions. Returns can be leptokurtic (fat tails with extreme high and low returns occurring more often than consistent with a normal distribution). The return patterns show periods of both positive and negative skew in the returns. Daily returns can be extreme and make up most of the annual return.
- Strong economic growth may not benefit existing shareholders. New share issuance increases equity market cap but dilutes existing shareholder value. Strong growth could already be priced into the stock price. Growth opportunities could be unfairly allocated by the government and not be available to publicly owned companies or disproportionately benefit labor with higher compensation. Corporate governance to protect shareholders can be weak.
- Contagion has been exhibited when a crisis in one emerging market or in developed markets spreads to other emerging markets (essentially just another example or rising correlation during crisis).
- Currency devaluations as emerging market governments devalue their currency (creating a negative LCR) or restrict the ability of an investor to repatriate the funds back to their own market. A currency crisis in one emerging market has been observed to lead to contagion (the crisis in one emerging market leads investors to flee other emerging markets, causing the crisis to spread). Despite these crises, the evidence suggests declines in emerging market currency value can be offset by rising stock prices over time.
- Inefficient markets may allow better informed and capitalized institutional investors or those with local presence to earn excess returns.

LOS 19.n: Explain expected effects on share prices, expected returns, and return volatility as a segmented market becomes integrated with global markets.

CFA® Program Curriculum, Volume 3, page 211

As markets integrate and move through emerging market status to developed market status, the general progression is:

- Equity share prices rise as (1) capital can now flow into the formerly uninvestable market, and (2) to reflect declining stand-alone risk.

- Expected returns increase as capital flows into the market but then declines after the initial inflow to be consistent with the now higher stock prices and lower risk going forward.
- Long-run return volatility should decline as prices reflect information that is more freely available and political risk declines.
- Diversification benefits can decline despite the fall in stand-alone risk as correlation and covariance with world markets increases.
- Market microstructure and efficiency improve as transaction costs fall, liquidity increases, and prices are more informationally efficient.
- Capital costs fall with higher stock prices and lower risk. Lower capital costs finance higher economic growth.

STEPS IN ASSET ALLOCATION

LOS 19.o: Explain the major steps involved in establishing an appropriate asset allocation.

CFA® Program Curriculum, Volume 3, page 213

The asset allocation process is basically the portfolio management process we have identified throughout the CFA curriculum (i.e., construct the portfolio, monitor its progress, and revise the portfolio as necessary).

As we saw in Study Sessions 4 and 5, the asset allocation process starts with determining the investor's return requirement and risk tolerance, subject to the investor's current wealth and constraints. The manager formulates long-term capital market expectations and their potential effects on the various asset classes. The job is then to determine the mix of assets (allocation) that best meets the objectives defined in the IPS, subject to any other limitations specified by the investor. For example, an investor might strictly forbid investment in cigarette companies or companies that do business with certain countries.

Once the strategic allocation has been implemented, it should be monitored regularly as specified in the IPS. The monitoring process should contain a feedback loop so that changes in long-term market factors can be incorporated back into the "model" and an assessment made to determine whether adjustments to the strategic allocation are justified. If the market changes are only short term in nature, the manager should consider implementing tactical allocation measures, which have been approved in the IPS.

APPROACHES TO ASSET ALLOCATION

LOS 19.p: Discuss the strengths and limitations of the following approaches to asset allocation: mean–variance, resampled efficient frontier, Black–Litterman, Monte Carlo simulation, ALM, and experience based.

CFA® Program Curriculum, Volume 3, page 215

The Mean-Variance Optimization (MVO) Approach

The mean-variance approach to strategic asset allocation is a static approach (versus a multi-period dynamic approach). The mean-variance frontier is the *outer edge* of a graphical plot of all possible combinations of risky assets. The efficient frontier is the portion of the mean-variance frontier that contains portfolios (combinations) with the highest expected return at each level of risk. Figure 1 shows an example of a mean-variance frontier and the efficient frontier.

The horizontal axis represents risk as measured by standard deviation. The vertical axis represents portfolio-expected return. All portfolios below the efficient frontier, even those on the mean-variance frontier but below the global minimum variance portfolio, are sub-optimal. This is because there is a portfolio (on the efficient frontier) that has a higher expected return for the same amount of risk.

Figure 1: Mean-Variance (Efficient) Frontier

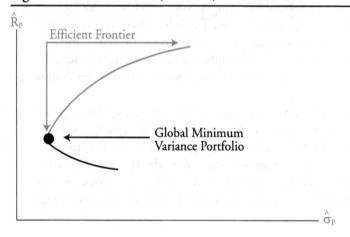

Efficient portfolios are essentially portfolios with varying allocations to the available asset classes. To determine an efficient portfolio with an expected return of *k* and given that there are *j* asset classes, we find the allocation that has the lowest standard deviation, such that:

$$\hat{R}_P = \sum w_i \left(\hat{R}_i \right) = k \text{ for } i = 1 \text{ through } j$$

where:
$\hat{R}_P$ = expected return on the portfolio
w_i = weight of class i and $\sum w_i = 1$
$\hat{R}_i$ = expected return for class i

MVO identifies at each level of return the portfolio with the lowest standard deviation and the asset allocation for that portfolio. The efficient frontier then starts with the portfolio with the lowest standard deviation and rises to the right. MVO and the EF can be constructed on either a constrained or unconstrained basis. Unconstrained allows short selling of asset classes, in other words negative asset weights, while constrained does not. In both cases the weights of the portfolio must total 100% (1.00). For the unconstrained version Black (1972) proposed a 2-fund theorem that the asset class weights of any minimum-variance portfolio can be found as a weighted average of the asset class weights of a pair of minimum-variance portfolios.

> *Professor's Note: This concept will be important later in this session as the basis of the corner portfolio theorem. Both here and later the correlation between the pair is ignored, which is equivalent to making it 1.0 so no diversification benefit occurs.*
>
> *This simplification is reasonable when the pair is a set of corner portfolios, but not when it is any random pair as implied in 2-portfolio theorem. The 2-portfolio theorem will not be discussed again in the CFA curriculum but the same calculations will be used with corner portfolios. Know them by exam day. It is just a weighted average calculation.*

Example: Efficient frontier

Assume only four asset classes combined into Portfolio A ($w_1 = 0.25$, $w_2 = 0.15$, $w_3 = 0.20$, $w_4 = 0.40$) and Portfolio B ($w_1 = 0.30$, $w_2 = 0.20$, $w_3 = 0.35$, $w_4 = 0.15$), which lie on the efficient frontier. Portfolio A has an expected return of 10%, and Portfolio B has an expected return of 15%. **Calculate** the asset class weightings (combination of Portfolios A and B) for the efficient portfolio with an expected return of 11%.

Answer:

We solve for w in the following equation:
$$\hat{R}_P = w_A\hat{R}_A + w_B\hat{R}_B \Rightarrow \text{letting } w_B = (1-w_A)$$
$$0.11 = w_A(0.10) + (1-w_A)(0.15)$$
$$w_A = 0.80, \text{ so } w_B = 0.20$$

Thus, the weights of the individual asset classes in the resulting efficient portfolio allocation with an expected return of 11% are:

Asset class 1: $(0.80 \times 0.25) + (0.20 \times 0.30) = 0.26$

Asset class 2: $(0.80 \times 0.15) + (0.20 \times 0.20) = 0.16$

Asset class 3: $(0.80 \times 0.20) + (0.20 \times 0.35) = 0.23$

Asset class 4: $(0.80 \times 0.40) + (0.20 \times 0.15) = \underline{0.35}$

$$\sum = 1.00$$

Cash Equivalents: Is There a Risk-Free Asset?

MVO is a 1-period model (generally one year) and essentially assumes the inputs will remain constant over time. Over a single, discrete time period it is generally possible to identify a risk-free asset with a known return, zero standard deviation, and correlation to other asset returns of zero. A discount government security normally approximates the requirements of risk free. When such an asset exists it leads to the concept of CALs and the CML. A CAL is a line between the risk-free asset and a portfolio of risky assets while the CML is the line between the risk-free asset and the market portfolio of risky assets. It is important because if an investor can borrow and lend at the risk-free asset rate the investor can construct any portfolio on the CML and these optimal portfolios on the CML then dominate (are superior to) the otherwise optimal portfolios on the EF of risky assets. The market portfolio is the only portfolio common to the CML and EF.

While correct as stated, there are conceptual and practical problems with using the CML to construct an SAA:

- For the multiple and often ongoing time periods of a typical portfolio there is no risk-free asset that meets the required definition of known return with zero standard deviation and correlation. The single-period government security will have a changing return over time and a standard deviation of return. The typical MVO may or may not include a cash equivalent asset class. If included it would be a risky asset with an expected return, standard deviation, and correlation. It will be treated as any other asset class to construct an EF but not a CML.

- Even if a risk-free asset existed for a client concerned with only a single period, there could be practical problems. Consider a client seeking a return higher than the market; the CML would require borrowing on an ongoing basis to take a leveraged position in the market. Generally borrowing creates risk and imposes obligations to the lender that are unacceptable to most investors as a long-term strategy. Even the low-risk client who on the CML would invest in the market and a risk-free asset may have issues as a long-term strategy with paying active management fees for this approach.

Professor's Note: Be well familiar with the concepts of the EF, CALs, and CML, plus borrowing and lending at the risk-free rate to construct efficient portfolios on the CML. This is well covered at all CFA levels. Be prepared to articulate and explain any of these issues in a constructed response question. Be able to give a short answer or a longer answer with additional details and maybe an illustration to meet the minutes and point value of the question.

Levels I and II have briefly discussed the limitations of the CML concept. At Level III, assume the CML approach is not relevant for SAA and portfolios should be selected from the EF unless the question clearly states borrowing and lending at the risk free rate is acceptable or the question directly asks for a CML solution.

Resampled Efficient Frontier (REF)

A significant drawback to generating an efficient frontier through traditional mean-variance optimization methods is the *sensitivity* of the frontier to changes in the inputs. Because the inputs themselves (e.g., expected returns, covariances) are estimates, reliance on an efficient frontier developed through a traditional, single mean-variance optimization is questionable.

In response, Michaud[3] developed a simulation approach utilizing historical means, variances, and covariances of asset classes, which, combined with capital market forecasts, assumes they are fair representations of their expectations. His *resampling* technique is based on a Monte Carlo simulation that draws from the distributions to develop a simulated efficient frontier. Because the simulation is run thousands of times, the efficient portfolio at each return level, and hence the resulting efficient frontier, is the result of an averaging process.

Rather than a single, sharp curve, the resampled efficient frontier is a blur. At each level of return is a simulated efficient portfolio at the center with a distribution of portfolios above and below it. Think of the portfolio in the middle as being at the center of a normal distribution. The asset mix at any point on the resampled efficient frontier is an average of many portfolios that might have been constructed to meet that return. It is not possible to know the single exact portfolio that is optimal and like any average, the average is more stable than any single portfolio that might be generated by a single MVO calculation.

By utilizing this resampling technique, a portfolio manager is able to judge the need for rebalancing. For example, if the manager's portfolio is within a 90% confidence interval of the most efficient portfolio, it could be considered *statistically equivalent*. That is, rebalancing to the most optimal weights would not produce a statistically significant change in its risk-return profile.

Resampling has *advantages* over traditional MVO:

- It utilizes an averaging process and generates an efficient frontier that is more stable than a traditional mean-variance efficient frontier. Small changes in the input variables result in only minor changes in the REF.

3. Michaud, Richard, 1989. "The Markowitz Optimization Enigma: Is Optimized Optimal?" *Financial Analysts Journal*, January.

- Portfolios generated through this process tend to be better diversified.
- By comparing any asset mix of an existing portfolio to the range of asset mixes across the multiple portfolios on the REF that could have generated the required return, it is possible to see if the current mix is within the boundaries of what is acceptable. This is likely to lead to less portfolio turnover and lower transaction costs.

A *disadvantage* of resampling is its lack of a sound theoretical basis. There is no theoretical reasoning to support the contention that a portfolio constructed through resampling should be superior relative to another constructed through traditional mean-variance analysis. In addition and like MVO, the inputs are often based on historical data that could lack current relevance.

Black-Litterman

With the same motivations as Michaud (resampling), Black and Litterman developed two models for dealing with the problems associated with estimation error, especially expected return: (1) the unconstrained Black-Litterman model (UBL) and (2) the Black-Litterman model (BL). Hint: The assigned reading focuses primarily on BL (i.e., constrained for no short selling).

The **unconstrained Black-Litterman model** (UBL) starts with the weights of asset classes from a global index. Applying a Bayesian process, the manager increases or decreases the weights based upon her views of expected asset class returns and the strengths of those views with no constraint against short sales (negative weights are allowed). The UBL is intuitive in that the manager starts with market weightings and directly increases or decreases those weights based on the manager's opinion of what will outperform or underperform. If the manager has a strong opinion domestic equity will underperform, the manager can shift significant assets out of domestic equity to a specific asset class expected to outperform or broadly across all other classes if the manager has no specific views on what will outperform.

UBL does not define how to make these adjustments to weights, but in practice most managers select relatively diversified portfolios without negative weights.

The **Black-Litterman (constrained) model** (BL) allows no negative asset weights, also produces well-diversified portfolios that incorporate the manager's views on asset class returns, and is a more defined process. It is a rigorous mathematical process starting with reverse optimization. BL can be used to both calculate the market's consensus expectations of returns by asset class and then construct an MVO portfolio adjusted for the manager's views of those returns. The BL model requires several steps:

- Select a relevant, global market index. Input the market weights for the asset classes in that index and a covariance matrix for those classes.
- Use reverse optimization to back-solve for the implied, expected returns of those asset classes. Having started with a market index and the market's weightings, these will be consensus returns expectations.
- The manager then reviews the implied returns and expresses any opinions regarding the returns and the strength of those opinions.

- The manager then resets any implied returns up or down to reflect the manager's opinions and conviction level. For example suppose the back-solving implies Spanish equities have an expected return of 12% while the manager expects 14% but with low confidence. This could be expressed as a 14% expected return but with a high standard deviation.
- A new MVO is run using the adjusted returns where the manager had an opinion and the market consensus return where the manager has no opinion. The new MVO produces the recommended asset mix.

Like UBL, the manager's opinions and level of conviction are incorporated, but BL then uses MVO to also factor in asset volatility and correlations in a disciplined process to find the optimal mix. BL tends to be less sensitive to changes in inputs and less likely to produce the under diversification common in traditional MVO.

Example: Asset allocation using BL

A portfolio manager has asked the quantitative department of his firm to reverse engineer the expected returns of a global index. The quant department has provided the following data:

Table A: Global Asset Class Weights

Assets	Class 1	Class 2	Class 3	Class 4	Class 5	Class 6	Class 7
E(R)	9.5%	4.5%	5.1%	4.7%	6.2%	5.6%	6.9%
% weights	10%	15%	5%	25%	20%	10%	15%

a. Assuming the manager has no market views and the client has *average risk tolerance*, **determine** the optimal portfolio asset class allocations.

(2 minutes)

b. Now, assume the manager expects asset class 1 and 3 to have equal returns of 8%, while class 5 outperforms class 2 by 1%. **Describe** the most likely affect of the manager's views on the weightings of the classes where the manager has a view and the next steps the manager would take if using the Black-Litterman model for asset allocation.

(9 minutes)

Answer:

a. If the manager has no particular expectations or is otherwise uncomfortable adjusting asset class expected returns and the risk tolerance of the client is average, the market portfolio would be held. She would weight the asset classes in the portfolio the same as their global weights shown in Table A.

b. The market-implied returns of 1 and 3 are 9.5% and 5.1%, respectively. The view adjusted return is 8% for both. Running a new MVO with a lower 8% return for #1 would likely lower its weight. A higher 8% return for #3 would produce a higher weight.

The market-implied returns for 5 and 2 are 6.2% and 4.5%, respectively, a difference of 1.7%. The view adjusted is only a 1% difference so the relative return of #5 will shift down for a lower weight and #2's relative return shifts up for a higher weight.

The next steps would be to quantify the return levels for #5 and #2 consistent with a 1% difference and indicate confidence in the views. Then run a new MVO using the manager-adjusted returns to establish the new optimal portfolio weights.

Monte Carlo Simulation (MCS)

MCS is a statistical modeling tool often used to complement MVO or other asset allocation tools. For example a manager could begin by selecting several optimal portfolios using MVO that have acceptable risk and return for the client and then use MCS to generate multiple simulated paths displaying how these portfolios would perform over time. The MCS can consider path dependency effects on the portfolio, such as a constant nominal or real amount of funds withdrawn periodically or taxes paid on the returns. The MCS paths could be ranked in order of value to facilitate answering such questions as: Will the portfolio be exhausted? When? How bad or good could it be?

Professor's Note: This is another nice discussion of MCS to complement the earlier discussions. Remember that in SAA, MCS does not replace MVO and the other techniques. MCS further analyzes the SAA output of the other models for path dependency issues and statistical analysis.

Surplus Asset Liability Management

The allocation methodologies discussed thus far attempt to identify the strategic allocation that achieves the best long-run results (i.e., the best asset-only allocation). Asset liability management (ALM), on the other hand, considers the allocation of assets with respect to a given liability or set of liabilities. The ALM approach searches for the set of allocations, which maximize the *difference* (the *surplus*) between assets and liabilities at each level of risk (much like the efficient frontier represents the maximum return at each level of risk).

Figure 2 shows an example of an ALM efficient frontier[4] for a generic defined benefit pension plan.

Figure 2: The Asset Liability Management (ALM) Efficient Frontier

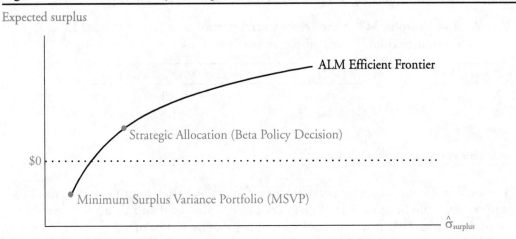

The vertical axis in Figure 2 is the value of the expected surplus (assets minus liabilities), and the horizontal axis represents the associated risk, measured by standard deviation of surplus. As with any *efficient* frontier, there is a minimum-variance portfolio, which in this case is the minimum variability of surplus. With the lowest risk it will also generate the minimum expected surplus. As you move to the right on the frontier, both the expected surplus and the risk increase. There is no assurance the MSVP will have a positive surplus. In this case the MSVP has a negative surplus.

The choice of any portfolio on the frontier is a client and manager decision; they accept more and more risk as they move out on the frontier. In Figure 2, management has selected the allocation labeled Strategic Allocation. Because it is a risker decision than selecting the MSVP it could be called a beta policy decision. Because the MSVP is negative, the client and manager could choose to be somewhat more aggressive and move up and out the frontier (a beta decision) or the client could increase funding to increase the assets and the surplus.

The ALM efficient frontier could also be presented in terms of the funding ratio (i.e., the value of plan assets divided by the value of plan liabilities). In that case, the ratio is presented along the vertical axis, as either a percentage or a ratio, and risk is plotted along the horizontal axis. Other than the way the vertical axis is labeled, the analysis is the same.

As with other optimization procedures, ALM requires estimations of all associated mean-variance parameters and thus suffers from the same estimation biases. Of course this now also includes estimating the liabilities as well. To help avoid these inherent limitations of MVO, the manager can utilize a resampling technique or the Black-Litterman approach for ALM. Monte Carlo simulation could then be added as a compliment to examine path dependency and gain statistical probability insight to the behavior of the surplus over time.

---

4.   The ALM efficient frontier is sometimes referred to as the *surplus* efficient frontier.

Example: Surplus ALM with simulation as a complement

A pension plan or any other portfolio with definable and quantifiable liabilities (future payouts) can benefit from ALM and further benefit from MCS analysis.

Step 1: Run a surplus MVO and select several portfolios from the surplus EF that provide acceptable risk and return combinations.

Proposed SAA	E(R) of Surplus	Standard Deviation of Surplus
A	1.0%	0.0%
B	1.5%	3.1%
C	2.0%	6.4%
Current Portfolio	1.6%	5.3%

It should be clear the current portfolio is inefficient. A better combination of risk and return could be achieved with a linear combination of B and C. 80% invested in portfolio B plus 20% in C will have a weighted average return of 1.6% and a lower weighted average standard deviation. The current portfolio will plot on the interior of the efficient frontier.

Step 2: Use Monte Carlo simulation to examine the future performance of the assets, liabilities, and resulting surplus of the selected portfolios over time. Each curved line on the graph represents the max value of the surplus at some probability as time passes. For example, the 90% line indicates that 90% of the time the surplus will be at or below the line and 10% of the time the surplus could be higher.

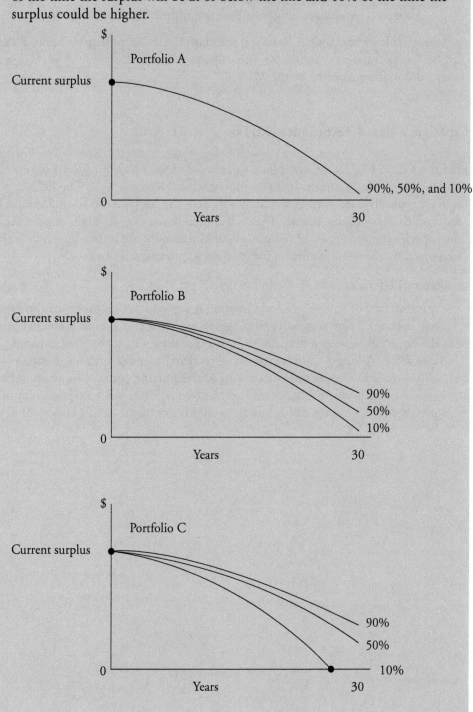

Step 3: Examine the output and determine the next steps. The manager determines the current portfolio is unacceptable and rejects C as too risky for the client because at the 10% probability it would be exhausted prior to the 30-year horizon and require additional funding by the client. The manager decides A, which is the MSVP and has a zero standard deviation of surplus, is too conservative and recommends B as the appropriate portfolio.

It is reasonable to conclude A has a 0.0 standard deviation of surplus because the surplus has no variability at 90, 50, and 10% probability. Because 0.0 is the lowest standard deviation, A must be the MSVP.

Experience-Based Techniques (EBTs)

For the Exam: EBT is just the process of elimination, which is covered in more detail in the earlier study sessions. It is commonly tested. Know it well. The EBT approach is more typically used with individuals who lack the background to understand the more mathematical approaches. This is less of an issue than it might appear because the experience-based rules of the process of elimination are in fact generally well supported by the more mathematically based approaches.

Common EBT rules include the following:

- A 60/40 mix of equity and fixed income is a good starting point for the average risk investor. More aggressive (less aggressive) investors should increase (decrease) the equity allocation and make the corresponding adjust the fixed income allocation. A longer time horizon is generally consistent with more equity.
- 100 – investor's age is sometimes used as the starting equity allocation. (Hint: I would not put much reliance on this last one as it has not been used very much in past answers. The concept is fine but other factors have to be considered as well.)

Summary of the Six Approaches

Figure 3: Strengths and Limitations of Asset Allocation Approaches

Asset Allocation Approach	Strengths	Limitations
Mean-variance optimization (MVO)	• Optimization programs used to generate the efficient frontier are inexpensive and readily available. • Identifies portfolios with the highest expected return at each level of risk and the associated asset allocation. • It is typically sign constrained to prevent negative weights (short selling). • Cash equivalents are modeled as a risky asset class if included. • Widely understood and accepted. • Easily adapted to model risk as downside risk or tracking error, return as excess return over some minimum threshold return, constrain the deviations of asset weights versus some relevant benchmark, model the correlation to change over time and converge during periods of stress (high volatility). • The modeling of the EF can be simplified with the use of corner portfolios. • Commercially available software.	• The number and nature of estimates required (e.g., expected returns, variances, covariances) can be overwhelming as the number of asset classes increases • Expected returns are subject to estimation bias. • Static (1-period) approach. • Can yield under-diversified (concentrated) portfolios unless constrained. • MVO output can be very sensitive to the inputs, making the resulting output unstable.
Resampled efficient frontier	• EF is more stable than traditional MV. • Small changes in inputs produce only minor changes in SAA. • Portfolios tend to be better diversified than traditional MVO. • Commercially available software.	• No theoretical basis for the approach. • Inputs often based on historical data.
Black-Litterman	• Theoretically justified way to address the sensitivity of inputs problem and incorporate manager views. • Typically generates more stable SAA and better diversification. • Can be constrained or unconstrained though constrained is the more useful and rigorous approach. • BL (constrained) quantifies and begins with market consensus expected returns and allows the manager to systematically diverge from this starting point. • Commercially available software.	• Often the inputs are based on historical data. • Complicated.

Figure 3: Strengths and Limitations of Asset Allocation Approaches (Cont.)

Asset Allocation Approach	Strengths	Limitations
Monte Carlo simulation	• Statistical analysis tool to further analyze the SAA output of the other approaches. • Models path dependency issues. • Generates statistical probabilities of meeting or not meeting return objectives. • Can also model liabilities and surplus. • Used to complement the other approaches. • Commercially available software.	• Can be complex to implement. • Can generate false confidence; the output is only as accurate as the inputs.
ALM	• Considers the allocation of assets with respect to liabilities. • Can generate a surplus frontier that shows the combinations of risk and return. • Otherwise similar to MVO. • Commercially available software.	• Same issues as MVO.
Experience based	• Incorporates decades of asset allocation experience. • Easy to understand and consistent with the more complex approaches. • Inexpensive to implement. • Useful on the exam.	• Allocation rules may be too simple for some investors. • Experience-based rules can be contradictory in some applied settings.

CONSTRAINTS AGAINST SHORT SALES

LOS 19.q: <u>Discuss</u> the structure of the minimum-variance frontier with a constraint against short sales.

CFA® Program Curriculum, Volume 3, page 216

When short selling is constrained (prohibited) all asset class weights will be positive or zero and must of course sum to 1.00. In the constrained situation the earlier 2-portfolio theorem leads to the much more useful corner portfolio theorem. This allows the EF to be closely approximated by linear combinations of a small number of corner portfolios. The global minimum-variance portfolio is by definition a corner portfolio and is the left-most point of the EF. All other "corners" are set when the weight of an asset class changes from zero to positive or from positive to zero for a portfolio on the EF. In addition whichever corner has the highest Sharpe ratio can be modeled as being the market portfolio.

Professor's Note: MVO modeling is still needed to initially identify the corner portfolios, those portfolios where the weights of some assets in the portfolio go from positive to zero or the weights of others go from zero to positive as you "pass" a corner portfolio.

However once the corners are identified, simple linear math (no correlation needed) can interpolate the points in between.

This kind of math is easily tested on the exam.

Figure 4 shows an example of an efficient frontier with six corner portfolios and one additional portfolio. Portfolio A is the global minimum-variance (GMV) portfolio, which is always included as one of the corner portfolios. To approximate any portfolio on the efficient frontier, we only need the two *adjacent* corner portfolios. For example, Portfolio L is a weighted average of Portfolios B and C.

Figure 4: Efficient Frontier with Corner Portfolios

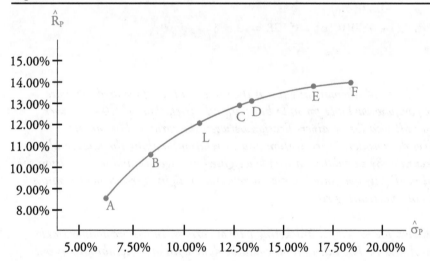

Corner Portfolios and Interpolating Points Between

Mathematically, calculating the standard deviation of an efficient portfolio, given the adjacent corner portfolios' standard deviations, is identical to the calculations we use when we calculate the weights of a portfolio necessary to achieve an expected return.

Example: Standard deviation using corner portfolios

An analyst has selected the two adjacent corner portfolios A and B. Their expected returns are 10% and 15% respectively, while their standard deviations are 12% and 16%. Calculate the weights of A and B to construct a portfolio with an 11% expected return. Calculate this new portfolio's standard deviation.

Answer:

First calculate the required weight of Portfolio A is 0.80 and the weight of Portfolio B is 0.20. Without knowing the correlation of A and B, the standard deviation of the weighted portfolio is closely approximated by a weighted average of A's and B's standard deviations:

$$\hat{R}_P = w_A\hat{R}_A + w_B\hat{R}_B \Rightarrow \text{letting } w_B = (1 - w_A)$$
$$0.11 = w_A(0.10) + (1 - w_A)(0.15)$$
$$w_A = 0.80, \text{ so } w_B = 0.20$$
$$\sigma_P = 0.80(\sigma_A) + 0.20(\sigma_B)$$
$$\sigma_P = 0.80(0.12) + 0.20(0.16) = 0.128 = 12.8\%$$

Professor's Note: Mathematically this is the same result as if we used the more complex portfolio variance formula but with all correlations of 1.0—in other words, we allowed for no diversification between the corners. The corners themselves do consider diversification and correlation, making the final results quite accurate. By calculating a simple weighted average of standard deviation the risk will be slightly overstated, not by much, and a slight overstatement is much better than understating risk.

Hint: Always use the closest bracketing pair of corners. In the previous example that was A and B. The calculations could be done with other combinations but the estimations of standard deviation will be higher, less accurate, and therefore wrong.

LOS 19.i: <u>Select</u> and <u>justify</u> an appropriate set of asset classes for an investor.

CFA® Program Curriculum, Volume 3, page 197

LOS 19.r: <u>Formulate</u> and <u>justify</u> a strategic asset allocation, given an investment policy statement and capital market expectations.

CFA® Program Curriculum, Volume 3, page 223

Professor's Note: The following example looks intimidating. Take the time to go through it a step at a time. Taking it one step at a time it is not so bad.

Example: Strategic asset allocation

Jim Sheehan is the portfolio manager for the $200 million Brent Industries defined benefit pension fund. Jim is planning on making a presentation to the trustees of the pension plan. His firm has come up with the long-term capital market expectations as shown in the following figure.

Capital Market Expectation

Asset Class	Expected Return	Expected Std. Dev.	Correlations				
			1	2	3	4	5
U.S. equity	12.00%	16.00%	1.00				
U.S. bonds	8.25%	6.50%	0.32	1.00			
Int'l equities	14.00%	18.00%	0.46	0.22	1.00		
Int'l bonds	9.25%	12.25%	0.23	0.56	0.32	1.00	
Alternative inv.	11.50%	21.00%	0.25	0.11	0.08	0.06	1.00

Using the capital market expectations, Jim identifies an efficient frontier with the six corner portfolios (see the following graphic) with the characteristics shown in the following table.

Corner Portfolio	Expected Return	Expected Std. Dev.	Sharpe Ratio	Asset Class Weights				
				U.S. Equity	U.S. Bonds	Int'l Equities	Int'l Bonds	Alt. Inv
1	14.00%	18.00%	0.639	0.00%	0.00%	100.00%	0.00%	0.00%
2	13.66%	16.03%	0.696	0.00%	0.00%	85.36%	0.00%	14.64%
3	13.02%	13.58%	0.775	21.69%	0.00%	56.56%	0.00%	21.75%
4	12.79%	13.00%	0.792	21.48%	0.00%	52.01%	5.24%	21.27%
5	10.54%	8.14%	0.988	9.40%	51.30%	26.55%	0.00%	12.76%
6	8.70%	6.32%	0.981	0.00%	89.65%	4.67%	0.00%	5.68%

Efficient Frontier for Brent Industries Pension Fund

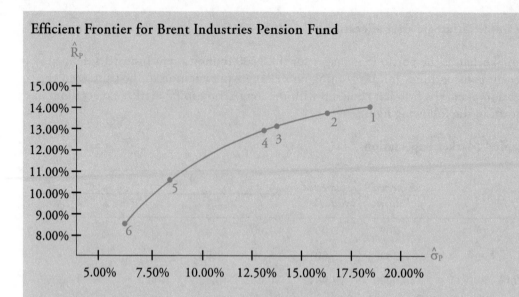

The following additional information is available about the pension fund:

- The trustees have established a spending rate of 8.50%. Inflation is expected to be 2% per year, and the cost of managing the fund is expected to be 0.40%. The trustees would like to preserve the purchasing power of the fund and are concerned with multi-period compounding issues.
- The majority of plan participants are young, so additional liquidity needs are minimal.
- The trustees would like to limit risk (as defined by standard deviation) to no more than 10% per year.

A.   **Calculate** the fund's required rate of return and **determine** the appropriate strategic asset allocation.

(10 minutes)

B.   **Calculate** the Sharpe ratio of the market and the risk-free rate.

(4 minutes)

C.   **Discuss** whether a risk-free asset should have been included as an asset.

(4 minutes)

Answer:

A.   The required return is 11.11% [= (1.085)(1.02)(1.004) − 1], which lies between Corner Portfolios 4 and 5 with their expected returns of 12.79% and 10.54%. We solve for w in the following equation:

$$0.1111 = w_4(0.1279) + (1 - w_4)(0.1054)$$

$$w_4 = 0.25 \Rightarrow w_5 = 0.75$$

In other words, the efficient portfolio with an expected return of 11.11% has 25% weight of Corner Portfolio 4 and 75% weight of Corner Portfolio 5. With respect to asset classes, the weights are then derived as follows:

U.S. equity $= (0.25)(0.2148) + (0.75)(0.0940) = 0.1242 = 12.42\%$

U.S. bonds $= (0.25)(0.0000) + (0.75)(0.5130) = 0.3848 = 38.48\%$

Int'l equity $= (0.25)(0.5201) + (0.75)(0.2655) = 0.3292 = 32.92\%$

Int'l bonds $= (0.25)(0.0524) + (0.75)(0.0000) = 0.0131 = 1.31\%$

Alt. invest. $= (0.25)(0.2127) + (0.75)(0.1276) = 0.1489 = 14.89\%$

Additional comments, not for the answer on exam day:

- Adding the return components is incorrect given the trustee's statements.
- In the above computation for U.S. equity, 0.25 (the weight of Corner Portfolio 4) is multiplied by 21.48% (the proportion of U.S. equity in Corner Portfolio 4). Similarly, 0.75 (the weight of Corner Portfolio 5) is multiplied by 9.40% (the proportion of U.S. equity in Corner Portfolio 5). We then add these together to arrive at 12.42% as the weight of U.S. equity in the efficient portfolio with an expected return of 11.11%. We repeat the same process for each asset class.

1. Sum of weights should be 100%:

    $$0.1242 + 0.3848 + 0.3292 + 0.0131 + 0.1489 = 1.00 = 100\%$$

2. Also, check that the sum of the weights of each asset class multiplied by their expected returns adds up to 11.11%:

    $$\hat{R}_P = (0.1242)(0.12) + (0.3848)(0.0825) + (0.3292)(0.14)$$
    $$+ (0.0131)(0.0925) + (0.1489)(0.1150)$$
    $$= 0.1111 = 11.11\%$$

Also note that the standard deviation of this portfolio is (approximately) the weighted average of the standard deviations of Corner Portfolios 4 and 5, which satisfies the risk requirement of the fund:

$$\sigma_P = (0.25)(0.13) + (0.75)(0.0814) = 0.09355 = 9.36\%$$

B.   The corner portfolio with the highest Sharpe ratio will approximate the market portfolio. That is Corner Portfolio 5 in the table. Therefore the Sharpe of the market is 0.988. No other data is provided for calculating the market Sharpe directly.

This can be used to derive the risk-free rate as we know Corner Portfolio 5 (the market) has a Sharpe of 0.988, expected return of 10.54% and standard deviation of 8.14%. Therefore:

Sharpe of market = MRP / standard deviation of market = MRP / 8.14 = 0.988

MRP = 8.04%

MRP = return of market – risk-free return = 8.04 = 10.54 – risk-free return

risk-free return = 2.50%

C.   Over the multi periods of a pension plan there is no effective risk-free asset with known return over all periods. It would be possible to model cash equivalents as a risky asset class with an estimate return and standard deviation but it is not essential. A wide range of global equity and fixed income and alternatives is already being considered.

Special Considerations

The IPS may specify near-term liquidity needs. For example, an individual investor may consider providing for retirement her primary investment goal. However, she may have a secondary goal of taking a vacation in six months and wants to have a specific dollar amount available toward that planned expense. In such a situation, the present value of the projected cash flow should be invested in cash equivalents. The remainder of the portfolio is allocated according to the weights previously established.

Example: Planned cash outflow

Suppose a question stated $20,000,000 is required as a liquidity reserve to fund retiree pension buyouts planned in the next year. **Determine** the appropriate strategic asset allocation for the fund.

Answer:

Determine the appropriate SAA using any of the tools available. Then set aside the necessary cash equivalents of $20,000,000 before applying the SAA to the remaining funds.

For the Exam: This is a frequent situation on the exam. Now suppose the question states the expenditure will be in one year and the one-year interest rate is 5%. Set aside the PV at 5% of $20,000,000.

The Capital Allocation Line

The capital allocation line (CAL) is the straight line drawn from the risk-free rate to the **tangency portfolio** on the efficient frontier, where *the tangency portfolio is the corner portfolio with the highest Sharpe ratio*. If the investor's required rate of return is lower than the expected return on the tangency portfolio, the investor will invest a portion of the funds in a risk-free asset and the remainder in the tangency portfolio. If, on the other hand, the investor's required rate of return is higher than the tangency portfolio's expected rate of return, the investor will use margin (borrow at the risk-free rate) to leverage the return. If the IPS specifically prohibits borrowing, then we select different corner portfolios above the tangency portfolio. The new corner portfolios will be the ones that bracket the investor's required rate of return.

Example: Determining the tangency portfolio

Continuing the previous example (the figure from the previous example is reproduced for your convenience).

Corner Portfolio	Expected Return	Expected Std. Dev.	Sharpe Ratio	Asset Class Weights				
				U.S. Equity	U.S. Bonds	Int'l Equities	Int'l Bonds	Alt. Inv
1	14.00%	18.00%	0.639	0.00%	0.00%	100%	0.00%	0.00%
2	13.66%	16.03%	0.696	0.00%	0.00%	85.36%	0.00%	14.64%
3	13.02%	13.58%	0.775	21.69%	0.00%	56.56%	0.00%	21.75%
4	12.79%	13.00%	0.792	21.48%	0.00%	52.01%	5.24%	21.27%
5	10.54%	8.14%	0.988	9.40%	51.30%	26.55%	0.00%	12.76%
6	8.70%	6.32%	0.981	0.00%	89.65%	4.67%	0.00%	5.68%

1. **Determine** which portfolio is the most suitable candidate for the tangency portfolio.

2. Assuming no constraint against leverage and a risk-free rate of 2.5%, **determine** the asset allocation for the pension fund if management chooses an available corner portfolio.

3. Assume you are not allowed to leverage. **Determine** the asset allocation if management chooses an available corner portfolio.

Answers:

1. Corner Portfolio 5 with an expected return of 10.54%, has the highest Sharpe ratio (0.988) and would be the most suitable candidate for the tangency portfolio. Because it has the highest Sharpe ratio, Portfolio 5 is the tangency portfolio for the capital allocation line. If allowed to borrow and lend at the risk-free rate, the investor will combine Portfolio 5 with the risk-free asset to attain the desired expected return.

2. The fund's required rate of return is 11.11%, the risk-free rate is 2.50%, and the expected return of the tangency portfolio is 10.54%. Let w_{RF} denote the weight of the risk-free asset and $(1 - w_{RF})$ denote the weight of the tangency portfolio:

$$0.1111 = (w_{RF})0.0250 + (1 - w_{RF})0.1054$$
$$0.1111 = 0.0250w_{RF} + 0.1054 - 0.1054w_{RF}$$
$$0.0804w_{RF} = -0.0057$$
$$w_{RF} = -0.07; (1 - w_{RF}) = 1.07$$

Therefore, we borrow 7% and invest 107% in the tangency portfolio.

3. In the situation where using margin is not allowed (i.e., cannot borrow at the risk-free rate), the investor will combine the two corner portfolios adjacent to the required return. We will assume the investor has a required return of 11.11% and no borrowing is allowed. In this situation, Corner Portfolios 4 and 5 (expected returns of 12.79% and 10.54%, respectively) will be combined.

Let w_4 be the weight of Corner Portfolio 4 in the combination of 4 and 5:

$$11.11 = w_4(12.79) + (1 - w_4)(10.54)$$
$$11.11 = 12.79w_4 + 10.54 - 10.54w_4$$
$$0.57 = 2.25w_4$$
$$w_4 \approx 0.25$$
$$w_5 \approx 0.75$$

Investing 25% of our funds in Corner Portfolio 4 and 75% in Corner Portfolio 5, the asset class weights in the final portfolio are:

Asset class weight	$= (w_4)$(wt in 4)	$+ (w_5)$(wt in 5)	
U.S. equity	$= (0.25)(21.48)$	$+ (0.75)(9.40)$	$= 12.42\%$
U.S. bonds	$= (0.25)(0.00)$	$+ (0.75)(51.30)$	$= 38.48\%$
International equity	$= (0.25)(52.01)$	$+ (0.75)(26.55)$	$= 32.91\%$
International bonds	$= (0.25)(5.24)$	$+ (0.75)(0.00)$	$= 1.31\%$
Alternative investments	$= (0.25)(21.27)$	$+ (0.75)(12.76)$	$= 14.89\%$

STRATEGIC ASSET ALLOCATION ISSUES

LOS 19.s: <u>Compare</u> the considerations that affect asset allocation for individual investors versus institutional investors and <u>critique</u> a proposed asset allocation in light of those considerations.

CFA® Program Curriculum, Volume 3, page 225

For the Exam: The CFA® text devotes 33 pages to this last section. Treat it as a cursory review of important topics: IPS, SAA, and human capital covered earlier and in more detail. The CFA® text does discuss TAA, but that was defined earlier in this assignment and will be covered in more detail in a later study session.

We are intentionally keeping this section brief in order to utilize candidate time effectively. I recommend reading the next few pages, verify it is familiar, and review the earlier write-ups as needed. Do review the section on TAA, as it is a nice preview of material that will come in later study sessions.

Individuals. Individuals' goals include meeting living expenses, funding children's educational expenses, funding retirement, setting up trusts, et cetera. In other words, the individual typically looks primarily at wealth accumulation to meet required as well as *desired* expenditures. This does not preclude applying the concepts of ALM if the goals can be numerically quantified and treated as quasi-liabilities.

Another primary difference between an individual investor and an institutional investor is the patterns of income generation and wealth accumulation. Unlike the institutional investor, the typical individual's wealth is accumulated over many years, while the ability to generate income reaches a peak and falls to zero at retirement. The individual's *human capital* (the total present value of future employment income), therefore, is greatest at an early age, while his financial capital (accumulated wealth) increases over time and reaches a maximum at retirement.

The individual's human capital can be a major component of her total assets and must be considered in determining an appropriate strategic asset allocation. Think of the individual's human capital as an allocation to bonds (i.e., return comes in the form of income and isn't as risky as equities). As the young professional starts out, her earnings potential (human capital) is considerable and more than likely comprises the vast majority of her total portfolio (human capital plus financial capital).

At younger ages, then, she has a considerable allocation to *bonds* (her human capital) and the allocation of her financial assets should be toward riskier, higher-return assets like equities. As she ages and accumulates financial capital, her human capital becomes a smaller and smaller component of her total portfolio, and the financial assets require more protection (i.e., an allocation to safer assets).

Another factor that separates individuals from institutions is **longevity risk**. This is the possibility of living longer than planned. For example, the individual might do a very good job of planning for a 25-year retirement at the age of 60 and then live to be older than 100. In this situation, the accumulated wealth is probably not going to be sufficient to fund the extra years. The inverse (sort of) of longevity risk is **mortality risk**; the risk of dying younger than expected. Mortality risk is usually mitigated by purchasing life insurance. Note that the individual bears at least part of the longevity risk, but the individual's spouse and other heirs bear the mortality risk.

Figure 5 presents hypothetical asset allocations for an individual according to age. The client has a changing mix of human capital (HC) and financial capital (FC) as she ages. Her goal is to maintain a SAA of total wealth (TW) at 50/50 between equity and bonds. The table shows how the allocation of equity/bond within FC will change over time to maintain TW at her goal of 50/50. It shows she retires at age 60.

Figure 5: Mix of Human and Financial Capital and Financial Asset Allocation by Age

Age	Proportions of TW	Characteristic of HC	Allocation of FC for Desired 50/50 Allocation of TW	Allocation of TW Achieved
30	10% FC & 90% HC	100% bond like	100% equity	10% equity & 90% bond
50	60% FC & 40% HC	100% bond like	83.33% equity & 16.67% bond	50% equity & 50% bond
60	100% FC	n.a.	50% equity & 50% bond	50% equity & 50% bond

The table shows that her goal of 50/50 for SAA in the early years is not possible. Her 90% of TW in HC that is bond-like only allows her to achieve a 10% allocation of TW to equity even with 100% of FC in equity. As her HC proportion declines, it is possible to allocate the FC to achieve her SAA of 50/50. The table illustrates that there are limits to achieving her SAA goal when HC is taken into account. There is no particular reason her HC had to be viewed as 100% bond-like or that her SAA goal had to be 50/50 or could not change over time. These are simply assumptions that can be changed.

Institutional investors. Institutional investor may be concerned with meeting liabilities, increasing wealth, or both. An insurance company must fund liabilities and grow surplus. Banks must meet reserve requirements, make loans, and manage the investment portfolio to correct the imbalance between loans and deposits with respect to duration, credit quality, and liquidity; while seeking a return. Entities with definable, measurable liabilities should evaluate portfolios from an ALM perspective.

Defined benefit pension plans. Defined benefit pension plans are concerned foremost with meeting pension obligations, so an ALM process is generally employed. The pension fund manager estimates the minimum acceptable (inflation-adjusted) return and then searches for the appropriate strategic allocation. Any future changes to the strategic allocation for the pension fund are based on several factors.

- The proposed allocation must meet the plan's risk and return objectives. Potential allocations are often compared on a risk-adjusted basis using the Sharpe ratio.
- The volatility of the plan surplus must be maintained within established bounds.
- The allocation must meet liquidity requirements.

Models, such as Monte Carlo simulation, can be employed to determine the long-term effects of the proposed allocation.

Endowments. The primary goal of an endowment is meeting spending requirements while protecting the fund principal. Note that the relevant rate of inflation for an endowment is the rate that affects its institutional beneficiary. For example, a university's costs typically rise at a higher rate than the overall economy, so its endowment fund must incorporate this higher rate into return calculations. Risk is a very important concern for an endowment because its funding is usually critical to the beneficiary.

Because bonds, especially Treasuries, are incapable of meeting their long-term return requirements, endowments usually allocate to a mix of debt for income and stability and equity for long-term returns and growth.

Professor's Note: When you think about a successful university endowment, you realize that the endowment must (1) meet a portion of the university's current spending needs, (2) keep up with inflation to protect the fund's principal, and (3) meet increased future needs caused by enrollment increases.

Foundations. Although not usually tied to a single beneficiary, foundations are formed to provide grants to individuals, communities, and/or organizations. Depending upon their legal status, foundations are required to make minimum annual payouts based on a percentage of fund assets. The primary goal is to cover the spending requirement while protecting the fund's principal. From a strategic asset allocation standpoint, foundations and endowments are very similar. On the exam, be sure to select an allocation that meets the spending requirements, covers expected inflation, and provides for sufficient growth to fund anticipated growth.

Insurance companies. A characteristic that distinguishes insurance companies from most other institutional investors is the need to *segment* their portfolio. The portfolio is segmented along product lines, as each line has risk and return objectives related to its specific constraints.

Portfolio constraints can differ significantly across segments. For example, if the segment funds fixed-annuity products, the fund should be allocated in fixed-income securities. A segment that funds variable annuities and variable life products indexed to equity markets should be allocated to equities. Of course, as we discussed in Study Session 5, the surplus portfolio is usually invested heavily in equities to provide necessary growth.

While segmenting the portfolio by line of business is useful and became popular some years ago for insurance companies, it can be overdone. Companies that created too many segments created control issues and sub-optimal results. Companies have moved toward limiting the number of segments of the total portfolio. Each segment is then viewed in isolation versus its liabilities, but the total aggregate portfolio is also analyzed to determine the final optimal allocation of assets.

For the Exam: On the exam, the specifics of the individual segments would have to be provided and you would select a suitable allocation for each based on its return and risk objectives and its constraints. Tax laws vary considerably from country to country, so any tax differences will have to be clearly noted for you on the exam. Also be prepared to discuss, if asked, why companies have moved to limit the segmentation. As is common at Level III, the basic core issues are generally well-tested. Occasionally, some of the sub-details will be tested.

Banks. The strategic allocation for banks is determined by their product mix and the goals of the securities portfolio. As we discussed in Study Session 5, the primary goals for a bank's securities portfolio are:

- Provide liquidity.
- Manage credit risk.
- Manage duration (gap management).
- Generate income.

Of the listed goals, managing duration (interest rate risk) is the most important, although managing credit risk and providing a source of liquidity are also very important. The strategic allocation is determined through an ALM process. You saw in Study Session 5 that bank portfolios are allocated primarily to fixed-income securities, and the equity (surplus) duration (asset duration minus liability duration) is managed by altering the duration of the securities portfolio.

TACTICAL ALLOCATION

LOS 19.t: Formulate and justify tactical asset allocation (TAA) adjustments to strategic asset class weights, given a TAA strategy and expectational data.

CFA® Program Curriculum, Volume 3, page 279

Tactical asset allocation (TAA) involves short-term deviations from the strategic asset allocation in an attempt to capitalize on capital market disequilibria (mispricing). The goal is to add value relative to an already established SAA or benchmark. A primary challenge is whether the expected benefits will outweigh the upfront costs to implement the TAA deviation away from SAA. The TAA could be undertaken at infrequent intervals or as part of a regular tactical allocation program that monitors market conditions, sectors, or asset classes, and reacts accordingly. TAA can be performed by internal personnel or by outside firms that specialize in TAA.

A disciplined approach to TAA could consist of:

- Periodically review market prices and expected returns for asset classes. For fixed income, the YTM is often taken as an initial proxy for expected return. If the manager believes the market return is attractive (unattractive), fixed income can be overweighted (or underweighted). Estimating market expectations for equity tends to be more difficult but the manager might take observed stock index prices and back-solve for the implied return using a dividend discount model or other valuation model. The managers can then react to the implied return and under- or overweight the asset class.

©2013 Kaplan, Inc.

- These expected returns could be adjusted for the manager's perception of risk. For example, if the manager believes current conditions are more risky than normal, the manager could assess expected returns as needing to be higher than normal just to maintain a neutral weight.
- Many TAA approaches (but not all) are based on an assumption that returns are mean reverting to some long-term level.

Adding value through TAA is challenging and should be used as an increment to SAA, not a replacement for SAA. The decision to pursue TAA must consider both expected value added but also cost.

Example: Adjusting Global Allocation

Foundations Ltd., manages the portfolio of a large endowment fund with a strategic allocation of 70% to equities. The 70% is split with 40% in UK equities and the remaining 30% in international equity. The firm's economics staff has made the following return projections.

Asset Class	Long-term E(R)	Short-term E(R)
UK Equity	8%	4%
International Equity	9%	7%

1. **Calculate** the long- and short-term expected return for equity.

(4 minutes)

2. The manager is not willing to change the SAA to equity of 70%. Is there a TAA opportunity? If so, what is it?

(2 minutes)

3. The same portfolio normally holds a laddered portfolio of bonds as a 20% allocation to fixed income. A tactical band is established by policy of 5% around this (a maximum of 25% and a minimum of 15%). The current allocation is 20%. The portfolio manager expects the central bank to loosen monetary policy, resulting in a small reduction in real interest rates and a large increase in inflation expectations. The manager proposes to tactically move 10% of the portfolio from bonds to alternative investments. Is the action appropriate? What other information should be considered? If the action is not appropriate, could it be made appropriate? How?

(6 minutes)

Answer:

1. LT: $(40/70)(8\%) + (30/70)(9\%) = 8.42\%$

   ST: $(40/70)(4\%) + (30/70)(7\%) = 5.29\%$

2. Yes, there is an opportunity. The short-term view of equities is less attractive with the larger shortfall for UK equity. The manager could tactically asset allocate funds from UK to international equity but keep the total equity at 70%.

3. The small fall in real rates and large increase in inflation expectations will raise interest rates and reduce bond prices and returns. Reducing bond exposure may make sense, but a reduction from 20% to 10% is too large and exceeds the tactical band.

   The manager needs to compare the projected bond returns to alternative investment returns and consider the costs of the trade before making a smaller shift. The often high transaction cost and low liquidity of alternative investments makes this an important consideration.

   After this is done, the action may be appropriate. Change in risk should also be evaluated.

Professor's Note: This is a broad and rather open-ended question that draws on multiple study sessions, some of which have not yet been covered. Such questions have appeared on the exam. When they do, give answers that are solidly based on the CFA® curriculum, answer all parts of the questions, and pay attention to the assigned point values to decide how much detail to include in the answers.

KEY CONCEPTS

LOS 19.a

Strategic asset allocation combines capital market expectations (formally represented by the efficient frontier) and the investor's risk, return, and investment constraints [from the investment policy statement (IPS)]. Strategic asset allocation is long-term in nature, and hence the weights are called *targets* and the portfolio represented by the strategic asset allocation is called the *policy portfolio*.

Each asset class has its own quantifiable systematic risk. Strategic asset allocation is a conscious effort to gain the desired exposure to systematic risk via specific weights to individual asset classes. Each asset class represents relatively similar investments (e.g., long-term corporate bonds) with similar systematic risk factors. Exposure to specific asset classes in specific proportions enables portfolio managers to effectively monitor and control their systematic risk exposure. In other words, strategic asset allocation reflects the investor's desired systematic risk exposure.

LOS 19.b

Tactical asset allocation is the result of active management wherein managers deviate from the strategic asset allocation to take advantage of any perceived *short-term* opportunities in the market. Hence, tactical asset allocation introduces additional risk, which should be justified by additional return (i.e., positive alpha).

LOS 19.c

Strategic allocation responds to the interaction of the investor's long-term strategic needs and long-run capital market expectations. The investor's goals are in terms of investment policy statement (IPS) objectives and constraints.

It should be remembered that the strategic allocation is based on long-run goals and capital market expectations. Tactical allocation may be used if the market experiences short-term disruptions or the manager recognizes mispriced assets, whereby they can change the allocation for short periods.

Because managers are the *experts* at selecting investments, the question is whether strategic allocation is worth the time and effort. The first response is that without a clearly defined strategic allocation, the portfolio may not reflect the investor's desires. Also, the importance of strategic asset allocation has been well-established empirically. One study showed that 94% of long-term performance is explained by strategic asset allocation.

LOS 19.d

ALM strategic asset allocation is determined in conjunction with modeling the liabilities of the investor. For investors with specific liabilities (e.g., defined benefit pension plans or insurance companies), asset allocation is tailored to meet liabilities and to maximize the surplus, given an acceptable level of risk. This usually results in a relatively high allocation to fixed-income assets. Strategic asset allocation involves specifically modeling liabilities and determining the asset allocation appropriate to fund them. Even for those investors who don't have specific (contractual) liabilities, future obligations (e.g., providing for post-retirement living expenses for an individual investor) can be modeled as liabilities, and an ALM approach to strategic asset allocation can be applied.

In asset-only strategic asset allocation, the focus is on earning the highest level of return for a given (acceptable) level of risk without any consideration for liability modeling. The liability (explicit or implied from future expected cash outflows) is indirectly taken into consideration through the required rate of return. Because the asset-only approach does not specifically model liabilities, the risk of not funding liabilities is not accurately controlled.

LOS 19.e

Dynamic asset allocation takes a multi-period view of the investment horizon. In other words, it recognizes that asset performance in one period affects the required rate of return and acceptable level of risk for subsequent periods. Dynamic asset allocation is difficult and costly to implement. However, investors who have significant liabilities, especially those with uncertain timing and/or amount, find the cost acceptable. Usually, investors who undertake the asset-liability approach to strategic asset allocation prefer dynamic asset allocation.

Static asset allocation ignores the link between optimal asset allocation across different time periods. For example, the manager using a static approach might estimate the necessary mean-variance inputs at a point in time and then construct the long-term portfolio accordingly. The manager using dynamic allocation allows for changing parameters over time using such techniques as Monte Carlo simulation. This allows the manager to build in expected changes to inputs as well as model unanticipated changes in macroeconomic factors.

LOS 19.f

Individuals display *loss aversion* rather than risk aversion and approach investing from a segmented perspective. Because of *mental accounting,* they meet goals one at a time. Their overall asset allocation is likely to be different from their optimal strategic allocation and inconsistent with their risk tolerance.

LOS 19.g

The portfolio's return objective is based on portfolio size, liquidity needs, time horizon, and maintenance of the principal. Unless stated otherwise, we always assume the investor will maintain the principal, so the portfolio must not only meet spending needs but expected inflation and management fees as well.

The risk objective should be specified in light of the investor's risk aversion. Investors can be classified using a numerical scheme, such as scoring investors from 1 to 10 based on their risk tolerance, with 1 indicating very high tolerance and 10 indicating very low tolerance.

The utility-adjusted (risk-adjusted) return the investor will realize from the portfolio can be found by using the following equation:

$$U_P = \hat{R}_P - 0.005(A)\left(\sigma_P^2\right)$$

where:

$\hat{R}_P$ = portfolio expected return
A = investor's risk aversion score
σ_P^2 = portfolio variance

In addition to standard deviation as a measure of risk (volatility), the acceptable level of risk can be stated in terms of *downside risk* measures such as shortfall risk, semivariance, and target semivariance.

LOS 19.h

Asset classes have been appropriately specified if:
- Assets in the class are similar from a descriptive as well as a statistical perspective.
- They are not highly correlated, so they provide the desired diversification.
- Individual assets cannot be classified into more than one class.
- They cover the majority of all possible investable assets.
- They contain a sufficiently large percentage of liquid assets.

LOS 19.i, 19.r

The capital allocation line (CAL) is the straight line drawn from the risk-free rate to a tangency portfolio on the efficient frontier, where the tangency portfolio is the corner portfolio with the highest Sharpe ratio. If the investor's required rate of return is lower than the expected return on the tangency portfolio, she will invest a portion of the funds in a risk-free asset and the remainder in the tangency portfolio.

If, on the other hand, the investor's required rate of return is higher than the tangency portfolio expected rate of return, she will use margin (borrow at the risk-free rate) to leverage the return. If the IPS specifically prohibits borrowing, then we select different corner portfolios above the tangency portfolio. The new corner portfolios will be the ones with the highest Sharpe ratios that bracket the investor's required rate of return.

For example, an endowment's return objective is 7% with a maximum standard deviation of 11%, and no risk-free asset is available.

Given the corner portfolio returns below, determine the standard deviation and asset weights for the portfolio that will meet their objective.

Corner Portfolio	E(R)	σ	Sharpe Ratio	Asset A Weight	Asset B Weight	Asset C Weight
1	9.0%	16.0%	0.438	100%	0%	0%
2	7.5%	11.5%	0.478	80%	20%	0%
3	5.5%	7.7%	0.455	0%	40%	60%
4	5.3%	7.6%	0.434	0%	0%	100%

7% lies between corner portfolios 2 and 3. Solving for the weights of corner portfolios 2 and 3: $7.0 = W_2(7.5) + (1 - W_2)(5.5)$, $7.0 = 7.5W_2 + 5.5 - 5.5W_2$, $7.0 - 5.5 = 2W_2$, $1.5 = 2W_2$, $1.5 / 2 = W_2$, $.75$ or $75\% = W_2$ and $.25$ or $25\% = W_3$.

The approximate standard deviation of the portfolio is a weighted average of the standard deviations of Corner Portfolios 2 and 3:

$$\sigma_p = 0.75(0.115) + 0.25(0.077) = 0.1055 = 10.55\% \text{ (less than the maximum of 11\%)}$$

To calculate how much the strategic portfolio invests in assets A, B, and C, use the 75/25 weights in corner portfolios 2 and 3:
- Portfolio 2 has weights 80/20/0 in assets A, B, and C.
- Portfolio 3 has weights 0/40/60 in assets A, B, and C.

Our portfolio has weights in A, B, and C of:
- Asset A: 0.75(80) + 0.25(0) = 60%
- Asset B: 0.75(20) + 0.25(40) = 25%
- Asset C: 0.75(0) + 0.25(60) = 15%

LOS 19.j

There are advantages and disadvantages to adding different asset classes to a portfolio:
- Inflation-protected securities provide protection against inflation and automatically increase or decrease portfolio cash flows with inflation and deflation. U.S. Treasury Inflation Protection Securities (TIPS) are highly liquid and virtually risk free.
- The theoretical justification for adding global securities is the potential to increase return at all levels of risk. The practical implications of including global securities relate to other concerns associated with global investing that are not experienced in a domestic-only setting.
- The primary benefit to including alternative investments in an asset allocation is the diversification benefit. However, the practical drawbacks include the typically large amount of capital required and the need to carefully select out-performers.
- In some cases, information on alternative investments can be sparse or even nonexistent.

LOS 19.k

A decision rule based on the new investment's Sharpe ratio, the current portfolio Sharpe ratio, and the correlation of the returns on the two is used. If the Sharpe ratio of the new investment is greater than the current portfolio Sharpe ratio multiplied by the correlation of the new investment's returns with the portfolio's returns, adding the investment to the portfolio will improve the portfolio Sharpe ratio:

If $S_i > S_p \times \rho_{i,p}$ adding the investment will improve the portfolio Sharpe ratio

where:
S_i = Sharpe ratio of proposed investment
S_p = current portfolio Sharpe ratio
$\rho_{i,p}$ = correlation of the returns on the proposed investment with the portfolio returns

Sharpe Ratio is the: (expected return of the asset less the risk free rate) divided by the standard deviation of the asset.

LOS 19.1

Currency risk: Investing in a foreign-denominated security exposes the investor to changes in value of foreign asset and changes in value of the foreign currency. This has implications for the return of the asset and for its volatility.

> Empirical evidence suggests that the standard deviation of currency is only about half the standard deviation of stock prices. It is the less important determinant of risk. (In the bond market, the currency volatility is generally higher than bond volatility, reflecting bonds are generally less volatile than stocks, making it a more important consideration for bond investors).

Political risk: Exists when a country has (1) irresponsible fiscal and/or monetary policy, and/or (2) lacks reasonable legal and regulatory rules to support but not stifle financial markets. It could arise if a government confiscates property without compensation, unduly restricts foreign investment or suspends capital and currency movement, manipulates the currency or taxes foreign investors unfairly, is unstable or defaults on its debt, and allows or requires companies to be managed for goals inconsistent with those of the shareholders.

Home country bias: Refers to the observation that investors tend to overweigh investments in their own country, creating a suboptimal portfolio allocation.

Costs in International Assets

- Transaction costs can be higher and liquidity can be lower.
- Withholding taxes on foreign investors may not be fully offset by tax treaties.
- Free-float can be an issue. The stated market capitalization may include shares held by the government or other investors who will not sell.
- Inefficient market infrastructure can result in high costs for security registration, settlement, custody, management, or information.

Opportunities in International Assets

1. Foreign markets could be undervalued and, thus, offer better expected return.

2. While the investor's home market may have had the best returns in the past, that is not a reliable indicator of future returns.

3. Even if correlations rise in the short run during crises, the long-run benefits of diversification can remain.

4. Correlations among bond markets tend to be lower than among equity markets. Adding international bonds to domestic-only portfolios can be particularly beneficial in reducing risk for risk averse investors.

LOS 19.m

A mean-variance based approach that assumes correlations and standard deviations are stable over time. The observation that correlations increase during financial crises is inconsistent with this assumption and indicates **conditional return correlations** (i.e., correlations that depend on market volatility and conditions). Diversification benefits fail when they are most needed.

Alternative methods exist to calculate correlation conditioned on the level of return. A portfolio could be optimized both assuming normal conditions and assuming crisis conditions.

A simpler method to determine what is happening to correlation is to plot rolling correlations between markets over time. The plot reveals:

- Correlations have been rising over time, and potential diversification benefits have decreased as markets integrate.
- Correlations did rise during crises periods and then fell back after the crises, within a generally rising upward trend.

LOS 19.n

As markets integrate and move through emerging market status to developed market status, the general progression is:

- Equity share prices rise as (1) capital can now flow into the formerly uninvestable market, and (2) to reflect declining stand-alone risk.
- Expected returns increase as capital flows into the market but then declines after the initial inflow to be consistent with the now higher stock prices and lower risk going forward.
- Long-run return volatility should decline as prices reflect information that is more freely available and political risk declines.

LOS 19.o

The asset allocation process is essentially the portfolio management process that has been identified throughout the CFA curriculum. The steps are as follows:
- Determine the investor's return requirement and risk tolerance, subject to the investor's current wealth and constraints.
- Formulate long-term capital market expectations and their potential effects on the various asset classes.
- Determine the asset allocation that best meets the objectives defined in the investment policy statement (IPS), subject to any other limitations specified by the investor.
- Monitor the portfolio regularly as specified in the IPS. A feedback loop should be included so changes in long-term market factors can be incorporated into the *model* and to determine whether adjustments to the strategic allocation are justified. If market changes are short-term, tactical allocation measures should be considered.

LOS 19.p

Mean-Variance Approach

The **mean-variance approach** to strategic asset allocation is a static approach. Efficient portfolios are essentially portfolios with varying allocations to the available asset classes.

Resampled Efficient Frontier

There can be many different combinations (by varying the weights) of a given set of assets that will yield the same expected return and standard deviation, so the computer is asked for many sets of mean-variance efficient portfolios (a resampled efficient frontier) using the same set of returns and standard deviations.

The average weights for each asset are used to represent the weights of the assets in the resampled efficient frontier.

Black-Litterman

The Black-Litterman measure uses asset returns implied by a value-weighted global market index. The analyst can then adjust the model-generated returns using personal return expectations (and confidence in those expectations).

Monte Carlo Simulation

Using different strategic allocations (including the investor's current allocation), the program incorporates the effects of various assumed capital market factors (inflation, yield spreads, recession, etc., and their expected changes) in the next period as well as their compounding effects *over several future periods*. This way the model overcomes the static (1-period) nature of the typical mean-variance analysis.

Asset-Liability Management

Asset-liability management considers the allocation of assets with respect to a given liability or set of liabilities. The ALM approach searches for the set of allocations, which maximize the *difference* (the *surplus*) between assets and liabilities at each level of risk.

Experience-Based Techniques

Experience-based techniques have come about through decades of experience.

LOS 19.q

Each efficient portfolio represents weights on each of the asset classes. The only constraint was that the sum of all the weights should be equal to one. If we add an additional constraint of no short sales, we restrict the value of the weights to be greater than or equal to zero.

Here we have an additional constraint that the weight of each asset class be *non-negative*. In the case of a *constrained optimization* (no short sales in this case), the minimum-variance frontier changes from a smooth curve to one with corner portfolios.

LOS 19.s

Institutional investors. The typical institutional investor is concerned more with meeting liabilities than with generating wealth.

Individuals. Individuals' goals include meeting living expenses, funding children's educational expenses, funding retirement, setting up trusts, etc. In other words, the individual typically looks primarily at wealth accumulation to meet required as well as *desired* expenditures.

Unlike the institutional investor, the typical individual's wealth is accumulated over many years, while the ability to generate income reaches a peak and falls to zero at retirement. The individual's *human capital*, therefore, is greatest at an early age, while his financial capital increases over time and reaches a maximum at retirement.

At younger ages, then, he has a considerable allocation to *bonds* (his human capital) and the allocation of his financial assets should be toward riskier, higher-return assets like equities. As he ages and accumulates financial capital, his human capital becomes a smaller and smaller component of his total portfolio, and the financial assets require more protection (i.e., an allocation to safer assets).

Two other factors that separate individuals from institutions are **longevity risk** and **mortality risk**.

LOS 19.t

Tactical asset allocation (TAA) involves short-term deviations from the strategic asset allocation in an attempt to capitalize on capital market disequilibria (mispricing). If used it should be a compliment to SAA and expected added value should be compared to cost of implementation.

CONCEPT CHECKERS

1. Jack Manning, CFA, and Tess Brown, CFA, have just joined a financial planning firm. They will work as a team assessing and managing the portfolios of individual clients. Manning will specialize in forming long-term capital market expectations. Brown will assess each client's risk and return objectives as well as constraints. Based upon this, we would define the focus of:
    A. both Manning and Brown as tactical asset allocation.
    B. both Manning and Brown as strategic asset allocation.
    C. Manning as strategic asset allocation and Brown as tactical asset allocation.

2. Deviation from strategic asset allocation due to short-term capital market expectations is called:
    A. active risk assessment.
    B. tactical asset allocation.
    C. policy reallocation.

3. North East Fellowship University's endowment fund has $20 million in assets. The fund has a targeted spending rate of 4.50%. The fund has been incurring 0.75% as management costs. The trustees would like to preserve the purchasing power of the fund and curtail the risk in terms of standard deviation to no more than 10%. Inflation expectation is 2% per year over the foreseeable future. The fund's required rate of return is *closest* to:
    A. 7.25%.
    B. 7.39%.
    C. 8.02%.

4. Tom Wright is evaluating the following portfolios for his retirement. The risk-free rate is 3%, and Wright is moderately risk averse with a numerical ranking of 5.

Portfolio	Return	Std. Dev.
A	15.50%	19%
B	10.85%	12%
C	8.50%	14%
D	14.25%	16%

    The utility adjusted return for the portfolio Wright will *most likely* accept is *closest* to:
    A. 6.48%.
    B. 7.25%.
    C. 7.85%.

Use the following information to answer Question 5.

Portfolio	Exp. Return	Std. Dev.	Asset Class Weights			
			1	2	3	4
A	12.00%	10.50%	65%	–20%	35%	20%
B	16.50%	15.00%	15%	20%	50%	15%
C	18.00%	20.00%	30%	20%	25%	25%
D						

5. Given that Portfolio D is composed of 35% Portfolio A and 65% Portfolio B, the asset class weights in Portfolio D (in percent) are *closest* to:

	1	2	3	4
A.	32.50	20.00	30.75	16.75
B.	14.85	6.00	32.50	46.65
C.	32.50	6.00	44.75	16.75

Use the following information to answer Questions 6 through 9.

Alpa Singh, 56, was recently widowed. She was married to Robert Singh, MD, for 29 years and has two daughters, a 26-year-old and a 23-year-old. Upon the death of her husband, Mrs. Singh received $2 million from his life insurance policy. The Singhs had also set aside $1,350,000 towards their retirement. Mrs. Singh has no income of her own and was dependent on her husband. They lived comfortably, and Mrs. Singh estimates that she would need about $100,000 next year, after taxes. Even though her daughters are not dependent on her, she would like to gift them each $15,000 next year out of the after-tax return on the portfolio. She also would like to be able to pay $200,000 for the younger daughter's wedding in one year. As she will set aside the appropriate amount in T-bills, it will not be considered part of her investable portfolio. Her house is completely paid for, and she would like to leave it to her daughters upon her death as part of their inheritance. She would also like to leave a sizable inheritance for her grandchildren.

Mrs. Singh would like to keep her investments in the United States and not use any leverage in her portfolio. She considers herself to be moderately risk averse but recognizes that she has a long-term time horizon after taking gifts to her grandchildren into account. Her numerical risk aversion is 6. Her tax bracket is 30%, and inflation is estimated to be 1.50% per year. To be conservative, she and her advisor assume 100% of all return is taxed at 30% each year.

David Wells has been the financial adviser for the Singhs. To plan for changes in her portfolio and to invest the proceeds from the life insurance policy, he has prepared the following long-term capital market expectations:

| | Asset Class | Expected Return | Exp. Std. Dev. | Correlations | | | |
				1	2	3	4
1	U.S. Lg Cap	14.23%	14.74%	1.00			
2	U.S. Sm Cap	13.36%	17.32%	0.793406	1.00		
3	U.S. LT corp	9.47%	6.90%	0.317803	0.097134	1.00	
4	U.S. LT Gov	9.55%	8.99%	0.325103	0.075176	0.95754	1.00

The risk-free rate is assumed to be 2%. Using the long-term capital market expectations, the mean-variance optimization yields four corner portfolios as follows:

| Corner Portfolio | Expected Return | Exp. Std. Dev. | Sharpe Ratio | Asset Class Weights | | | |
				1	2	3	4
1	9.90%	6.60%	1.197	0.00%	11.10%	88.90%	0.00%
2	10.06%	6.64%	1.214	0.00%	14.90%	85.10%	0.00%
3	12.10%	9.58%	1.054	55.22%	0.00%	44.78%	0.00%
4	14.23%	14.74%	0.830	100.00%	0.00%	0.00%	0.00%

The efficient frontier from the same data is shown in the following graph:

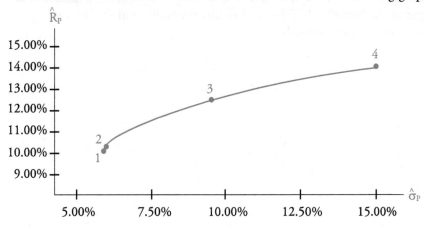

6. Assuming Mrs. Singh wants to protect the real value of her portfolio, the required nominal, before-tax rate of return her portfolio must generate to meet her combined expenses next year is *closest* to:
    A. 6.21%.
    B. 7.45%.
    C. 8.03%.

7.   Suppose that Mrs. Singh agrees with her adviser to seek a required rate of return of 11%. Wells then calculates the asset class weights of the efficient portfolio that has an expected return of 11%. His results are *closest* to (with weights given in percentages):
     A.   weights = 35.43; 6.32; 58.25; 0.00.
     B.   weights = 27.26; 7.25; 65.49; 0.00.
     C.   weights = 25.44; 8.03; 66.52; 0.00.

8.   Wells then determines the efficient portfolio that provides the highest level of utility for Mrs. Singh and calculates the utility she will derive from it. He decides on:
     A.   Portfolio 2 with $U_2 = 0.0879$.
     B.   Portfolio 3 with $U_3 = 0.0935$.
     C.   Portfolio 1 with $U_1 = 0.0859$.

9.   Using Roy's Safety-First Measure, **determine** which of the corner portfolios is the *most appropriate* given that the minimal acceptable return on the portfolio is 6%.

10. **Explain** the key assumption of the Black-Litterman approach in forming market expectations and how an analyst uses that assumption to form the expectations. **Explain** one of the benefits that the final results generally exhibit when using this approach over other methods.

Use the following information to answer Questions 11 and 12.

Bill Mosley is the Chief Investment Officer for Trinity Endowment Fund. The trustees of the fund have asked Bill to recommend a strategic asset allocation for the fund. The trustees have determined that the required rate of return for the fund should be 12% and that the fund standard deviation should not exceed 15%. Further, the fund should be diversified in broad asset categories including foreign equities and precious metals. The fund charter does not allow negative weights in any asset classes.

Bill has developed the following long-term capital market expectations:

| | Asset Class | Expected Return | Exp. Std. Dev. | Correlations | | | | |
				1	2	3	4	5
1	U.S. LT Corp	9.47%	6.90%	1.00				
2	U.S. LT GOV	9.55%	8.99%	0.96	1.00			
3	MSCI Eur	13.34%	16.13%	0.15	0.18	1.00		
4	MSCI PAC	12.51%	24.37%	0.03	0.02	0.55	1.00	
5	MSCI U.S.	14.29%	14.65%	0.32	0.33	0.67	0.25	1.00
6	Gold	2.04%	12.27%	−0.24	−0.24	−0.14	0.13	−0.32

The risk-free rate is assumed to be equal to 1.50%.

Based on the above capital market expectations, Bill ran a constrained optimization, and the results are shown below:

| Corner Portfolio | Expected Return | Exp. Std. Dev. | Sharpe Ratio | Asset Class Weights | | | | | |
				1	2	3	4	5	6
1	7.86%	5.05%	1.259	59.59%	0.00%	4.90%	0.00%	6.87%	28.63%
2	8.52%	5.18%	1.355	61.11%	0.00%	6.56%	0.00%	9.74%	22.58%
3	10.88%	7.23%	1.297	66.65%	0.00%	7.47%	4.78%	20.78%	0.32%
4	14.10%	13.96%	0.903	0.00%	0.00%	4.75%	8.22%	87.03%	0.00%
5	14.18%	14.19%	0.894	0.00%	0.00%	0.07%	6.33%	93.60%	0.00%
6	14.29%	14.65%	0.873	0.00%	0.00%	0.00%	0.00%	100.00%	0.00%

The efficient frontier is shown below.

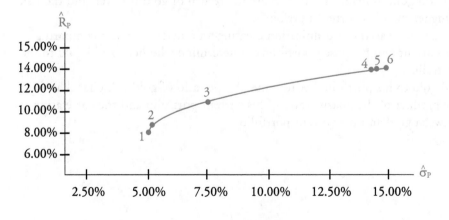

11. What would be the asset class weights of the efficient portfolio that would be recommended for the endowment fund?
    A. Weights = (43.47%; 0%; 6.52%; 5.98%; 43.82%; 0.21%).
    B. Weights = (35.22%; 0%; 6.23%; 5.67%; 21.71%; 0.32%).
    C. Weights = (45.98%; 0%; 6.21%; 5.45%; 33.72%; 0.21%).

12. **Discuss** and **contrast** asset-only versus asset-liability portfolio management.

13. **Describe** expected return estimation bias associated with traditional mean-variance allocation and **describe** a method that can be used to help solve the problem.

14. Due to the recent decline in gold prices, Thomas Goetz, a banking executive in Spain, is considering adding gold to his portfolio, which currently contains no precious metals. Goetz has gathered the following information:
    - Risk free rate = 3%.
    - Correlation between gold and his current portfolio = 0.42.
    - Expected return of his current portfolio = 11%.
    - Expected return of gold = 8%.
    - Standard deviation of his current portfolio = 15%.
    - Standard deviation of gold = 20%.

    Goetz has two objectives: (1) to make the right decision regarding whether to add gold to the portfolio, and (2) to make the decision in the most efficient manner possible. Considering both objectives, he should:
    A. not add gold to his portfolio because the return of gold is lower, and the risk is higher than his current portfolio.
    B. run a mean-variance optimization creating an efficient frontier comparing the current and proposed portfolios to determine whether to add gold to the portfolio.
    C. add gold to his portfolio because the Sharpe ratio of gold is higher than the product of the Sharpe ratio of his current portfolio and the correlation between gold and his current portfolio.

15. Hannah Tremblay is a Canadian investor who has the following asset allocation in her portfolio:
    - 30% invested in a mixture of Canadian bonds of different maturities and risk levels.
    - 10% invested in a foreign bond index fund.
    - 40% invested in Canadian equities.
    - 15% invested in foreign stocks.
    - 5% invested in alternative investments.

    Which of the following is an issue she should be most concerned with in her portfolio?
    A. Political risk.
    B. Currency risk.
    C. Lack of diversification.

16. **Explain** conditional return correlation and its implication on asset allocation in the portfolio construction process.

17. Which of the following is *least accurate* regarding what happens to stocks in an emerging market when it becomes a developed market?
    A. Volatility decreases as information flows more freely and political risk decreases.
    B. Expected return will be higher when the economy reaches developed market status.
    C. Equity prices rise as investors are able to buy the stock that was previously unavailable.

ANSWERS – CONCEPT CHECKERS

1. **B**   Strategic asset allocation uses long-term capital market expectations as well as the client's risk and return objectives and constraints.

2. **B**   Short-term deviations from the strategic asset allocation to take advantage of short-term capital market expectations are called tactical asset allocation.

3. **B**   Required rate of return = $(1.045)(1.02)(1.0075) - 1 = 0.0739 = 7.39\%$

    Ordinarily, either adding or compounding the components would be acceptable. In this case, the curriculum specifies the compounding method.

4. **C** $U_A = \hat{R}_A - 0.5(R_Z)(\sigma_A^2) = 0.1550 - 0.5(5)(0.19)^2 = 0.0648 = 6.48\%$
    $U_B = \hat{R}_B - 0.5(R_Z)(\sigma_B^2) = 0.1085 - 0.5(5)(0.12)^2 = 0.0725 = 7.25\%$
    $U_C = \hat{R}_C - 0.5(R_Z)(\sigma_C^2) = 0.0850 - 0.5(5)(0.14)^2 = 0.0360 = 3.60\%$
    $U_D = \hat{R}_D - 0.5(R_Z)(\sigma_D^2) = 0.1425 - 0.5(5)(0.16)^2 = 0.0785 = 7.85\%$

    Because U_D is the highest of all four, Tom gets the highest utility by investing in Portfolio D with a utility-adjusted return of 7.85%.

    Hint: Remember this function can also be presented as –0.005 instead of –0.5. If –0.005 is used, the inputs must be in whole numbers. For example, $U_A = 15.5\% - 0.005(5)(19)^2$ = 6.48%. Either approach is acceptable on the exam.

5. **C**   Investing 35% of our funds in Corner Portfolio A and 65% in Corner Portfolio B, the asset class weights in Portfolio D are:

    $$\text{asset class weight} = (w_A)(\text{wt in A}) + (w_B)(\text{wt in B})$$
    $$\text{weight of 1} = (0.35)(65) \quad + (0.65)(15) = 32.50\%$$
    $$\text{weight of 2} = (0.35)(-20) \quad + (0.65)(20) = 6.00\%$$
    $$\text{weight of 3} = (0.35)(35) \quad + (0.65)(50) = 44.75\%$$
    $$\text{weight of 4} = (0.35)(20) \quad + (0.65)(15) = 16.75\%$$
    $$\sum_{i=1}^{4} W_i = 100\%$$

6. **C**   The total value of Singh's portfolio is $3,350,000 ($2,000,000 life insurance proceeds + $1,350,000 retirement portfolio). To provide $200,000 in one year, she will set aside the present value of $200,000 at 2% = $196,078 in T-bills. Therefore, she has an investable portfolio of $3,350,000 – $196,078 = $3,153,922.

    Singh's after-tax living expenses and gifts over the coming year total $130,000. This represents an after-tax real spending rate of $130,000 / $3,153,922 = 4.12%. Adding 1.5% inflation to protect the real value of the portfolio, the required after-tax nominal return becomes 5.62%. The before-tax nominal return = 5.62% /(1 – 0.30) = 8.03%.

7. **C**   The expected return of 11% lies between Corner Portfolios 2 and 3 with expected returns of 10.06% and 12.10%, respectively. We solve for w in the following equation:

    $$0.11 = w_2(0.1006) + (1 - w_2)(0.1210)$$
    $$w_2 = 0.5392; w_3 = 1 - 0.5392 = 0.4608$$

In other words, the efficient portfolio with an expected return of 11% has 53.92% weight in Corner Portfolio 2 and 46.08% weight in Corner Portfolio 3. With respect to asset classes, the weights then are derived as follows:

US Lg Cap $= (0.5392)(0) + (0.4608)(0.5522) = 0.2544 = 25.45\%$
US Sm Cap $= (0.5392)(0.149) + (0.4608)(0) = 0.0803 = 8.03\%$
US LT Corp bonds $= (0.5392)(0.851) + (0.4608)(0.4478) = 0.6652 = 66.52\%$
US LT Gov bonds $= (0.5392)(0) + (0.4608)(0) = 0\%$

Note: The approximate standard deviation of the efficient portfolio with 11% expected return is the weighted average standard deviations of Corner Portfolios 2 and 3.

Standard deviation = $(0.5392)(0.0664) + (0.4608)(0.0958) = 0.08 = 8\%$

8. **B** Risk aversion is 6.

$$U_1 = \hat{R}_1 - 0.5(R_Z)(\sigma_1^2) = 0.0990 - 0.5(6)(0.0660)^2 = 0.0859$$

$$U_2 = \hat{R}_2 - 0.5(R_Z)(\sigma_2^2) = 0.1006 - 0.5(6)(0.0664)^2 = 0.0874$$

$$U_3 = \hat{R}_3 - 0.5(R_Z)(\sigma_3^2) = 0.1210 - 0.5(6)(0.0958)^2 = 0.0935$$

$$U_4 = \hat{R}_4 - 0.5(R_Z)(\sigma_4^2) = 0.1423 - 0.5(6)(0.1474)^2 = 0.0771$$

Portfolio 3 has the highest utility for Mrs. Singh.

9. Corner Portfolio 3 is the most appropriate. Roy's Safety-First criterion for Portfolio 3 is:

$$RSF_{P3} = \frac{\hat{R}_P - R_{MAR}}{\sigma_P} = \frac{12.1\% - 6\%}{9.58\%} = 0.637$$

Portfolio	Expected Return	Std. Dev.	Roy's Safety First Measure
1	9.90%	6.60%	0.591
2	10.06%	6.64%	0.611
3	12.10%	9.58%	0.637
4	14.23%	14.74%	0.558

10. *Key assumption*: Financial markets are in equilibrium.

Using this assumption and current market data, the analyst backs out the implied market risk premium and covariances of the assets from a value-weighted global market index. In other words, it gives the equilibrium values implied by the existing market prices. Also, the analyst can adjust the results using personal expectation.

Resulting benefit: Because the analyst uses a global index, the Black-Litterman approach tends to yield portfolios that are more diversified than those determined using other methods. It also yields returns for each asset, helping to avoid the associated input bias.

11. **A** The required rate of return of 12% lies between Corner Portfolios 3 and 4 with expected returns of 10.88% and 14.10% respectively. We solve for w_3 in the following equation:

$$0.12 = w_3(0.1088) + (1 - w_3)(0.1410)$$

$$w_3 = 0.6522$$

65.22% is in Corner Portfolio 3 and 34.78% is in Corner Portfolio 4, so the asset class weights are:

US LT Corp:	$(0.6522)(0.6665) + (0.3478)(0)$	$= 0.4347 = 43.47\%$
US LT Gov:	$(0.6522)(0) + (0.3478)(0)$	$= 0$
MSCI Europe:	$(0.6522)(0.0747) + (0.3478)(0.0475)$	$= 0.0652 = 6.52\%$
MSCI Pacific:	$(0.6522)(0.0478) + (0.3478)(0.0822)$	$= 0.0598 = 5.98\%$
MSCI US:	$(0.6522)(0.2078) + (0.3478)(0.8703)$	$= 0.4382 = 43.82\%$
Gold:	$(0.6522)(0.0032) + (0.3478)(0)$	$= 0.0021 = 0.21\%$

12. Asset-liability portfolio management allocates assets within the framework of funding liabilities. The optimal allocation is the one that maintains risk within an acceptable range while providing the return necessary to meet the liabilities. The manager can employ an ALM efficient frontier framework. The ALM frontier plots surplus at various levels of risk, and the manager selects the allocation on the frontier that produces an acceptable mix of expected surplus and risk.

    In contrast, asset-only allocation looks solely at risk and return with the goal of maximizing return for the acceptable level of risk. Although liabilities can be modeled into the required return, the surplus (assets minus liabilities) is not specifically considered. To avoid the estimation uncertainty associated with projecting expected returns, the Black-Litterman approach can be employed in an asset-only allocation.

13. The inputs to the traditional mean-variance allocation include expected returns, standard deviations, and correlations. The expected return bias arises from the requirement to estimate expected returns. This is a necessary first step in all of the asset allocation approaches, except one. The analyst may have intentional or unintentional bias to over- or understate expected return. This is unfortunate because expected return is a crucial input, and the models are very sensitive to this input.

    The one model that does not require the analyst to start with estimating expected return is the Black-Litterman (BL) approach. In this model, the inputs are the historical standard deviations, weights, and correlations of assets in a world index. Using a reverse optimization process, expected return is back-solved. The analyst must still react to these implied, market consensus, expected returns, and, bias is still possible, but the analyst must explicitly deal with market consensus expectations, which would help to mitigate biases.

> *Professor's Note: All models except BL start with expected return. Only BL is different in this regard, so it is the only acceptable answer to the question. The correct answer not only depends on knowing facts about each model, but also how you use good judgment in thinking about those facts in a somewhat creative fashion.*

14. **C**   If $Sharpe_G > Sharpe_P \times \rho_{G,P}$ then add gold to the portfolio:
Sharpe ratio = $(ER - R_f)$ / Std
Sharpe ratio of gold = (8 – 3) / 20 = 0.25
Sharpe ratio of current portfolio = (11 – 3) / 15 = 0.53
$Sharpe_P \times \rho_{G,P}$ = 0.53 × 0.42 = 0.22
0.25 > 0.22, therefore, add gold to the portfolio.

Note that generating a new efficient frontier including gold in the analysis will answer whether or not Goetz should add gold to his portfolio; however, it is a cumbersome process. The decision rule used by comparing Sharpe ratios and correlation was developed as a more efficient way to answer the question.

15. **B**   Tremblay should be considering the impact of foreign currency (non-Canadian dollars) on her portfolio risk and return. There is no indication of political risk, and she has reasonable diversification.

16.   Conditional return correlation means that correlation is dependent upon the amount of volatility in the global markets at any point in time. Evidence has shown that global markets become more highly correlated during times of crisis, with correlation decreasing after the crisis is over. Global markets have also become more highly correlated as they have become more integrated over time. In response to higher correlations among global markets and during times of crises, portfolios can be constructed using a conditional correlation calculated based on the magnitude of return instead of assuming correlation will be constant. The portfolio will be optimized using the conditional correlations reflecting both normal and abnormal market conditions.

17. **B**   As an emerging market transitions to a developed market, expected return increases at first when capital flows into the market causing stock prices to increase and then expected return falls. The expected return should remain positive in the newly classified developed market but at a lower level due to lower risk than during the transitional phase from developing to developed market.

Use the following information for Questions 1 through 6.

Tyler Robinson, CFA, a senior analyst at RNC Investments, is reviewing the investment policy statements (IPS) of two new RNC clients. The first client, Bob Carlson, is a 45-year-old seasoned investor who prefers to take a strategic approach to allocating his assets. The second client, Rick Olsen, is a 22-year-old recent college graduate who believes in monitoring his portfolio on a daily basis and capitalizing on perceived mispricings.

Carlson has just moved his account from Aggressive Investments (AI) to RNC because he was uncomfortable with the 12% return AI was promising their clients. Carlson knew that this return was only achievable with an increased level of risk-taking. Robinson interviews Carlson over the phone and inquires about his spending rate and his risk aversion score on a scale of 1 to 10, with 10 indicating the lowest tolerance for risk. Carlson thinks that a 3% after-tax return should cover his spending needs on an annual basis and believes that his risk aversion score would be 8 out of 10.

Olsen has just opened up his first investments account through RNC. RNC services were recommended to him by one of his college finance professors who has a son working at RNC. Although he would like to manage his own investments, Olsen's new job requires him to work 60 hours a week leaving him little time to day trade for his own account. For this reason, Olsen has handed investing responsibilities to RNC and consequently, Robinson. Robinson asks Olsen the same two questions that he asked Carlson. Olsen thinks a 5% after-tax return is enough to cover his spending needs and rates his risk aversion score at 2 out of 10.

Robinson begins to select a static asset allocation for each investor given the information he gathered from both interviews. His first step entails specifying asset classes. Robinson believes that the set of asset classes should provide a high level of diversification and they should have a large percentage of liquid assets. However, he does not think that a majority of all possible investable assets need to be included in a given portfolio analysis or that assets need to be classified into more than one class. A drawback to Robinson's asset allocation approach is that the number of estimates needed is overwhelming. Robinson evaluates the following asset classes as possible investments for Carlson and Olsen:

Asset Class	Expected Return	Expected Standard Deviation
U.S. Large-Cap	8.5%	15%
U.S. Small-Cap	12%	20%
U.S. Fixed Income	5.5%	3%
Real Estate	7.0%	12%

Robinson then creates four portfolios with the previous asset classes and calculates their expected returns, standard deviations, and Sharpe ratios. The portfolios are as follows:

Corner Portfolio	Exp. Return	Exp. Std. Dev.	Sharpe Ratio	Asset Class Weights %			
				A	B	C	D
1	6.50%	5.95%	0.756	12	13	5	70
2	7.25%	8.30%	0.633	22	5	21	52
3	8.00%	11.15%	0.538	32	18	15	35
4	8.75%	14.25%	0.474	42	21	22	15

Robinson is anticipating a round of client presentations. He is preparing some discussion points to use with his more sophisticated clients regarding issues associated with various approaches and techniques related to strategic asset allocation. He has prepared the following points:

A. Identifying the risk-free asset is important for most clients because combinations of the risk-free asset and the market portfolio generally produce superior return to risk ratios. Combinations of the risk-free and market normally dominate portfolios on the efficient frontier that are made up of only risky assets and are more appropriate for most investors.

B. Neither asset only nor asset-liability management is necessarily superior. In the end it depends on the client circumstances. For example, foundations and endowments normally focus on asset only management. This is also true for most individuals. On the other hand, banks are more suited to ALM approaches.

C. Both Black-Litterman and Resampled Efficient Frontier models are built from more basic mean-variance analysis. The constrained Black-Litterman approach uses the underlying mathematics of mean-variance but solves for expected returns by asset class. The Resampled Efficient Frontier also uses the same underlying mathematics but solves for weighted average combinations of assets classes for the various points on the efficient frontier.

1. Assuming Robinson recommended Portfolio 1 to Carlson and Portfolio 4 to Olsen, the utility-adjusted returns for both investors would be *closest* to:
   A. 5.08% for Carlson and 6.72% for Olsen.
   B. 6.72% for Olsen and 6.26% for Carlson.
   C. 6.26% for Carlson and 8.61% for Olsen.

2. Has Robinson appropriately specified the set of asset classes?
   A. No, because a set of asset classes does not need to provide a high level of diversification.
   B. No, because a set of asset classes does not need to contain a large percentage of liquid assets.
   C. No, because a set of asset classes should cover a majority of all possible investable assets.

3.   What approach to asset allocation is Robinson *most likely* using?
        A. Resampled efficient frontier.
        B. Mean-variance optimization.
        C. Black-Litterman.

4.   Given the four corner portfolios that Robinson developed, the standard deviation of a portfolio that is capable of achieving an expected return of 7.5% is *closest* to:
        A. 9.73%.
        B. 9.51%.
        C. 9.24%.

5.   Assuming a risk-free rate of 2.5% and no constraint against leverage, determine the weights that should be invested in the risk-free asset and the tangency portfolio to achieve an expected return of 7.5%.
        A. The risk-free asset would be –20% and the tangency portfolio would be 120%.
        B. The tangency portfolio would be 75% and the risk-free asset would be 25%.
        C. The risk-free asset would be –25% and the tangency portfolio would be 125%.

6.   Which of Robinson's presentation points is *least accurate*?
        A. Point A.
        B. Point B.
        C. Point C.

SELF-TEST ANSWERS: ASSET ALLOCATION

1. **A**   Portfolio 1 has an expected return of 6.5% and an expected standard deviation of 5.95%. Given Carlson's risk aversion score of 8, his utility-adjusted return would be:

    $$U_P = 6.5\% - 0.005(8)(5.95^2) = 5.08\%$$

    Portfolio 4 has an expected return of 8.75% and an expected standard deviation of 14.25%. Given Olsen's risk aversion score of 2, his utility-adjusted return would be:

    $$U_P = 8.75\% - 0.005(2)(14.25^2) = 6.72\%$$

2. **C**   Asset classes have been appropriately specified if:
    - Assets in the class are similar from a descriptive as well as a statistical perspective.
    - They are not highly correlated so they provide the desired diversification.
    - Individual assets cannot be classified into more than one class.
    - They cover the majority of all possible investable assets.
    - They contain a sufficiently large percentage of liquid assets.

    Robinson was incorrect to not include a majority of all possible investable assets in a given portfolio analysis. This was evident in his choice to not consider an international asset class during his development of client portfolios.

3. **B**   Mean-variance optimization uses a static approach as opposed to a dynamic approach. Also, the primary drawback to mean-variance optimization is the overwhelming number of estimates needed (e.g., expected returns, standard deviations, correlations).

4. **C**   An expected return of 7.5% lies between Corner Portfolios 2 and 3, with expected returns of 7.25% and 8%, respectively. First, determine the weight that should be invested in these two corner portfolios to achieve the expected return.

    $$7.5\% = w_2 \times 7.25\% + (1 - w_2) \times 8\%$$

    $$w_2 = 67\%, \text{ therefore } w_3 = 33\%$$

    The standard deviation of the portfolio is the weighted average of the standard deviations of Corner Portfolios 2 and 3.

    $$\sigma_P = (0.67)(0.083) + (0.33)(0.1115) = 9.24\%$$

5. **C**   With no constraint against borrowing the expected return is the weighted average of the risk-free asset and the tangency portfolio. The tangency portfolio is the portfolio with the highest Sharpe ratio which happens to be Portfolio 1. The expected return of Portfolio 1 is 6.5%. The weights in the risk-free asset and the tangency portfolio are as follows:

    $$7.5\% = w_{RF} \times 2.5\% + (1 - w_{RF}) \times 6.5\%$$

    $$w_{RF} = -25\%, \text{ therefore } w_T = 125\%$$

    In order to achieve the desired expected return of 7.5% with no constraint against leverage, 25% should be borrowed at the risk-free rate and 125% should be invested in the tangency portfolio.

6. **A**   Statement A is least correct because the CML concept of combining the market portfolio and the risk-free asset is not relevant to most clients. For an ongoing portfolio there is no true risk-free asset with a known return along with zero standard deviation and zero correlation to other assets. Most clients are concerned with ongoing and multiple time periods. In addition, few clients will accept a long-term strategic allocation to the risk-free asset or borrowing (leverage). The rest of the statement is true but not the premise that the CML is relevant to most clients' SAA.

Point B is true as most individuals, foundations, and endowments do not have the specifically measurable, dateable liabilities to support the ALM approach. In contrast, ALM is the appropriate approach for defined benefit, insurance companies, and banks.

Point C is also true. Both methods are variations and extensions on basic mean-variance mathematics. Constrained Black-Litterman solves for market consensus expected return by asset class. The manager can then view and selectively adjust these expected returns. The view adjusted returns are then generally re-input into mean-variance analysis to solve for the efficient frontier. The Resampled Efficient Frontier overcomes the instability of the basic mean-variance model by running multiple passes of the model with slight variations of the inputs, then an average of possible asset allocations for various points on the EF are generated. These average asset allocations are more stable in that their makeup is less likely to change and less portfolio rebalancing will be required over time for minor changes in market conditions.

FORMULAS

---

endowment spending rules:

$$\text{spending}_t = S(\text{market value}_{t-1})$$

$$\text{spending}_t = (\text{spending rate})\left(\frac{\text{market value}_{t-1} + \text{market value}_{t-2} + \text{market value}_{t-3}}{3}\right)$$

$$\text{spending}_t = (R)(\text{spending}_{t-1})(1 + I_{t-1}) + (1-R)(S)(\text{market value}_{t-1})$$

leverage-adjusted duration gap: $\text{LADG} = D_{\text{Assets}} - \left(\frac{L}{A}\right)D_{\text{Liabilities}}$

market volatility: $\sigma_t^2 = \theta\sigma_{t-1}^2 + (1-\theta)\varepsilon_t^2$

factor model based market return: $R_i = \alpha_i + \beta_{i,1}F_1 + \beta_{i,2}F_2 + \varepsilon_i$

factor model based market variance: $\sigma_i^2 = \beta_{i,1}^2\sigma_{F_1}^2 + \beta_{i,2}^2\sigma_{F_2}^2 + 2\beta_{i,1}\beta_{i,2}\text{Cov}(F_1,F_2) + \sigma_{\varepsilon,i}^2$

covariance of two markets:

$$\text{Cov}(i,j) = \beta_{i,1}\beta_{j,1}\sigma_{F_1}^2 + \beta_{i,2}\beta_{j,2}\sigma_{F_2}^2 + (\beta_{i,1}\beta_{j,2} + \beta_{i,2}\beta_{j,1})\text{Cov}(F_1,F_2)$$

price of a stock at time 0: $P_0 = \dfrac{\text{Div}_1}{\hat{R}_i - g} \Rightarrow \hat{R}_i = \dfrac{\text{Div}_1}{P_0} + g$

Grinold-Kroner expected return on equity: $\hat{R}_i = \dfrac{\text{Div}_1}{P_0} + i + g - \Delta S + \Delta\left(\dfrac{P}{E}\right)$

expected bond return:

$\hat{R}_B$ = real risk-free rate + inflation risk premium + default risk premium + liquidity risk premium + maturity risk premium + tax premium

ICAPM: $\hat{R}_i = R_F + \beta_i\left(\hat{R}_M - R_F\right)$

beta for stock i: $\beta_i = \dfrac{\text{Cov}(i,m)}{\sigma_M^2}$

correlation of stock i with the market: $\rho_{i,M} = \dfrac{\text{Cov}(i,m)}{\sigma_i\sigma_M} \Rightarrow \text{Cov}(i,m) = \rho_{i,M}\sigma_i\sigma_M$

equity risk premium for market *i*: $\text{ERP}_i = \rho_{i,M}\sigma_i\left(\dfrac{\text{ERP}_M}{\sigma_M}\right)$

target interest rate to achieve neutral rate:

$$r_{target} = r_{neutral} + \left[0.5\left(GDP_{expected} - GDP_{trend} \right) + 0.5\left(i_{expected} - i_{target} \right) \right]$$

Cobb-Douglas function (% change): $\dfrac{\Delta Y}{Y} = \dfrac{\Delta A}{A} + \alpha\dfrac{\Delta K}{K} + (1-\alpha)\dfrac{\Delta L}{L}$

Solow residual = %ΔTFP = %$\Delta Y - \alpha$(%ΔK) $- (1-\alpha)$(%ΔL)

H-model: $V_0 = \dfrac{D_0}{r-g_L}\left[\left(1+g_L\right) + \dfrac{N}{2}\left(g_s - g_L \right) \right]$

constant growth model: $P_0 = \dfrac{D_1}{r - \overline{g}}$

Fed model: $\dfrac{\text{S\&P earnings yield}}{\text{Treasury yield}}$

Yardeni model: $\dfrac{E_1}{P_0} = Y_B - d\left(LTEG \right)$

P/10-year MA(E): $\dfrac{\text{current level of the S\&P}}{\text{average S\&P earnings over last ten years (adjusted for inflation)}}$

Tobin's q: $\dfrac{\text{total asset value}}{\text{total replacement cost}} = \dfrac{\text{MV debt + MV equity}}{\text{total replacement cost}}$

equity q: $\dfrac{\text{market value of equity}}{\text{replacement value of net worth}} = \dfrac{\text{\# shares outstanding} \times \text{price per share}}{\text{replacement value of assets} - \text{liabilities}}$

$$U_P = \hat{R}_P - 0.005(A)\left(\sigma_P^2 \right)$$

Roy's Safety-First Measure (RSF): $RSF = \dfrac{\hat{R}_P - R_{MAR}}{\sigma_P}$

If $S_i > S_p \times \rho_{i,p}$ adding the investment will improve the portfolio Sharpe ratio

where:
S_i = Sharpe ratio of proposed investment
S_p = current portfolio Sharpe ratio
$\rho_{i,p}$ = correlation of the returns on the proposed investment with the portfolio returns

$$S_i = \dfrac{\hat{R}_i - R_F}{\sigma_i}$$

INDEX

501(c)(3) 20

A

accrued benefits 53
accumulated benefit obligation 8
active lives 8
ALM 21
ALM approach 174
ALM strategic asset allocation 152
alpha research 63
alternative investments 159
anchoring trap 68
appraisal (smoothed) data 65
asset allocation steps 167
asset class returns 95
asset duration 26
asset/liability management (ALM) 11, 152
asset marketability risk 22
asset-only approach 52
asynchronism 66

B

bank constraints 28
bank objectives 28
bank risk measures 27
banks 26, 192
beta research 63
Black-Litterman approach 172
Black-Litterman (constrained) model (BL) 172
bond yield plus risk premium approach 75
bottom-up forecast 129
build-up approach 75
business cycle 81, 82
business spending 85

C

CAL 170
capital allocation line (CAL) 187
capital flows approach 99
capital market expectations 63
capital stock 119
cash balance plan 9
cash flow volatility 21
cash instruments 95
changes in employment levels 88
changes in productivity 88
checklist approach 94

CML 170
Cobb-Douglas production function (CD) 119
commercial paper 95
commodity pools 29
common stock 97
common stock-to-surplus ratio 24
conditional return correlations 165
conditioning information 67
confirming evidence trap 68
constant growth dividend discount model 124
constant growth model 72
consumer and business spending 85
consumer spending 85
contagion 90
corner portfolio 181
corner portfolios 180
crediting rate 20
credit risk 22, 27
credit risk-free bonds 96
credit risky bonds 96
cyclical analysis 81

D

data measurement errors and biases 65
data mining 67
debt risk premium 77
defined-benefit 9
defined benefit pension plans 190
defined-contribution 9
deflation 84
demutualized 20
discounted cash flow models 72
disintermediation risk 21, 22
diversification 27
downside risk 157
dynamic asset allocation 153

E

early expansion phase 83
earnings per share (EPS) 129
econometric analysis 93
economic forecasting 93
economic growth trends 88
economic indicators 94
efficient frontier 151
eligible investments 23
emerging market economies 92
emerging market government bonds 96

Emerging markets 92
emerging market stocks 98
Employee Retirement Income Security Act
    (ERISA) 13
employee stock ownership plans 15
endowment constraints 19
endowment objectives 19
endowments 15, 191
equity q 135
equity risk premium 77
ESOP 15
excess return 157
exchange rates 91
exogenous shocks 90
expected income return 73
expected nominal earnings growth 74
experience-based approach 151
experience-based techniques 178
ex post data 66

F

factor covariance matrix 71
fear of regret 154
Fed model 131
fiduciary 13
financial capital 190
financial equilibrium models 75
financial status and profitability 10
fiscal policy 87
forecasting exchange rates 98
forecasting tools 69
formulating capital market expectations 63
foundation constraints 17
foundation objectives 16
foundations 15, 191
full integration 79
full segmentation 78
fully funded 8
funded status 8
future benefits 54
future wage liability 54

G

geometric spending rule 18
global minimum-variance (GMV) portfolio 181
global securities 159
Gordon growth model 72
Grinold-Kroner model 73

H

hedge funds 29
H-model 123
home country bias 78
human capital 189
hybrid plans 14

I

income 27
individuals 189
inflation 84
inflation adjusted securities 159
inflation and asset returns 84
inflation indexed bonds 97
inflation risk 24
inflection points 81
initial recovery 82
institutional investors 190
insurance companies 20, 191
interest rate differentials 91
International Capital Asset Pricing Model
    (ICAPM) 75
inventory cycle 81
investment companies 29

L

labor force participation 88
labor input 119
LADG 27
late expansion 83
legal and regulatory factors 13
leverage-adjusted duration gap 27
liability duration 26
liability-mimicking portfolio 56
liability noise 54
liability-relative approach 52
liability-relative approach in practice 56
life insurance companies 20
life insurance company constraints 22
life insurance company objectives 21
limitations of historical estimates 65
limitations to using economic data 65
links between economies 91
longevity risk 189
long tail 23
loss aversion 153

M

macroeconomic links 91
macro expectations 63
market exposures due to future benefits 54
market risk premium 69
mean-variance approach 151

Mean-Variance Optimization (MVO) 168
mental accounting 154
micro expectations 63
minimum acceptable return 157
minimum surplus variance portfolio (MSVP) 175
minimum variance frontier 168
minimum-variance portfolio 175
misinterpretation of correlations 67
model and input uncertainty 69
monetary policy 85
Monte Carlo simulation 153, 174
mortality risk 190
MRP 69
multifactor models 70
multi-period Sharpe ratio 78
mutual funds 29
mutuals 20

N

net interest spread 22
neutral rate 86
non-life insurance companies 23
non-life insurance company constraints 25
non-life insurance company objectives 24
non-market exposures 54
nonstationarity 66
nonstationary data 65

O

output elasticity 119
output gap 81
overconfidence trap 68

P

P/10-year MA(E) 134
panel method 80
partial correlation 68
pension liability exposures 53
plan features 10
plan surplus 8, 10
population growth 88
portability 9
positive repurchase yield 73
problems in forecasting 64
profit sharing plan 9
projected benefit obligation 8
projecting historical data 69
prudence trap 68
prudent expert rule 31
prudent investor rule 23, 31
psychological traps 68
purchasing power parity (PPP) 99

R

real estate 98
real interest rates 91
recallability trap 68
recession 83
regime changes 65, 66
regret 154
reinvestment risk 21
relative economic strength approach 99
relative value models 130
repricing return 74
resampled efficient frontier 171
retired lives 8
return objective 12
risk aversion score 156
risk-based capital (RBC) 25
risk objective 155
risk premium approach 75
risk tolerance 155
rolling 3-year average spending rule 18
Roy's Safety-First Measure 157

S

savings-investment imbalances approach 99
semivariance 157
Sharpe ratio 160, 198
shortfall risk 11, 157
shrinkage estimators 69
simple spending rule 18
slowdown 83
smoothing rule 17
Solow residual 120
specifying asset classes 158
specifying risk and return objectives 154
spending rate 17
spending rules 17
sponsor and pension fund common risk exposures 10
static asset allocation 153
statistical tools 69
status quo trap 68
stock companies 20
strategic asset allocation 151
strategic asset allocation issues 189
surplus asset liability management 174
survivorship bias 65

T

tactical asset allocation 151, 152, 192
tangency portfolio 187
target covariance matrix 70
target semivariance 157
Taylor rule 86

term life 21
time horizon 25
time period bias 67
time series analysis 70
Tobin's q 135
top-down forecast 128
total factor productivity growth 88
total factor productivity (TFP) 119
total future liability 8
total real economic output 119
total return 25
transcription errors 65
Treasury Inflation Protected Securities (TIPS)
    97

U

unconstrained Black-Litterman model (UBL)
    172
underwriting or profitability cycle 24
Uniform Management Institutional Fund Act
    (UMIFA) 20
unique circumstances 13
universal life 21
use of surveys and judgment 80
utility-adjusted return 156

V

valuation risk 21
value at risk 27
VAR 27
variable life 21
variable universal life 21
volatility clustering 70

W

whole life or ordinary life 20
workforce characteristics 10

Y

Yardeni model 131
yield curve 87